AN INTRODUCTION TO THE DESERT FATHERS

D1593389

Christian monasticism emerged in the Egyptian deserts in the fourth century AD. This introduction explores its origins and subsequent development and what it aimed to achieve, including the obstacles that it encountered, for the most part making use of the monks' own words as they are preserved (in Greek) primarily in the so-called Sayings of the Desert Fathers. Mainly focusing on monastic settlements in the Nitrian Desert (especially at Scêtê), it asks how the monks prayed, ate, drank and slept, as well as how they discharged their obligations both to earn their own living by handiwork and to exercise hospitality. It also discusses the monks' degree of literacy, as well as women in the desert and Pachomius and his monasteries in Upper Egypt. Written in straightforward language, the book is accessible to all students and scholars, and anyone with a general interest in this important and fascinating phenomenon.

JOHN WORTLEY is Professor Emeritus of Medieval History at the University of Manitoba. His publications include *The Anonymous Sayings of the Desert Fathers* (Cambridge, 2013) and *More Sayings of the Desert Fathers* (Cambridge, 2019).

AN INTRODUCTION TO
THE DESERT FATHERS

JOHN WORTLEY

University of Manitoba

CAMBRIDGE
UNIVERSITY PRESS

University Printing House, Cambridge CB 8BS, United Kingdom

One Liberty Plaza, 20th Floor, New York, NY 10006, USA

477 Williamstown Road, Port Melbourne, VIC 3207, Australia

314–321, 3rd Floor, Plot 3, Splendor Forum, Jasola District Centre, New Delhi – 110025, India

79 Anson Road, #06-04/06, Singapore 079906

Cambridge University Press is part of the University of Cambridge.

It furthers the University's mission by disseminating knowledge in the pursuit of education, learning, and research at the highest international levels of excellence.

www.cambridge.org
Information on this title: www.cambridge.org/9781108481021
DOI: 10.1017/9781108646116

First published 2019

Printed in the United Kingdom by TJ International Ltd., Padstow, Cornwall

A catalogue record for this publication is available from the British Library.

Library of Congress Cataloging-in-Publication Data
Names: Wortley, John, author.
Title: An introduction to the Desert Fathers / John Wortley.
Description: Cambridge, United Kingdom; New York, NY:
Cambridge University Press, 2019. | Includes bibliographical references and index.
Identifiers: LCCN 2019000694 | ISBN 9781108481021 (hardback) |
ISBN 9781108703727 (paperback)
Subjects: LCSH: Desert Fathers. | Monasticism and religious orders –
Egypt – History – Early church, ca. 30–600.
Classification: LCC BR190.W675 2019 | DDC 271.009/015–dc23
LC record available at https://lccn.loc.gov/2019000694

ISBN 978-1-108-48102-1 Hardback
ISBN 978-1-108-70372-7 Paperback

uxori carissimae

Contents

Preface

This little book is mainly intended for anybody who knows next-to-nothing about the Desert Fathers and would like to know more. Insofar as it is possible to do so, the Fathers' own tales and sayings (apothegms) have been used to illustrate what those elders believed, how they behaved and what motivated them. References have been provided throughout to English translations of the tales and sayings in order to permit the reader to do further searching on his or her own behalf, for to do the material adequate justice is more than a book of this size could accomplish.

It is well to keep in mind that by far the greater part of this book is of a legendary nature. That is to say that, for the most part, it is based on second-hand, third-hand and even remoter reports. It is pointless to ask whether this or that statement is true. What is true is that everything in this book was believed by some people (mostly monks) living at some time (mostly in the fourth to seventh century AD). What is also true is that most of the sources quoted here are the words of folk whose primary concern was to inspire others to live what they conceived to be virtuous lives. For the most part they were at pains solely to create models for emulation, with occasional examples of what was to be avoided. Insofar as this book qualifies to be called history, it is a history of how men's minds were working at the end of ancient times and the beginning of the Middle Ages. Times they certainly were a-changing: old values were collapsing and a new set of guidelines was only just emerging. That was indeed a dark age in which the lights that remained were burning rather low. The Desert Fathers were, in their way, the bearers of those lights – lights that might not be altogether useless for us as we seem to be entering another dark age.

All the evidence suggests that Christian monasticism (monachism) first arose in Egypt in the fourth century of our era. It is not impossible that it was also a spontaneous growth elsewhere, especially in Syria, though this has yet to be proved. But no matter how it began, over the course of the next millennium or so, Christian monachism was destined to become a great power in both church and state. Almost from its inception it spread throughout and even beyond the Roman Empire with remarkable alacrity. Monks being monks precisely because they withdraw from 'the world' to be alone (*monos*), for some considerable time the disassociation of monastery and world was carefully maintained. But gradually and perhaps inevitably that disassociation began to disintegrate, partly as a result of the establishment of monasteries in urban centres, partly because some monasteries attracted emigrants who peopled the surrounding countryside. As some monasteries evolved into immense powerhouses of great wealth and influence, a growing number of monks became persons of considerable importance, first in church, by assuming positions of responsibility and power, subsequently (especially in the west) in secular society, where they were often the only persons with any education. It is no exaggeration to say that by the end of the Middle Ages the monastic movement had entirely taken over the church in the west and almost completely in the east. One interpretation of the Protestant Reformation sees it as an attempt to rid the western church of its monastic elements. A similar aim has been attributed to the revolutionary movements of the eighteenth and nineteenth centuries and even to the Second Vatican Council. Yet the insistence on celibacy for most clergy in the Roman church and for the higher clergy in the east is one of the more obvious relics of monastic influence persisting to this day, even though the institution of monachism itself appears to be in decline. Appearances, however, can be deceiving. Undoubtedly fewer men and women are professing themselves in religious orders now than a century ago, but it may be (as Jesus said of Jairus' daughter) that 'the damsel is not dead but sleepeth' [Mk 5.39]. There is a surprising amount of interest these days in the Desert Fathers' and others' 'mystical' writings; more people than ever are now living (at least some of the time) alone. This writer hopes that readers of his book are able to discern something of the fire at the heart of the monastic movement in the elders' tales and sayings; also, that they find them as richly rewarding in as many ways as (or even more than) he continues to find them himself.

Acknowledgements

The author wishes gratefully to acknowledge the unstinting support and generosity of his good friends Robert Kitchen and Michael Montcombroux, *a fortiori* of Janice Roberts, to whom he has the good fortune of being married.

Glossary

Non-English Words Retained in the Translations

Abba	Father; a senior monk but not necessarily an *old* one.
Accidie	[*akêdia*] 'Sloth, torpor, especially as a condition leading to listlessness and want of interest in life' [*OED*], probably akin to depression. See Chapter 4.
Agapê	literally 'love', used to designate a common meal shared by monks on special occasions (hence 'love-feast'), possibly originally made possible by some freewill offering [*agapê*]; also a charitable donation, alms.
Amma	Mother.
Anchorite	[*anachorêtês*] one who withdraws: one who has abandoned 'the world' for the desert or has left a community to live alone.
Anthropomorphism	the attribution of human qualities to the Deity.
Apatheia	literally, 'unfeeling'; indifference to physical conditions, a term often found conjoined with *anorexia*, terms found rarely in the apothegms but common in later monastic writing.
Apothegm	[*apophthegma*] a concise saying or maxim, usually delivered by an elder.
Archimandrite	originally the same as *higoumen* but eventually one with superior authority. Nowadays an honorific title granted to a monastic priest.
Askêsis	literally, a formation or training, usually meaning the practice of asceticism: the discipline associated with the monastic way of life, often translated as 'spiritual discipline'.

Askêtês	ascetic one who practises spiritual discipline.
Coenobion	[*koinobion*] literally, 'common life'. A place or an institution where monks live together with shared worship, meals and responsibilities under the supervision of a *koinobiarch*, here translated as 'superior' or *higoumen*, q.v.
Dynamis	the healing 'power' believed to be given off by holy persons and their relics, etc. [cf. Mark 5.30].
Embrimion	'A bundle of coarse papyrus stalks bound at intervals of a foot so as to form long, slender fascines which were also used as seats for the brethren at the time of the office [Daniel 7 / 18.4, line 36] and on other occasions' [Cassian, *Conf* 1.23.4].
Hesychia	[*hêsuchia*] not merely (or necessarily) silence [*siôpê*], but an interior silence characterised by a tranquil acquiescence in the will of God, producing a profound calm and great peace within. See Chapter 5.
Higoumen	[*hêgoumenos*] the head of a monastic community.
Lavra	a grouping of monks' cells, i.e. 'of monasteries'.
Leviton	(i.e. 'Levites') the monk's garment for prayer, usually white.
Logismos, pl. *logismoi*	a word of many meanings: it can simply mean one's thinking process, but it can also mean everything that goes on in that process, good, bad and indifferent, from a mere whim to a serious temptation.
Monachism	the monastic way of life.
Porneia	any illicit sexual or erotic activity in thought, word or deed. See Chapter 4.
Semantron	a wooden plank struck with a mallet to summon monks for services or for other assemblies.
Synaxis, pl. *synaxeis*	literally, 'a gathering together', this word means an act of worship, by either one or a very few monks (the 'little synaxis', also called *liturgy*) or an entire community (e.g. at weekends and festivals) at a central location. The Holy Eucharist ('Offering') is often called *synaxis*.

English Words Used with Specific Meanings

Alienation	(also *voluntary exile* and *expatriation*) translates *xeniteia*, Latin *perigrinatio*; making oneself a 'stranger and sojourner' [1 Pet 2.11] usually in an uninhabited place or in a foreign land.
Ascetic, -ism askêtês,	*askêsis,* the practitioner and practice of spiritual discipline, perceived as a training or formation in travelling the way to perfection.
Burnt-faced-one	[*aithiops,* from which 'Ethiopian'] a devil or demon.
Dried loaf	[*paxamas,* named after the baker Paxamos] a small loaf of bread that has been sun-dried or baked hard (cf. *bis-cuit,* 'twice baked').
Elder	this word translates *gerôn,* often misleadingly rendered 'old man', but age is not necessarily implied (cf. 'elder' among Native Americans). An elder is one advanced, not so much in age, as in experience and in spiritual growth; hence a senior monk, as opposed to a junior (brother).
Eremitic	pertaining to the desert [*erêmos*].
Expatriation	see *Alienation.*
Loose-talk	[*parrhêsia*] 'outspokenness', 'familiarity', also in a good sense: 'freedom of access', e.g. to the Deity: cf. 1 Jn 2.28, etc.
Lord-and-master	translates *despotês.*
Monastery	'is the name of a dwelling and means nothing more than a place, a lodging that is, for monks' (even for only one monk) [Cassian, *Conf* 18.10].
Poverty	here inadequately translates *aktêmosynê,* literally 'without possessions'. In the apothegms the word means not only the voluntary abandonment of material possessions but, *a fortiori,* indifference to possessions even when they are accessible.
Sorrow for sin	here translates *katanyxis,* sometimes rendered 'compunction'.
Spiritual discipline	here indicates some ascetic practice, e.g. fasting, keeping vigil, etc., tending to spiritual growth and progress.
Spiritual gift	here translates *charisma.*

Worldling   'One who is devoted to the interests and pleasures
                       of the world' [*OED*]. This obsolescent English word
                       has been resurrected to represent the Greek *kosmikos*,
                       a person 'of the world' as opposed to one 'of the
                       desert', i.e. a person who is not a monk. *Kosmikos*
                       is sometimes translated 'layman', which means 'non-
                       clergyman' (but very few monks were clerics); some-
                       times 'secular', but that usually means a cleric who is
                       not a monk; not many worldlings were clerics.

Notes on the Text

Proper Names

Where there is an English equivalent, this has been used, e.g. John, Peter, James, Theodore, Elijah (for *Êlias*) and so forth.

The usual Latin forms have been used where there is an accepted transliteration (e.g. Macarius, Syncletica); otherwise the Greek names have been transliterated directly.

Where words are found in square brackets in the text, these are words that are not found in the Greek, but have been inserted to make the meaning clear.

Except for quotations from John Cassian's works, the author is responsible for all translations from Greek and Latin in this book.

References

Name + number	refers to *APalph*, e.g. Antony 17
Number only	refers to *APanon*, e.g. 475
Number with decimal	refers to *APsys*, e.g. 18.21
Letter + number	refers to *MSDF*, e.g. L4 = Latin 4

NB Some higher numbers in *APanon* have decimals and parts.

Abbreviations

AB	*Analecta Bollandiana*
AP	Sayings (apothegms) of the Desert Fathers
APalph	*The Alphabetic Sayings of the Desert Fathers*
APanon	*The Anonymous Sayings of the Desert Fathers*
APsys	*The Systematic Sayings of the Desert Fathers*
Asceticon	Isaac of Scêtê, *Ascetic Discourses*
BHG	*Bibliotheca Hagiographica Graeca*
Catechism	*Catechism of the Catholic Church* 1992
Conf	John Cassian, *Conferences*
HE	Ecclesiastical (i.e. church) history
HL	Palladius, *Lausiac History*
HME	Anon., *History of the Monks in Egypt*
Inst	John Cassian, *Institutes*
Instructions	Dorotheos of Gaza, *Instructions*
LXX	Septuagint (Greek Old Testament)
MSDF	*More Sayings of the Desert Fathers*
ODB	*The Oxford Dictionary of Byzantium*
OED	*Oxford English Dictionary*
PG	*Patrologia Graeca*
PL	*Patrologia Latina*
Pr	*Precepts of Pachomius*
PS	John Moschos, *The Spiritual Meadow* [*Pratum spirtuale*]
Ps	Psalm
Synag	Paul Evergetinos, *Synagogê*
SynaxCP	*Synaxarium Ecclesiae Constantinopolitanae* (Brussels 1902)
tr	translated by
VA	Athanasius, *Life of Antony* [*Vita Antonii*]
Vie	Lucien Regnault, *Vie Quotidienne*
VP	Jerome, *Life of Paul of Thebes* [*Vita Pauli*]

Maps

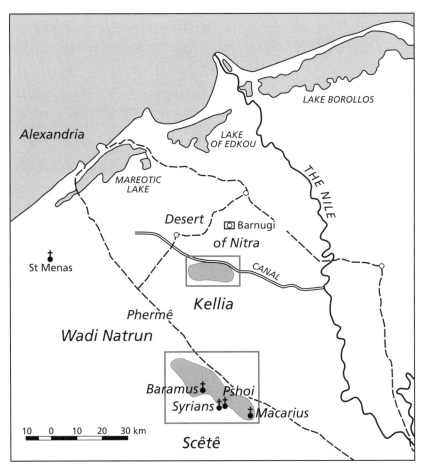

Map 1 The Nitrian Desert

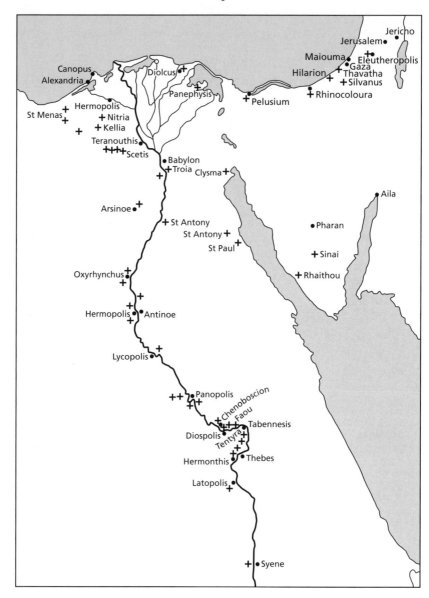

Map 2 Monastic Egypt

CHAPTER I

Desert Fathers

Riches are a trap of the devil. [E114]

Pachomius and Palaemon

About the year 312 AD, Emperor Constantine, fearing that the forces at his disposal might be insufficient for his self-imposed task of ruling the entire Roman world, proclaimed what today would be called a recruitment drive. He went about the task in much the same way as the Royal Navy used to enlist men in the eighteenth century: press gangs were sent out to capture as many promising young men as they could find and bring them in for training. One such gang sailed way up the River Nile, then performed its perfidious task on the way downstream. One of the young men they shanghaied was named Pachomius, of whom nothing more is known than that he was about twenty years old and that he was the son of pagan parents. It is not difficult to imagine the discomfort in which he and his fellow victims of this oppression were brought down the Nile, but:

> As he was being carried off with others on board ship to foreign parts, they docked one evening in a certain port where the citizens, on seeing how strictly the raw recruits were being guarded, enquired what their situation was and, motivated by the commandments of Christ, took great pity on their miserable plight and brought them some refreshments. Pachomius was very surprised at what they were doing and asked who these men were who were so eager and willing to perform such humble acts of mercy. He was told they were Christians, who were in the habit of doing acts of kindness to everyone, but especially towards travellers. He learned also what it meant to be called a Christian. For he was told that they were godly people, followers of a genuine religion, who believed in the name of Jesus Christ the only begotten son of God, who were well disposed to all people, and hoped that God would reward them for all their good works in the life to come. Pachomius' heart was stirred on hearing this, and, illumined by the

light of God, he felt a great attraction towards the Christian faith. [Life of
Pachomius 4]

Those Christians made such an impression on the young Pachomius
that, once he was able to leave the army (probably in 314), he resolved to
become one of them. Accordingly, he had himself baptised; but, rather
than living a normal civilian life, he then went off to embrace a solitary existence in the wilderness at a place called Chenoboskion, near his
Theban home.

He must have realised very soon that living alone was no easy matter;
that he needed a helping hand to do it successfully. Fortunately:

> He came to hear about a certain anchorite called Palaemon serving the Lord
> in a remote part of the desert. He sought him out in the hope of being able
> to live with him. He knocked on his door, asking to be let in. After a while
> the old man opened up to him. 'What do you want? Who are you looking
> for?' he asked. He was of a rather intimidating appearance because of the
> life of strict solitude he had been living for such a long time. 'God has sent
> me to you,' replied Pachomius, 'so that I may become a monk.' 'You would
> not be able to become a monk here. It is no light matter to entertain the
> idea of the chaste life of the true monk. There are many who have come
> in the past and have soon got wearied, strangers to the virtue of persever-
> ance.' 'Not everybody is like that', said Pachomius, 'so I beg you, take me
> in; and, in the course of time, to make trial of my will and see what I shall
> be capable of.'

Pachomius continued to insist and, finally, he overcame the old man's
resistance. He moved in with him and stayed there, sharing his austerities
and obeying his every command, for some years, until ... but that comes
later. (See Chapter 14.)

There is nothing remarkable about Pachomius' decision to seek Christian
baptism on his discharge from the army. Christianity had only recently
been legalised and was now becoming fashionable; many people, no doubt
for a variety of reasons, were seeking to align themselves with the new faith
at that time. What is remarkable is that, having embraced Christianity, a
very social religion ('Love your neighbour as yourself'), Pachomius headed
for isolation and solitude. It is even more remarkable that he was one of
many men and some women who were heading in the same direction.
Reliable statistics are lacking, but there is no doubt that literally hundreds
of people were looking for a new way of life (a solitary life), mainly in Egypt
so far as we know, but in other countries too. It may be an anachronism on
the part of the hagiographer to say that 'Palaemon was serving the Lord *in
a remote part* of the desert' (he was writing sometime later), but there is no

reason to doubt Palaemon's statement that 'There are many who have come [to me] in the past', come, like Pachomius, seeking to be taught how to lead the solitary life so they could practise their faith in isolation, away from the disturbances of 'the world'. Increasing numbers of folk must have been in search of persons like Palaemon, capable of instructing them in how to live and pray alone. And not by any means of all of them 'soon got weary' or turned out to be 'strangers to the virtue of perseverance'. On the contrary, many persevered until the day when each one could set up his/her own solitary dwelling (or cell) in some remote spot where, in due course, like Palaemon, he/she might be sought out by others seeking to learn the theory and practice of living a solitary life for the glory of God. The most successful ones we know nothing of, for they were wholly successful in the quest for solitude. Constantly in search of greater solitude, such people penetrated further and further into the wilderness.

Those are the people whom we call the Desert Fathers. They were the pioneers of Christian monasticism (or monachism), the first Christian monks. The term *monk* must not under any circumstances be taken at anything like its modern face value. Monk, monasticism and monachism ('living alone') all derive from the Greek word *monos*, meaning alone, single. In Syriac there is only one word, *īḥīdāyā*, for both *monk* and *solitary* – and this was entirely appropriate for the Desert Fathers. It is important to stress this because the early history of monasticism was at first largely dictated by the quest for solitude. Monasticism did rather quickly become a matter of 'brothers dwelling together in unity' [Ps 132/133.1] and eventually of addressing 'the world' (the Friars), but, in the beginning, it was not so. The first monks were hermits (from *eremos*, desert) and anchorites (from *anachorein*, to withdraw or retreat from the world of folk and activity). They were monks in that they dwelt *alone* in almost total isolation from the world and from each other. Even today it is tacitly assumed that the ultimate goal of the monk is to be alone. After the coenobites, 'the second type [of monks] is that of anchorites or hermits ... Well trained among a band of brothers for single combat in the desert ... they are ready, with God's help, to fight the vices of body and mind with hand and arm alone' [*Rule of St Benedict* 1.3–5].

Motivation

One may well ask: why did so many 'renounce the world' in that era that began with the cessation of persecution and ended with the explosion of Islam? What provoked the phenomenal rise of Christian monachism that saw considerable numbers of men and some women abandoning 'the world' for the fastnesses of, first, the Egyptian, then of the Palestinian, the Syrian and other deserts? Before he died in 373, Athanasius of Alexandria could write: 'The desert became a city of monks who, having abandoned their own, reproduced the heavenly way of life', 'and now the desert is filled with monks' [*VA* 14.7, 41.4, cf. 8.2].

What then motivated so many people to abandon home and family for a solitary life of penury? It is surely not insignificant that the rise of monachism more or less coincided with the legalisation of Christianity in the Roman Empire. That would have led to a large increase in the number of people openly professing the Christian faith. Most of the neophytes would have remained in their homes with their families and continued to enjoy such comforts as were at their disposal. Why then was a significant minority among them motivated to abandon all that, in order to embrace a life of spiritual discipline?

We have a very precise answer to this question in Antony's case. Visiting the local church shortly after his parents' death, he was already thinking about how the Apostles abandoned their normal way of life to follow Jesus and how the early Christians sold their goods and laid the proceeds at the Apostles' feet to feed the poor [Mt 4.20, 19.27; Acts 4.34–35]. Then he heard the Gospel being read where Jesus tells a rich man, 'If you want to be perfect, go, sell all you have and give to the poor then come and follow me' [Mt 19.21] and 'Take no thought for the morrow' etc. [Mt 6.34; *VA* 2, 3]. John Cassian says that Lk 24.26, 'Except a man hate ...' etc. was also read in his hearing [*Conf* 3.4.2], but there is nothing of this in *VA*. Antony was so inspired by what he is said to have heard that he promptly divested himself of all his possessions (including his home) and espoused the solitary life: ostensibly because he 'would be perfect'.

At least that is what Athanasius says, providing a very appropriate explanation of Antony's renunciation of 'the world', but it is not impossible that Athanasius fitted the Scripture to the event. For never again (at least in the early days) do we read of those words of Jesus inspiring a person to embrace the monastic life. In fact, those words hardly ever recur in the apothegms and they are never again said to occasion a vocation [cf. 46 / 14.32; 392 / 6.6; 566 / 15.117, etc.]. Babylas the actor is said to have been prompted to renounce the world by hearing the text: 'Repent for the Kingdom of Heaven is at hand' [Mt 3.2] and even that is exceptional. In fact, very rarely indeed is any spiritual reason given why a person chose to withdraw from the world. In most cases, except where there is a physical cause (such as to escape, e.g. from a persecution or a lover), it is simply stated that this or that person took the necessary steps to isolate him- or herself from society with no reason given.

How Can I Be Saved?

There may be doubt as to *why* a person withdrew from the world: there is no doubt what he or she hoped to gain by withdrawing. This is clearly revealed in many apothegms, the majority of which are set in the form of question and answer: a clear indication of their didactic purpose. Over and over again a neophyte or a junior monk approaches an elder (i.e. senior monk, who is addressed as abba, 'father') and asks a question. The question is often no more than a simple request for 'a word': 'Say something to me', meaning: 'Give me a phrase on which I can meditate.' Sometimes a specific question is asked concerning some aspect of the monastic life, e.g. 'Why am I continually discouraged?' or 'What am I to do under this burden that oppresses me?' [92 / 21.8; Poemen 145]. But in very many cases the question asked concerns one's personal salvation: 'How can I/we be saved?' or 'What should one do to be saved?' [91 / 21.6]. Amoun of Nitria knew very well what people were coming into the desert for: 'If they were many who came there *wanting to be saved*, he would assemble the entire brotherhood' [*HME* 20.10]. But the spirit had to be willing: 'We have it within ourselves to be saved, *if we want to be*,' one elder commented [226 / 10.148, last line].

It is not always clear who asks whom [e.g. Euprepius 7 / 10.24; 91 / 11.50; Ares 1 / 14.3; 143/ 6.20], but this is by no means always the case [Antony 19 / 16.1]. Even if it is usually a relatively junior monk who poses the question, salvation is by no means a matter of concern only for juniors, nor is the question of how salvation is to be attained asked once only: it was clearly an ongoing concern in monastic circles. Three fathers (not brothers, hence senior monks) are reported to have been in the habit of visiting Antony once a year to question him concerning their 'thoughts' (*logismoi* – the other great topic of monastic discourse; see Chapter 4) and about *salvation of the soul* [Antony 27 / 17.5]. Nearly all the fourth-century fathers are said to have been asked and to have responded to the question of how one is to be saved [e.g. Ares 1 / 14.3; Macarius the Egyptian 23 / 10.47, 747, 764]. On one occasion no less a person than Poemen is said to have approached Macarius 'with many tears', begging him: 'Say a something to me: tell me how can I be saved?' [Macarius the Egyptian 25].

There are many similar passages where the question is stated as clearly as that; there are several more where the question is implied by an answer that terminates in a phrase such as '… so that our soul might be saved' or

'… and thus you will be able to be saved' [Antony 33 / 3.1]. Here is one particularly striking such answer: 'If God were to take into account our inattention in prayer and psalm-singing, we could not be saved' [Theodore of Enaton 3 / 11.35]. Thus, whether explicit or implied, the question of salvation arises with remarkable frequency in the apothegms.

A very considerable amount of monastic time and effort appears to have been devoted to debating and answering the question of how one might be saved. When Antony had serious visitors, he would sit up all night long talking to them about the attainment of salvation [*HL* 21, 8–9]. When Macarius the Egyptian visited him, they would work away braiding rope out of palm-fronds, all the time 'speaking of what is advantageous to the soul' [Macarius the Egyptian 4 / 7.14]. This is hardly surprising, for Antony was of the opinion that 'The monk should think of *nothing other* than the salvation of his soul' [630]. One elder, when asked to explain the meaning of 'every careless word' [Mt 12.36], said: 'Every word uttered on a material subject is chatter and only that which is said concerning the salvation of the soul is not chatter' [555]. Another monk says in his prayer: 'Lord … you have brought me into the *order of this salvation*. Save me Lord for "I am thy servant and the son of thy handmaiden" as you will' [403 / 11.116, 12.28, cit. Ps 115.7 / 116.16]. Even the demons knew of the monks' concern with the question of salvation for, on one occasion, a demon disguised as a monk said, as he was setting out to visit a brother: 'I shall go to that man of God and discuss with him what might be conducive to the salvation of our soul' [7.31]. In that way he hoped to persuade the brother that he was a monk and no demon.

From one point of view the monks' concern about how they were to be saved is only what might be expected of those who were taking their religion seriously. Most people would agree that, in the Christian tradition, the goal for which the faithful aim, worldling and monastic alike – indeed the whole object of the Christian endeavour – is precisely to attain salvation. It is the will of God that 'all should be saved and come to the knowledge of the truth' [1 Tim 2.4] and it was to make salvation accessible for all that the Incarnation took place: 'Christ Jesus came into the world *to save sinners*' [1 Tim 1.15]. 'It was for you, O man, that Christ was born; it was for this that the Son of God came: that you might be saved' [81]. Monks, in common with all Christians, were right to be concerned about their eternal salvation.

Saved from What?

There are some clear indications that a monk was *not* enquiring directly about his eternal salvation when he posed the question: 'What shall I do to be saved?' – indications that he might well have had something else in mind. For example, when the jailor at Philippi discovered that Paul and Silas had not (as he feared) escaped, he asked them: 'Sirs, what must I do to be saved?' [Acts 16.30] – substantially the same question that is asked (sometimes *verbatim*) over and over again in the apothegms. The answer given by Paul and Silas is formal: 'Believe in the Lord Jesus and you shall be saved, you and yours' [Acts 16.31]. Yet, for all its clarity and precision, *not once* is that answer cited (or even obliquely referred to) when a question similar to the jailor's is answered in the apothegms. Scriptural quotations abound, but this is *never* one of them.

Second, although the expressions 'to be saved' and 'to have eternal life' are used more or less synonymously in the Christian Scriptures, the second of these terms is almost completely unknown in the apothegms [595 / 16.18 is a rare exception].

Third, it has to be borne in mind that many of the people asking the question 'How can I be saved?' had already renounced the world. In other words, they had already surmounted the obstacle that proved too much for the young man who approached Christ asking what he must do to inherit eternal life [Mt 19.16–22; Mk 10.17–22; Lk 18.18–23]. The surrender of one's earthly goods and connections, one's home and family, is not a sacrifice that is made (other than in very odd circumstances) without a considerable degree of commitment to the one who requires it. For this reason, it can be reasonably concluded that most of those asking what they could do to be saved already had their feet firmly on the golden ladder to the heavenly city.

Fourth, the monk is sometimes defined as 'one who is concerning himself with his own salvation' [*HL* 23 / 5.54 (*bis*); 135 / 3.38; 528 / 15.131; 70 / 10.178]. Indeed, there are many passages where the terms 'saving one's soul' and 'living the ascetic life' are used as though they were synonymous and interchangeable, as in some nineteenth-century Russian novels,[1] e.g. 'As he was rushing off to the city, a brother asked an elder for a prayer. The elder said to him: "Do not be in a hurry to get to the city, but rather to flee from the city *and be saved*." ' The robbers whom Abba Moses arrests embrace the monastic life with the words: 'Why should we reject salvation?' ' "What a fine thing is the order of monks" [one monk] said and,

[1] The verb used, e.g., in Dostoyevsky, *The Brothers Karamazov* 1.2, 1.4, 6 (twice), 8, 1.3, 7, 11, 2.6.2(c), etc. is спасаться, *lit.* 'to save oneself', always with a monastic meaning; cf. the charming story of the youth who told his mother he wanted to save his soul and, eventually, shut himself away to sit working out his own salvation [135 / 3.38].

the Lord being in favour of my salvation, I went off and became a monk'
[130; *HL* 19.4; 191 / 5.44]. Somewhat enigmatic is the case in which a father
who prays for a prostitute to be saved is said to have succeeded, in that she
proceeds to enter a monastery [Serapion 1 / 17.34]. The clearest statement
is probably that which was given to a brother who asked an elder: 'How
am I to be saved?' He was given a demonstration in which the elder tied
himself up in his own robe [*leviton*], saying: 'This is how the monk must
be: stripped of the material aspects of this world and crucified in warfare
[with the demons]' [143 / 6.20], which, being interpreted, is: you are to be
saved by becoming one of us, namely a monk.

Yet there are plenty of stories making it very clear that espousing the
monastic life by no means guarantees entry into the Kingdom of Heaven.
Quite the contrary, for monks are frequently and categorically warned that
their eternal salvation is by no means assured [e.g. *VA* 66; *HL* 21.16–17]
and that many secular persons may well enter the eternal abode ahead of
them, e.g. Abba Silvanus' warning: 'I was snatched away to the judgement
and I saw many of our kind going off to punishment and many worldlings
going into the Kingdom' [Silvanus 2 / 3.33; see also 489 / 20.21; cf. Antony
24 / 18.1]. Fully aware of this, one father remarked: 'It were a shame for a
monk to leave all his possessions and go into exile for the sake of God, then
afterwards to go to damnation' [110 / 21.30].

The Means and the End

From these considerations, it can be concluded there is no necessary
connection between salvation in the usual sense of the word ('The saving of
the soul; the deliverance from sin, and admission to eternal bliss, wrought
for man by the atonement of Christ,' *OED*) and its apparently esoteric
meaning in the dialectic of the early monks. This apparent duality of per-
ception is addressed by John Cassian in the first of his *Conferences*, 'The
goal and end of the monk.' In an attempt to state it rationally, Cassian
says that everybody has what later fathers would call 'the hope of glory'
[cf. Col 1.27; Eph 1.11], meaning salvation in the commonly accepted sense
of the word: attainable (through faith in Christ) in the world to come.
This Cassian designates the hoped-for τέλος / *finis* or end of every human
life. Then he goes on to speak of the σκοπός / *destinatio*, the 'goal' which
is the destiny of those who have embraced the monastic life, meaning
something to be aimed at in this *present* life. Just as a farmer hoping to
enjoy an abundant harvest at the end of the year (says Cassian) diligently
performs all those tasks which long experience has taught him are likely

to be conducive to a good crop, in that same way must the monk apply himself to the matter of attaining salvation. This is the monk's travelling to the desired end. If this be less than clear (as Cassian sometimes is), the matter is more simply expressed in the heading of a *Gerontikon of Sinai* in which it is asserted that the contents of that book exist 'for the imitation, zeal and instruction of those who (1) wish to live correctly the heavenly [i.e. monastic] way of life and (2) desire to enter the Kingdom of Heaven'. The ultimate goal is to enter the Kingdom of Heaven; the immediate goal is, simply put, to be a successful monk: to live the monastic life correctly, neither despairing of success and returning to 'the world' nor falling into the slough of uncaring, lack of zeal and lukewarm faith.

There is an anecdote concerning Antony in the earliest extant stratum of the apothegms where it is clearly Antony's *immediate*, not his ultimate, salvation that is in question:

> Once when the holy Abba Antony was residing in the desert he was over-come by *accidie* and a cloud of black thoughts. He said to God: 'Lord, *I want to be saved* but my thoughts will not leave me alone. What am I to do in my affliction? How can I be saved?' Going outside [his cell] a little way Antony saw somebody similar to himself sitting working, then standing up to pray, sitting down again to work at rope-making, then standing to pray once more. It was an angel of the Lord sent to correct Antony and to encourage him. He heard the angel saying: 'Act like this and you shall be saved.' He was greatly cheered and encouraged on hearing this and by doing [as he was told] he was saved. [Antony 1 / 7.1]

Other Meanings of 'Saved'

Although Antony asks more or less the same question as the jailor at Philippi, he is not using the same frame of reference. But then neither are the verb *to save* and its cognates always used in the jailor's sense throughout the Scriptures. In fact, often (indeed always in the Old Testament) they have a meaning *other* than the *OED* definition [see above]. Such words occur with greater frequency in Psalms than in any other book of the canon and, coincidentally, Psalms is the second most frequently cited book (after the First Gospel) in the apothegmatic literature. This is hardly surprising because, whereas some monks knew amazingly large tracts of Scripture by heart [e.g. 150 / 4.70; 222 / 10.135], even more could recite the entire Psalter, while every monk would know at least some of the Psalms, e.g. the twelve psalms said each morning and the twelve at sundown. Indeed, it was in the words of the Psalmist that the monk usually prayed.

This means that the verb *to save* and its cognates were frequently on his lips and in his mind.

Such words are used in a variety of ways in Psalms, but the most frequently occurring meaning is that of rescue from enemies (physical or spiritual) which oppress the Psalmist, obvious examples being: 'Save me O God for the waters are come in, even unto my soul' and 'Deliver me from the wicked doers and save me from the bloodthirsty men' [Ps 68/69.1; 58/59.2]. The Desert Fathers believed themselves to be assailed by a host of enemies, external (demons) and internal (temptations), which sought to drive them from their chosen path and way of life and to distance them from 'the God of our salvation'. The words of the Psalmist were appropriate for the anchorite in many ways that are not always easy to appreciate today. Indeed, the best way to gain an understanding of the monks' mentality is to study their prayer book: the Psalter.

In the New Testament too (especially in the Gospels), the verb *to save* is used not always in the sense of conferring eternal life, but rather to mean 'making whole', e.g. the many times when Christ, having accomplished a healing, says to the patient: 'Your faith has made you whole / has saved you' [Mt 9.22, etc.]. Jairus asks Jesus to lay hands on his daughter 'so she may be saved and live' [Mk 5.23]. When, in the passage cited above, Antony says he wants to be saved, he is using the word in both senses, the Psalmist's and the Evangelist's. He is asking both to be *rescued from* and to be *cured of* the affliction of *accidie*. In this way, he prays to be delivered from the wreck of his monastic endeavour that the attack of *accidie* might well entail if it continued too long: cf. the apothegm in which a monk thanks God for having prevented him from an irrevocable fall [52].

Antony's case is unusual in that it is one of only two occasions (in the extant literature) on which the question 'How am I to be saved?' is addressed directly to the Deity. In the other case it is not by a monk, but by a worldling that the question is asked, or rather by whom a prayer is uttered in which the question is implied. While the future Abba Arsenius [354–445; see *ODB* 187–188] was still serving as a senior minister in the government of the Emperor Theodosius I (possibly as tutor to Arcadius and Honorius), he prayed: 'Lord, lead me in such a way that I might be saved.' The reply was explicit: 'Flee from men and you shall be saved' [Arsenius 1 / 2.3], whereupon he left all and became a distinguished monk with John Colobus at Scêtê. What was Arsenius praying to be saved *from*? Presumably not from the wrath to come, since he was a man of faith prepared to take the ultimate step of renunciation. Saved, then, presumably, from 'the world' [1 Jn 2.15–17, 4.4–5, etc.], saved from secular society and all its impurities by withdrawing into the desert. Paul's expression 'this present wicked world' [Gal 1.4; see also 1 Jn 2.15–17, 4.4–5, etc.] seems to characterise exactly what the monks sought to be saved from: 'the vain world's golden store' and all that it entails. In the fourth century it entailed far more than we can imagine. Most of the religions we call *paganism* were alive and well, perpetrating a variety of customs and practices that were utterly abhorrent to Christians. How abhorrent can be judged from the avidity with which Christians gave themselves to the task of tearing down the pagan temples when the opportunity to do so presented itself.

'Flee from Men'

The instruction Arsenius received to flee from men frequently recurs, for 'the love of men obstructs us from the love of God', one father says [G6], and another: 'Let us flee from [worldlings] as one flees from a serpent' [G51]. 'Flee from the glory and repose of this world,' says Cronios [Cronios 5], while Antony goes even further: 'Hate the world and all that is in it' [Antony 33 / 3.1]. Poemen advises: 'Follow the good way, do justice, flee from this world entirely' [E178] and for those tempted to return there is this: 'Do not hasten to the city, but rather make haste to flee the city and be saved' [130].

Yet fleeing from the world was a relatively small thing compared with the very big thing of subsequently and for the rest of one's life *staying away* from the world and all its works. For some monks life must have been an ongoing struggle *not* to return to the world and most monks were probably afflicted with the same *logismos* at least some of the time, especially at difficult stages in their experience.

> One of the fathers came to Abba Theodore and said to him: 'Here such-and-such a brother has gone back to the world' and the elder said to him: 'Are you surprised at that? Do not be surprised; but do be surprised if you hear that somebody has been able to escape from the jaws of the Enemy.' [Theodore of Phermê 8 / 10.34]

For Theodore what was truly remarkable was that anybody ever does *not* give up and simply return to the world. Thus the first item in *APalph* cited above ('Once when the holy Abba Antony was residing in the desert …', etc.) [Antony 1 / 7.1] can be seen as a triumph over the temptation to abandon the cell and to leave the desert. Of course, Antony 'was greatly cheered and encouraged' by his encounter with the angel, for it showed him how he could be saved from being driven back into the world by the 'accidie and a cloud of black thoughts' that were afflicting him. The encounter with the person 'similar to himself' had rescued his monastic career from disaster; he was being saved.

Staying the Course: Humility

'What is "progress" for a monk?' 'It is humility that leads a monk to progress.' [381 / 15.97]

Although the texts seem to speak of the Royal Road (see Chapter 7) as single and unique, a bewildering variety of answers is given on how to stay on that road and to proceed along it. This is not surprising: one director of souls characterised himself and others in a similar position as 'those who have a number of brethren dependent upon us whom we guide *in different ways* towards salvation' [70 / 10.178]. This is borne out by the texts: when asked how one might be saved, Ammoes (for instance) replies: 'Verily, if you have a good heart, you will be saved' [E121]. That is unusual; the fathers usually list three virtues (occasionally four) which are essential to salvation/safe passage. Some confusion arises as the three or four virtues named are rarely the same. But there is one feature common to most of the fathers' prescriptions: the virtue of humility, or 'humble mindedness' (probably two translations of the same Coptic word). Humility is not universally prescribed; witness the monk who asked an elder: 'What should I do that I may be saved?', and the elder answered: 'The work of your hands together with divine service will deliver you' [E188]. But that is truly exceptional; humility features far more frequently than any other virtue, as in the following examples: 'If a man have *humility*, poverty and refrains from judging others, the fear of God shall come upon him' [Euprepius 5 / 137 / 1.29]. 'Fear, love and *humility* are what God requires' [222 / 10.135; cf. Euprepius 6 / 1.18 / 1.30]. 'Abba Mark said he who wished to pass the "intelligible sea" [an expression not found elsewhere] is long-suffering, *humble*, watchful and abstinent' [2.21]. When a brother phrased his request in this rather unusual way (for the apothegms): 'Tell me, father, how can I acquire Jesus?' he was told: 'Labour, *humility* and ceaseless prayer acquire Jesus; all the holy men from first to last were saved by these three' [10.129].

Humility then is the most frequently required condition for that salvation to which the monk aspires; humility is also the virtue which was held in highest esteem by the Desert Fathers. For them humility was the foundation on which all else rested: 'The ground on which God demanded that sacrifice should be offered is humility,' one elder remarked [*Synag* 1.44.1.45], while another had a striking vision demonstrating the impossibility of entering the Kingdom of Heaven for one lacking humility [Arsenius 33 / 18.3].[2] It is no exaggeration to say that humility is the very keystone and lynchpin of the Desert Fathers' teaching. They found unequivocal support for this in the Gospel: 'John of the Thebaid said a monk must practice humility *before all else* because this is the first commandment of the Lord' [John of Kellia 2 / 15.36; cf. *HME* 1.59]. By 'the first commandment' he was referring to the first of the *Beatitudes*: 'Blessed are the poor in spirit' [Mt 5.3].

> Abba Longinus was asked: 'Which virtue is greater than them all, father?' and the elder said: 'If pride is worse than all [other sins,] to the point that it cast some ones out of the very heavens, I think that humility is certainly strong enough to bring a man out of the very abyss, even if the sinner is like a demon. Thus the Lord pronounces "blessed" "the poor in spirit" before all else.' [558]

Abba Longinus clearly assumes that by 'poverty of spirit' the Lord meant humility, which is indeed the usual interpretation of this beatitude in Patristic hermeneutics. This beatitude is also the only one with the promise: 'For theirs is the Kingdom of Heaven.' But Longinus is by no means the only father to speak of the salvific force of humility:

> Humility has often saved many people, even without [their] effort. We have the Publican and the Prodigal Son as witnesses, for they only said a few words and were saved. A man's good works will lead him to perdition if there is an absence of humility, for many are led into pride by their great efforts, like the Pharisee. [552; cf. Lk 18.10–14, 15.11–23; Epiphanius 6]

So humility is the *sine qua non* of monastic life and anybody who is without it had better run away and keep silent [305A / 15.81]. Syncletica,[3] practical as ever, says: 'Just as it is impossible for a ship to be built without nails, so a monk is incapable of being saved without humility' [Syncletica 59 /15.66]. Sisoes, the disciple of Antony and his successor at the Inner Mountain, says: 'Fasting is the mother of all virtues ... but humility of spirit is itself greater than all the virtues' [E155]. John Colobos used to

---

[2] 'He saw a temple and two persons on horseback carrying a piece of wood crossways, one beside the other. They wanted to enter through the gate but could not because the piece of wood was crossways. One would not humble himself to carry the wood lengthwise behind the other; for that reason they remained outside the gate.' (This one of three figures.)

[3] All the apothegms attributed to Syncletica in *APalph* are extracts from her fifth-century *Life*, *BHG* 1694, see St Athanasius, *The Life and Regimen of the Blessed and Holy Teacher Syncletica*, tr Elizabeth Bryson Bongie, Toronto 1995. Born to a rich family in Macedonia she embraced the monastic life in Alexandria where she was frequently consulted by the sisters of the region. Her sayings are singularly astute.

say: 'Humble-mindedness and the fear of God are indeed superior to all the virtues' [John Colobos 36, 22 / 15.35].

A truly remarkable anonymous saying (which appears only to have survived in Latin) takes the matter a little further by explaining exactly why humility is so crucial to the Christian endeavour: 'All labour lacking humility is done in vain, for humility is the forerunner of charity. Just as John [the Baptist] was the forerunner of Jesus, drawing everybody to him, so humility draws [one] towards love; that is, to God himself, for God is love' [*PL* 73;1036D]. In this way might the 'poor in spirit' acquire the Kingdom of Heaven, hence the pursuit of humility must be the first concern of all who would be saved. 'Every day, every year, every week, examine what progress you have made in prayer, in fasting, in *hesychia* and, above all, in humility for that is the true progress of the soul ... [Without humility,] even if a man perform prodigies and raise the dead, he is far from God' [592 / 27]. Sisoes even says that it is no great thing that your thought be with God; 'What *is* great is to see yourself as inferior to all creation, because that and physical labour are what produce humility' [Sisoes 13 / 15.65]. Humility is acquired by continence, prayer and considering oneself to be the least of men [Tithoes 7 / 15.61]; it is one of the principal 'instruments of the soul' [Poimen 36 / 15.50]; indeed, 'The crown of the monk is humility' [Or 9 / 98 / 21.15].

Such is the power of humility that the humble monk is a menace to the demons. One demon confesses to Macarius the Egyptian that he was beaten 'by your humility alone and, because of that, I can have no power over you' [Macarius 11 / 15.40]. 'Humility neutralises all the power of the enemy for I have myself [*anon*] heard [the demons] saying: "When we assail the monks, one of them turns about and makes an act of obeisance [or "apologises"'] thus wiping out all our strength' [77 / 15.112]. When an elder who has been struck 'turns the other cheek' [Mt 5.39], 'the demon retreats, unable to endure the burn' [298 / 15.71]. Abba Moses says: 'He who has humility humiliates the demons; but he who has no humility is tossed around by them' [499 /15.44] and Antony says: 'I beheld all the snares of the devil deployed on earth. "Whoever might negotiate a way through them?" I groaned and I heard a voice which said: "Humility"' [Antony 4 / 15.3]. In a word, humility seems to be the key to the other virtues. When a brother says: 'Tell me some practice I can observe by doing which I can seek *all other virtues*,' he is told: 'He who can endure being set at naught, despised and wronged can be saved', for 'Humility is a great and a divine work' [323 /15.103].

It would be misleading to claim that humility is universally presented as the unique path to salvation. One father says that for the person who 'does unto others ...' it will suffice for his salvation [253 / 1.31], another states that it is possible to be saved by the prayer of somebody else [66 / 18.14], while a third tells of a brother who was saved by his patient endurance of a drunken elder's tantrums [27 / 16.27; cf. 339 / 16.28, saved by suffering theft]. In yet another instance, a difficult brother is saved by the long-suffering of Abba Isidore who takes him into his own cell [Isidore of Scêtê 1 / 16.6]. But all those acts required humility; so the answer to the question 'What can I do to be saved' (sc. from failing as a monk) is clearly: 'Acquire humility.' For the highway of (monastic) salvation is navigated by humility, not primarily by purity of heart (as John Cassian has it), but by the pursuit of humility. And in this Benedict followed the Desert Fathers, not John: witness the longest chapter (c.7) of the *Rule* that bears his name: 'The Ladder of Humility'.

CHAPTER 2

Beginnings

Flee from men and remain silent – and you shall be saved. [132D]

Alone-ness

Christianity appears to have existed for three centuries without monasticism, then, within a remarkably short time, to have acquired a monastic movement of significant proportions; a movement which would eventually transform the structure and the nature of the entire church, in both east and west, and alter the course of history. Few have been able to believe that such a movement arose *sui generis*, 'Without father, without mother, without descent' [Heb 7.3]. Hence the influence of various non-Christian quasi-monastic communities has been suggested as leading to the emergence of Christian monasticism, for instance the 'recluses' in the Serapeum at Memphis and the priestly ascetics at Heliopolis before Christ. Some have posited also the Gymnosophists, ten of whom Alexander the Great is said to have encountered on the banks of the Indus in what is now Pakistan. These 'naked philosophers' (probably Digambara Jain monks) were later mentioned with approval by both Philo the Jew and Clement of Alexandria, but there is little or no evidence of them ever having any influence in the west. Despite a general absence of monastic practice in Judaism and an active antipathy to it, two Jewish communities have been cited as possible models for early Christians to emulate: the Essenes of Qumran-fame on the shores of the Dead Sea and the Therapeutae, a Hellenistic Jewish sect that flourished in suburban Alexandria for some years. But as neither survived very long into the first century of our era, any connection with Christian monasticism must remain purely hypothetical.

Most of the proposed predecessors of Christian monasticism appear to have manifested certain characteristics of coenobitic monasticism, i.e. the sharing of a life in common. That was indeed the distinguishing characteristic of the monachism of Upper Egypt, allegedly the invention of

Pachomius (see Chapter 14). But commonality was a secondary development in Lower Egypt. There, the earliest Christian monachism was not in the least coenobitic: it was solitary. Antony, Pachomius, Amoun, Macarius the Egyptian – these all started out endeavouring to lead a solitary existence. It was in spite of themselves that each became the focal point of a settlement and (eventually) of a community. Hence if the origins of Christian monachism are to be found, they are to be sought among individuals who were already practising voluntary solitude, not where brethren were 'dwelling together in unity' [cf. Ps 132.1 / 133.1].

A few such persons there appear to have been in so many societies that it might not be presumptuous to view voluntary solitude as a universal phenomenon. It was well known in ancient China; the Hindu 'Third Ashram' required it and many Buddhists still practise it. Presumably some Greeks did too, for when Aristotle wrote, 'A man who lives alone is either a lower animal or a god' [*Politics* 1253a] he must have known (or known of) some folk who were (or had been) living in self-imposed isolation. It would be good to know whether it was indeed the case that, as Charles Kingsley states, 'Similar anchorites might have been seen in Egypt 500 years before the time of St Antony, immured in cells in the temples of Isis or Serapis',[1] for, if there were any such folk in pre-Christian Egypt, it is no surprise that Egypt appears to be where Christian monachism first emerged. As we already noted, all the known earliest Christian solitaries carefully sought out others who had embraced the solitary life before them, in order to receive instruction from them. The question arises: from whom did *they* receive instruction in how to lead the solitary life? Who taught the person who trained Pachomius' Palaemon? Who had taught *him*? And where did *his* teacher acquire the necessary knowledge? Eventually the line has to go back before any Christian opted for the solitary life, to persons serving other gods (or none at all) who were practising the art of living alone. It is not difficult to see how attractive such a way of life would seem to some Christians, given the examples of e.g. Elijah and John the Baptist, and the presence in the Gospels of phrases such as this: 'Very early in the morning, while it was still dark, Jesus got up, left the house and went off to a solitary place, where he prayed' [Mk 1.45] – with all of which they would have been familiar. Baltasar Gracian may have caught the spirit of the earliest Christian solitaries when he re-phrased Aristotle's dictum (above): 'He who can live alone resembles the brute beast in nothing, the sage in much

---

[1] Charles Kingsley, *The Hermits*, London 1869.

and God in everything.' Maybe there were solitary sages in Egypt who were able to point their Christian emulators to godliness.

It should be noted in passing that the known early Christian solitaries were not true solitaries: they did not isolate themselves completely. For those who placed themselves in voluntary confinement there was always some casement through which they could receive the necessities of life and also communicate with their fellow beings. Persons in remote locations must have maintained some similar connection with 'the world'. The true solitary detached him/herself completely from the rest of humanity and contrived to be totally self-sufficient, e.g. the 'grazers' who lived off the land (see Chapter 9). The successful solitary would remain totally unknown, or would only become known at the very end of his/her life when somebody stumbled across the dying person only to bury the corpse [e.g. 132 C / 20.12]. One could say the earliest Christian solitaries of whom we know were *failed* solitaries for, as their fame spread, the numbers of visitors increased and, of those, a growing number installed themselves willy-nilly not too far away from where the solitary lay. In due course, a degree of communality gradually developed among those disciples.

Antony the Great

Assuming that Jerome's *Life of Paul of Thebes* is indeed largely fictitious, the earliest Christian monk known to us by name is Antony 'the Great', *c.* 250–356. Around the year 270 Antony divested himself of the property he had inherited from his parents, then (having made provision for his sister) began to lead a solitary existence of spiritual discipline. Without going far from his former home, he lived alone, but in consultation with persons living in the area who were already experienced in the solitary way of life. Fifteen years later he took the step which more than any other earned him the (incorrect) title of being the first Christian monk. He left the inhabited world and went into the desert, traditionally into the Nitrian Desert, about 95 kilometres south-west of Alexandria. He stayed there for thirteen years, suffering fearful temptations. His hermitage could not have been very far into the desert and must not have been totally isolated, for friends from a local village are said to have come and rescued him when he became seriously ill. But Antony was not giving up; he sought out an abandoned Roman fort at Pispir (Der-el-Memun, to the east of Arsinoe). There he walled himself in and led a strictly enclosed life for some twenty years, afflicted by even worse temptations and visions than before. There was a small opening in the wall through which he received what meagre supplies he required and by means of which he communicated with those who came to him, but nobody was allowed to enter his cell.

Eventually, presumably *c.* 303, some people broke down the door and brought Antony out; to their amazement, they found him fit and well in spite of his privations. He now became increasingly famous and much sought after. In spite of himself, a community of disciples accumulated around the fort (to which he had returned). Determined to find greater solitude, he retreated into the Eastern Desert, probably *c.* 313. He travelled for three days, then came to a small oasis where there was a spring of water and some palm trees. He chose to settle there, but his flight was in vain: visitors and would-be disciples soon found him again and there too a community developed in association with his retreat. Antony came out a number of times, to visit other communities and even to intervene against heresy in Alexandria, but he always returned to his retreat at 'the Inner Mountain' and there he died in 356.

The 'Mountain' of Nitria

Meanwhile other developments were taking place elsewhere. We should note that the Coptic word *tô-ou* that we translate *mount[ain]* also means a community or settlement. Hence that is the way it should be understood when we speak (e.g.) of the Mount of Pispir or of 'the Inner Mountain'; now we come to 'the Mount of Nitria'. This name caused some confusion in the past, for the edge of the Western Desert (where it was supposed to be located) is relatively flat. However, the location of Nitria has now been definitely identified with that of the modern village of Al Barnuji, formerly known as Pernoud.

Describing the origins of Nitria, Palladius tells [*HL* 8; see also *HME* 22] how a certain Amoun [Ammonas] was obliged to marry by an uncle. For eighteen years bride and groom lived together but apart, he 'spending all day in the garden and in the balsam patch, for he was a balsam-grower. In the evening he would come in, offer prayers and eat with her. Then again, after offering the night-time prayer, out he would go' [*HL* 8.3]. Eventually the wife suggested they separate so he could embrace the solitary life. In around 325, 'Out he went and came to the inner part of the Mountain of Nitria (for at that time there were not yet any monasteries there) and he built himself a cell consisting of two domed chambers … He used to see his blessed partner twice a year' [*HL* 8.5]. For twenty-two years they lived like that, then Amoun died. It is hard to say exactly when, but it was prior to the death of Antony in 356, for Antony had a vision of Amoun being taken up [*VA* 60.1–4]. If Amoun hoped to be alone when he withdrew to Nitria, he must have been disappointed, for he too was assailed by an ever-increasing number of visitors and by persons wishing to emulate his way of life, living in proximity to him. More came after his death, and the loose collection of solitary monks established there began to evolve into an organised community with bankers, merchants and church services. By the end of the fourth century Nitria was famous, frequently visited by people from Alexandria and the Delta region. Consquently, some of the monks began focusing their attention on the visitors' needs rather than on saving their own souls.

Kellia

Already before Amoun died, the need for more space for some monks and possibly the increasing secularisation of others led to an inevitable reaction. Amoun may have appealed to Antony for advice, for there are several indications that the two were acquainted with each other, including this rather touching question and its equally enigmatic answer:

> Abba Amoun of Nitria visited Abba Antony and said to him: 'I observe that I labour harder than you do, so why is your name held in higher honour among folk than mine?' Abba Antony said to him: 'It is because in my case I love God more than you do.' [Amoun of Nitria 1 / 17.3]

This apparent *contre-temps* notwithstanding, the two were to have another meeting that was to have far-reaching consequences:

> Abba Antony once visited Abba Amoun at the Mountain of Nitria and, when they had met with each other, Abba Amoun said to him: 'Since, thanks to your prayers, the brothers have become numerous and some of them want to build cells far away so they may live in *hesychia*, how far from here do you bid the cells to be built?' 'Let us eat the ninth-hour meal,' he said, 'then let us set out and walk through the desert in search of the place.' When they had travelled the desert until the sun was about to set, Abba Antony said to him: 'Let us offer a prayer and set up a cross here so that they who want to build might build here. Thus, when the [brothers] over there visit those here, setting out after taking their collation at the ninth hour, they might in that way make their visits – and those going the other way likewise. In this way they can remain undistracted in their visits to each other.' The distance is 12 miles. [Antony 34]

That is how the soon to be celebrated monastic settlement known as Kellia ('The Cells') allegedly came into being. Located almost 18 kilometres into the desert to the south of Nitria, it was not exactly easily accessible. But its establishment, whenever and however that took place, certainly attests to the success of Amoun's leadership at Nitria. He had attracted a significant body of men desirous of the solitude for which he had trained them but which Nitria could no longer provide. There is good reason to suspect that here also was a cultural split: that many of those who moved to Kellia were not simple Coptic folk like the majority of monks, but sophisticated Hellenised men from the Delta and beyond, well acquainted with Hellenistic philosophy.

Outstanding among these was Macarius of Alexandria. Born at the end of the third century like his more famous namesake, Macarius the Egyptian, this Macarius became known as 'the city-dweller' because he retained something of his urban culture. 'He sold dried fruit in his youth and probably retained throughout his life the characteristics still to be observed in the young merchants who people the streets of Cairo today: their politeness, dynamism and care-free nature, but also their audacity even their calculating,' wrote Dom Lucien. Converted and baptised *c.* 330 Macarius became a monk at Nitria. He subsequently served as the priest at Kellia and there he died in 393/394, at almost one hundred years old. [For his alleged visit to Pachomius, see Chapter 14; *APanon* 488–494 for anecdotes.]

Even better known, and by no means the only foreigner who resided at Kellia, was Evagrius Ponticus, 'the philosopher of the desert' (345–399), later stigmatised (as were other monks of Kellia) for being too much under the influence of Origen, hence their antipathy to anthropomorphism. (See Chapter 13.) The visitor from the Mount of Olives in 394–395 was almost certainly speaking of the men at Kellia when he wrote this description of what was probably tending to become the usual disposition of a monastic settlement:

> They inhabit a desolate place and the cells are at such a distance that nobody can be recognised by another or be seen with ease; neither can one's voice be heard but they live in profound *hesychia*, each one in solitary confinement. Only on Saturday and Sunday did they congregate in the churches and encounter each other. [*HME* 20.7]

There were probably about five hundred monks living at Kellia by the end of the fourth century, rising to thousands in the next two centuries, then steadily declining until the site was abandoned in the ninth century and lost. It was, however, rediscovered by Antoine Guillaumont in 1964 and has since been partially excavated, so far revealing 1,500 structures of various kinds, mostly cells for one, two or more persons and other structures suggestive of a society of some complexity. At some point Kellia itself put out a satellite settlement at Phermê, 11 kilometres to the south east. That site has been excavated to a certain extent, revealing about 115 cells. More recently a team using the geophysical method of magnetic prospection has made further discoveries there.

Scêtê

Even further into the desert, south of Kellia, lies Wadi al Natrun, where Scêtê, the most renowned site of monastic settlements in Egypt, is located. Wadi al Natrun is a chain of eight saline lakes lying north-west to south-east, about 34 kilometres in length with about 240 square kilometres of its surface lying below sea level. Nitron salt was harvested there from dried-up lake beds to be used in mummification and in the manufacture of Egyptian faience, and later by the Romans as a flux for glass-making. There are springs of fresh water in the Wadi that feed vast mosquito-infested marshes [Macarius the Egyptian 21], with abundant growth of reeds and bushes along the shores. The reeds (which were thick enough to hide in, Moses 8 / 8.13) provided monks with the raw materials for some of their handiwork, but the sound of the wind in them was disturbing for some fathers [Arsenius 25 / 2.8].

Of Scêtê (possibly from Coptic ϢⲒϨⲦ, *Šihēt*, 'Measure of the Hearts'), the writer of *HME* has this to say, in spite of the fact that he never went there:

> Scêtê is a desolate place, at a distance from Nitria of a night-and-a-day [journey] into the desert and there is great danger for those who go there. For if you make a small error you are in danger of wandering off into the desert. All the men there are advanced; nobody who is not can remain in that place for it is savage, lacking in all the necessities of life. [*HME* 23.1]

John Cassian (who *did* go there) wrote: 'In the Desert of Scêtê is the habitation of the most experienced among the fathers of the monks; it is a place of complete perfection' [*Conf* 1.1].

The pioneer-monk at Scêtê was Macarius the Egyptian [*c.* 300–391], of whom Palladius gives a brief biography and some anecdotes [*HL* 17]. In his youth he was a modest camel-driver, transporting nitre across the desert, and that may be how he became acquainted with the Wadi el Natrun. ('Abba, when you were a camel-driver and you used to steal nitre to sell it, did the guards not beat you?') [Macarius the Egyptian 31]. Then around 330, for unexplained reasons, he retired to a cell near a village on the Delta. He transferred himself to another village but had to flee from it on account of false accusations, and that was when he took up residence at Scêtê. Already as a young man he was held in high esteem and attracted disciples. Between 330 and 340 he made at least one visit to Antony, on whose advice he was ordained priest. Thus he was able to function as both priest and leader of a community that appears to have flourished vigorously for a time.

It is a little difficult to gain a clear idea of what Scêtê was like. Obviously, it was very remote, probably as far into the desert as anybody had gone, for 'Macarius used to say to the brothers at Scêtê when he was dismissing the congregation: "Flee, brothers!" One of the elders said to him: "Where can we flee to that is more remote than this desert?"' [Macarius the Egyptian 16 / 4.30]. Yet there must have been something of a village in the vicinity:

> Some brothers once visited Abba Macarius at Scêtê and they found nothing in his cell but some stale water. They said to him: 'Come up to the village Abba and we will refresh you.' The elder said to them: 'You know the bakery of so-and-so in the village, brothers?' 'Yes,' they said, and the elder said to them: 'I know it too. Do you know the property of so-and-so, there where the river flows?' 'Yes,' they said to him and the elder said to them: 'I know it too. So when I want [to go there] I will not need you: I will go up myself.' [Macarius the Egyptian 30]

Apart from a period of exile by the Arians in 373–375, Macarius spent the rest of his life at Scêtê; his reputation grew even more on his return from exile. People flocked to him, for healings, prophecies and sayings; consequently, the community grew. He was an honoured guest at Nitria at least once before he died at Scêtê, *c.* 390 [Macarius the Egyptian 2 / 20.4]. To what extent Antony influenced Macarius is not at all clear. This is the full description of their only known meeting, a passage to which we alluded in Chapter 1:

> Abba Macarius the Great visited Abba Antony at the mountain. When he knocked at the door [Antony] came out to him and said to him: 'Who are you?' 'I am Macarius,' he said, whereupon [Antony] closed the door, went in and left him. But when he saw his patience he opened up to him and, taking delight in him, said: 'I have been wanting to see you for a long time for I have heard tell of you.' He received him as his guest and gave him refreshment, for he was extremely exhausted. When evening fell, Abba Antony steeped some palm-fronds for himself; Abba Macarius said to him: 'Let me steep some for myself too,' and [Antony] said: 'Steep [some].' He made a great bundle and steeped it. From evening on they sat braiding [fronds], speaking about salvation of souls. The cord went out of the window down

into the cave. When the blessed Antony came in at dawn and saw the extent of the cord of Abba Macarius he said: 'Great power is coming out of these hands.' [Macarius the Egyptian 4 / 7.14; presumably Macarius 26 describes the same visit]

There is mention elsewhere of brothers from Scêtê visiting Antony [Antony 18 / 4.1], but he does not appear to have had any relationship with Macarius of Scêtê like that he had with Amoun of Nitria. It does appear that Scêtê, to a large extent, developed independently into the most significant of the Egyptian monastic communities, rather than under Antony's influence.

The 'Four Churches' of Scêtê

Monastery of Baramûs

To speak of Scêtê as a community conceals the fact that there appear to have been four separate communities there, once referred to as 'churches' [Isaac of Kellia 5 / 10.44], once as 'lavras' [*PS* 113]. There are four lavras at Scêtê to this day, but only one of the four, Deir Abu Makar (Abba Macarius' Monastery), is still a functioning monastery. Their location is mentioned in this apothegm: 'There is a marsh beside Scêtê, there where the churches were built and where the sources of water are located' [Carion 2].

The names of the four 'churches' at Scêtê are well known, but their origins are wreathed in the mists of legend, none more colourful than the one known as Baramûs. Macarius is alleged to have said:

> Once when I was living at Scêtê two young strangers came down there. One of them had a beard, the other was beginning to have a beard. They came to me saying: 'Where is Abba Macarius' cell?' and I said to them: 'Why do you want him?' 'We heard about him and about Scêtê,' they said, 'and we have come to see him.' 'I am he,' I said to them and they prostrated themselves, saying: 'We want to stay here.' But, seeing they were delicate and as though from affluent [circumstances], I told them: 'You cannot live here.' The older one said: 'If we cannot live here we will go somewhere else.' I said to myself: 'Why am I sending them off and offending them? The toil will make them run away of their own accord.' I said to them: 'Come, make yourselves a cell if you can.' 'Show us a place and we will make it,' they said. The elder gave them an axe and a basket full of bread and salt. The elder showed them some hard rock, saying: 'Get some stones here and bring yourselves wood from the marsh; set up a roof and live here,' for I thought (he said) they were going to run away because of the toil. But they asked me: 'What work do they do here?' 'Rope-making,' I told them.

Taking some palm-fronds from the marsh, I showed them the elements of rope-making and how one has to sew [it]. 'Make some baskets; deliver them to the guardians and they will bring you loaves,' I told them; and so I went my way. But for their part, they patiently performed everything I had said to them and for three years they did not visit me. I went on doing battle with my *logismoi*, saying: 'What on earth is their activity that they have not come to enquire of me about a *logismos*?' There are those from far away who come to me but these who are near have not come, nor were they going anywhere else – other than to church in silence to receive the sacrament. For a week, I fasted and prayed to God to show me their activity. After a week, I got up and went to them to see how they were living. When I knocked they opened [the gate] and greeted me – in silence. I offered a prayer and sat down. The older one gave a sign to the younger one to go out, then he sat there, braiding rope, not saying a word. At the ninth hour, he knocked; the younger one came and prepared a little gruel, setting a table at the older one's prompting. He placed three dried loaves on it, then stood in silence. 'Get up, let us eat,' I said; we got up and ate. He brought the bottle and we drank. When evening fell, they said to me: 'Are you going?' 'No,' I said; 'I am sleeping here.' [... In the course of the night the holiness of the young men was revealed to him. Next morning:] 'As I was leaving I said: 'Pray for me,' but they prostrated themselves in silence; I discovered that the older one was perfect while the enemy was still in combat with the younger one. A few days later the older brother died: the younger one the third day after. When some of the fathers visited Abba Macarius, he would bring them to their cell saying: 'Come and see the martyrs' shrine of the young strangers.' [Macarius the Egyptian 33 / 20.3]

The 'young strangers' were eventually identified (almost certainly incorrectly) as Maximus and Domitius, sons of Emperor Valentinian I (364–375), whence the name of the shrine, *Pa-Romoes* in Coptic ('Monastery of the Romans'), hence Baramûs. What this probably means is that the burial place [*martyrion*] of the strangers was (or became) the place where the weekly synaxis of Macarius' entourage took place, hence the focal point of that community.

Monasteries of Abba Macarius, John Colobos and Bishôi

The foundation of the next monastery, the one that actually bears Macarius' name and is still functioning, came about in much the same way that Antony's 'Inner Mountain' was his retreat from Pispir. Possibly as a consequence of the establishment of the shrine of the Strangers, Macarius' original settlement became increasingly popular. So, in quest of greater solitude and under supernatural guidance, that elder established a grotto for himself on top of a rock (presumably an eminence) to the south of the marsh. Even there he was assailed by those who would imitate his way of life and remain near him. Very little else is known, except that a church was eventually built below the eminence for the convenience of an ageing community, presumably well established by then.

The third community at Scêtê bears the name of a well-attested father, John Colobos, 'the Little' or 'the Dwarf', a person of many endearing qualities. 'Who is John who has the whole of Scêtê hanging on his little finger on account of his humility?' one father asked [John Colobos 36]. We learn that John had consideration for others' feelings:

> Once when Abba John was going up from Scêtê with other brothers their guide lost his way and it was night. The brothers said to Abba John: 'What shall we do, abba, for the brother has lost the way; maybe we will wander off and die?' The elder said to them: 'If we tell him he will be grieved and ashamed. But look here: I will pretend to be sick and will say: "I cannot travel [further] so I am staying here until dawn,"' and so he did. The rest of them said: 'Neither are we going on; we are staying with you.' They stayed [there] until dawn and did not offend the brother. [John Colobos 17 / 17.10; cf. Sisoes 30]

As a very young man, c. 357, John came to Scêtê where for twelve years he patiently served a sick and testy elder named Ammoes [Ammoes 3 / 4.11], an elder who eventually acknowledged the servant as his spiritual father [John the Theban / 16.5]. John Colobos is best known for his obedience. The most famous story about his obedience is that Pambo gave him a piece of dry wood with orders to plant and water it. John obeyed and went on watering it twice a day even though the water was about 12 Roman miles (almost 18 kilometres) from where they lived. After three years, the piece of wood sprouted and grew into a fruitful tree. Pambo took some of this tree's fruits and went around to all the elders, saying: 'Take, eat from the fruit of obedience' [John Colobos 1 / 14.4; see also Ares / 14.3].[2] (A 'Tree of Obedience' is still shown to visitors.) Around 380–385, John went into seclusion in a grotto close by the Tree of Obedience [John Colobos 1 / 14.4]. People flocked to him and thus a third community came into existence, the one that bears his name. It should be noted in passing that a journey of 12 miles for water was not unknown, but had its reward:

> An elder was living in the desert twelve miles distant from water. Once when he was coming to fill [his water-pot] his spirit failed him and he said: 'what

---

[2] A much longer version of this tale in which the stick does *not* take root is told by John Cassian of Abba John of Lycopolis [*Inst* 4.24].

is the need of this labour? I am coming to live near to the water.' As he said this, he turned around and saw somebody following him, counting his footsteps. 'Who are you?' he asked him. 'I am an angel of the Lord,' he said; 'I was sent to count your footsteps and to give you the reward.' The elder was much encouraged and more eager on hearing this; he moved five miles farther in[to the desert]. [199 / 7.38]

The founder of the fourth community was Bishôi (Pshoi,) probably not to be confused with the Greek name Paësius as it sometimes is. Bishôi was Egyptian, the youngest of seven sons. He was sent to Scêtê in obedience to a revelation his mother received. There he became the disciple of Amoi (called Pambo in the Greek *Life*) and the spiritual brother of John Colobos. When Amoi died, Bishôi joined John at the Tree of Obedience, where they studied the Scriptures together, especially Jeremiah. In due course the friends agreed to part, whereupon Bishôi went to live alone in a cave two miles further north. Word of his sanctity and of his miracles attracted followers who gradually coalesced into a community, even though Bishôi appears to have spent extended periods of time at remote locations. Today the remains of the Monastery of Bishôi are located approximately two miles north of the ruins of the Monastery of John Colobos.

We have now described what appears from the apothegms to have been the epicentre of early monachism, the Desert of Nitria. Within the apothegms there are mentions of monastic activity further afield: on the coast at various mile-posts west of Alexandria and also at points to the east, to say nothing of the two locations established by Antony at Pispir and the 'Inner Mountain'. But it is well to bear in mind that, meanwhile, something on a much larger scale was developing further up the Nile (see Chapter 14). Significantly more important (for it had far-reaching long-term effects) was the diffusion of 'Nitrian' monachism. Exported mainly by refugee monks, this was able to establish itself in Palestine, Syria and still further afield. The literature some of those settlements bequeathed to posterity (on which this study is based) consists largely of memories of the homeland and how it used to be in the old days; hence, it has to be treated with great caution.

CHAPTER 3

Becoming a Monk

If a man do good, he will moor his boat in a good port. [E128]

Finding a Mentor

A person wishing to embrace the solitary life in the early days might start out by simply removing him/herself to some remote location, but a much wiser path would be to seek out somebody who had already learned something of how to live the lonely life. In the same way that Pachomius sought out Paësius to guide him (and apparently stayed with him for seven years), Antony also looked for guidance: 'There was an elder in the village close by at that time who had practised the spiritual discipline of a solitary life from his youth up. Antony strove to be like him when he saw him . . . And if he heard about somebody else who was practising seriously, he would go and search him out' [*VA* 3.3–4]. Cases are recorded of persons trying to 'go it alone', e.g.:

> There was a brother who withdrew [from the world,] took the habit and immediately went into seclusion, saying: 'I am an anchorite.' When the elders heard of this they came and made him come out, obliging him to do the round of the brothers' cells, apologising and saying: 'Forgive me, for I am not an anchorite but a beginner.' [243 / 10.172]

Presumably it was to such cases that this apothegm referred: 'If you see a youngster rising up to heaven of his own volition, seize his foot and pull him back from there; it is to his advantage' [III, 244 / 10.173]. The solitary life had to be learned from one who had already mastered the art of living alone; and since some persons may always have aspired to live alone, it seems unlikely that the first Christians who sought to do so were destitute of persons who could point them the way.

How was a person who wished to embrace the solitary life to find one who was already engaged in it? As we said, those who had been wholly successful in the quest for solitude would be totally unknown, while those who were known probably regretted the degree to which they had become known, for that was the extent to which they were failing to realise their ideal of total isolation. Abba Alonios, one of Poemen's associates, said: 'Unless a person say in his heart: "I alone and God are in the world" he will not experience repose' [Alonios 1 / 11.13]. And when another elder (name unknown) was asked what sort of person a monk should be, he replied somewhat enigmatically: 'In my opinion, one on one'[1] [89 / 21.4]. Both fathers meant that there was no room for any third person. So, predictably, a true monk would be unreceptive to any proposal of human company and very reluctant to share his alone-ness with anyone. A further consideration is voiced by Paësius when Pachomius approaches him with a request to learn from him: he has seen others come with a similar request. Having disturbed his solitude, they had then taken off again. Hence, if a would-be monk were able to find the place where a desert elder was in retreat, he might not be able to make contact with him. Apart from the fact that the elder might be out visiting, he would be quite capable of ignoring the visitor by keeping his door firmly bolted for days on end.

This would not discourage a truly determined aspirant; eventually even the most austere father would open up to him and hear his request: 'Abba, let me stay with you.' He would probably not reply immediately, for an important concomitant of the solitary life was silence. (See Chapter 5.) Not that the true monk would *never* speak (other than when a special order were given to him), but he would never utter one more word than was absolutely necessary. When he finally did speak, it would be to offer a prayer with the visitor.

Then the monk would invite the visitor to sit down on the rush mat that was both sofa and bed – and proceed to do his best to discourage that person. He would describe the rigours and privations of the solitary life in some detail. And if it became clear that the neophyte could not be discouraged by argument, the elder would put him to a severe test by giving him a taste of those privations. This would be a double test: of the candidate's ability to *endure*, and of his readiness to *obey*. For one of the most important qualities in a monk was total and unquestioning obedience to his abba, his spiritual father, obedience which both *requires* and *generates* the crowning virtue of humility. 'Abba Moses said to a brother: "Let us acquire obedience which begets humility and brings endurance and long-suffering and

---

[1] ... *monos pros monon*, which Jean-Claude Guy translated: 'seul en face du seul', 'the alone confronting the Alone'.

grief-for-sin and brotherly love and charity, for these are our weapons of war" ' [14.6]. Sometimes an aspirant's obedience was sorely tried:

> One elder had his slave as his disciple and, wishing to dominate him, he trained him to be perfectly obedient, so that the elder could say to him: 'Go, light a good fire in the oven; take the book which is read at the *synaxis* and throw it into the oven.' He went and did so without question; and when the book was thrown [in] the oven was extinguished, so we might know that obedience is good; for [obedience] is a ladder to the Kingdom of Heaven. [53]

The following is a remarkably similar but more alarming tale:

> Abba Elijah of Scete recounted: 'When I fled to Scêtê I importuned Abba Hierax: 'Allow me to be your son so I may be your disciple and sit at your feet.' To test me he said to me: 'Will you obey me and do everything I tell you?' 'Yes, I will,' I said. 'Absolutely.' He lit a fire and, to put me to the test, said to me: 'If you want me to have you at my side and if you will obey me, stick your hand in this fire.' So I put my hand in the fire. I left it there until it was black and, if he had not taken my hand and lifted it off, I would no longer have it.' It was us to whom he told the miracle of his hand. [c24]

At his abba's command, one monk even threw his own son into an oven full of fire, 'but the furnace became immediately like the morning dew' [14. 28 / 295].

The Monastic Habit

Once an elder was convinced that the aspirant was a worthy candidate, he would give him the habit [*schema*]. 'There was a great elder who had the second-sight; he made this affirmation: "The force [*dynamis*] I beheld standing by at a baptism, that same force I also beheld at the clothing of the monk, when he received the habit" ' [365 / 18.36]. Antony is alleged to have attested to the *dynamis* of the monastic habit:

> While the brothers were sitting around him, Abba Antony said, 'Let us fight. Truly, the very habit of the monk is worthy of being hated in the presence of the demons. One time I wanted to test them concerning this matter: I brought a short garment, dalmatic, and scapular and hood. I threw them on a dummy; I dressed it; I set it up; I saw the demons standing around it in the distance. They were shooting arrows at it. I said to them, "You, you evil spirits – what is this you are doing to it? It is not a person! It is a dummy!" They said to me, "We know that. We are not shooting arrows at *it*. No, we are shooting at the clothing it is wearing and the monastic habit." I said to them, "What evils are these you are doing to it?" They said to me, "These

are the implements of war of those who afflict us and beat us all the time. It is this clothing that gives us all this trouble!" When I heard what they were saying, I gave glory to God who saves those who have faith in him, that he will rescue them from the evil spirits of the Devil, these who fight against the saints day and night as God brings their counsels to nothing.' [C61]

The nature of the clothes themselves was of small account: 'Abba Isaac said that Abba Pambo used to say: "The monk ought to wear the sort of clothing that, if he threw it out of the cell, for three days nobody would take it"' [Isaac of the Cells 12 / 6.11]. Isaac also said: 'Our fathers and Abba Pambo wore old, patched up clothes made of palm-fibre' [Isaac of the Cells 7 / 6.10], while 'Four [monks] from Scêtê dressed in skins once came visiting Pambo the Great' [Pambo 3 / 14.14].

The process of clothing an aspirant was fairly simple; this is recorded of Abba Patermuthius:

> One young man came to him wanting to be a disciple. Straightaway he put a *leviton* on him and a cowl on his head, then began leading him towards spiritual discipline when he had placed a sheepskin on his shoulders and girdled his loins with a belt. [*HME* 10.9]

Although the *leviton* is mentioned first, this was not normal garb unlike the rest of the items. It was a long-sleeved ankle-length garment, usually white, not unlike the *thawb* that Arabs wear. It was called *leviton* because it was the dress of the Levites, reserved for use in worship. A monk would carefully preserve the *leviton* in which he was clothed for use at his burial. Thus Abba James at Kellia:

> He secluded himself in *hesychia* at a cell outside the lavra, wearing his grave clothes as though he were about to die. It is the custom of the Egyptian fathers to keep the *leviton* in which they received the sacred habit and the cowl until they die and then to be buried in them. They only put them on for Holy Communion on Sunday then take them off right away. [Phocas 1]

Nevertheless this legend seems to suggest one father travelled with his *leviton*:

> One of the fathers went off to the city to sell his handwork. He was moved to compassion at the sight of a naked pauper and gave him his own *leviton*. But the pauper went and sold it. The elder was distressed when he learnt what he had done and regretted that he had given him the garment. But that night Christ appeared to the elder in a dream wearing the *leviton* and said to him: 'Do not be distressed for see: I am wearing what you gave me.' [358]

It is not so much the *leviton* as the sheepskin [*mêlôtê*] which is mentioned as a monk's characteristic possession. Sometimes it seems to signify a monk's entire (meagre) possessions, e.g. 'When you see children, take your sheepskins and get away' [Macarius the Egyptian 5 / 18.16], and 'for my part I [Isidore the priest] am packing up my sheepskin and going off to where there is adversity and there I will find repose' [Poemen 44 / 7.20]. *Mêlôtê* is a supercharged word, for this is the *mantle* which Elijah cast upon Elisha [1/3 Kgs 19.19] and with which each in turn divided the waters of the Jordan [2/4 Kgs 2.8, 13–14]. Abba Paul may have been thinking of that when, faced with an intransigent demon, 'he took his sheepskin and struck him on the back, saying: "Abba Antony has said: 'Get out'"' [HL 22.11].

In Upper Egypt (see Chapter 14) monks appear to have worn sheepskins all the time:

> In the Thebaid we saw another man whose name was Ammôn, the father of three thousand monks called Tabbenesiotes. They had a great way of life; they wore sheepskins and ate with their faces hidden, looking down so no-one could see another. [HME 3.1]

More usually monks are said to put the sheepskin on to go out, like an overcoat [cf. Motios 2]: 'As he was preparing his sheepskin to go out' [Mk 4]; 'When the elder heard of this he took his sheepskin and went out' [Silvanus 8]. Thus a visitor was to be relieved of his sheepskin on arrival somewhere [Bessarion 4 / 12.3, 20.1; John the Coenobite]. Antony certainly travelled in a sheepskin: 'Now (as Cronius related) it fell out that the Great One came next day, late in the evening, wrapped in a sheepskin mantle' [HL 21.8], but the sheepskin was not worn only in the cool of the evening: 'Then out of the great desert there came Piôr just at the sixth hour, in the burning heat, an old man wearing his sheepskin cloak [HL 39.4]. Presumably it afforded some protection from the heat, for one elder 'immediately took up his sheepskin and went out into the desert' [526], while another 'used to get up, take his sheepskin, come out, walk around his cell and go [back] in' [394 / 10.171]. It is not clear whether it is wearing sheepskins or moving around that is being blamed in the following passage: 'Said Abba Sisoes to him: "If the brothers of those times had met us, the elders, wearing sheepskins in our own time and moving here and there, they would have mocked us, saying: 'These people are possessed by demons'"' [E137].

The sheepskin could also serve as a kind of receptacle. Speaking of 'the brother who has been my companion from my youth until today', Palladius says: 'I am aware of him having three times received the bread he needed from an angel. One day when he was in the remotest desert and did not even have a crumb, he found three warm loaves in his sheepskin'

[*HL* 71.3] and it is said of the brothers at Nitria: 'each would fill his sheep-skin or a basket with loaves' [*HME* 20.11]. The *mêlôtê* could serve as a vessel too: 'The elder took my sheepskin and went about a stone's throw away from me. After he had prayed, he brought it to me full of water' [Bessarion 4 / 12.3].

Obedience

Once he was clothed, a monk's real apprenticeship began. Total and unquestioning obedience was of course required. Joseph of Thebes [1 / 1.14] said it was something precious in the sight of the Lord when someone living in submission to a spiritual father renounced all his own desires. Isidore the priest at Scêtê used to say: 'Persons under instruction must love those who are their instructors like fathers and fear them like rulers, neither diminishing fear through love nor obscuring love through fear' [Isidore 5 / 10.42]. The best fathers taught by example. Poemen told one who was training a disciple: 'If you want to be beneficial to him, show him virtue by deed. He who pays attention to the word remains slow; but if you show him by deed, that stays with him' [G70].

> Abba Isaac said: 'As a young man I was staying with Abba Cronios and he never told me to do a task even though he was aged and tremulous. Of his own accord he would get up and offer the water bottle to me and likewise to all. After that I stayed with Abba Theodore of Phermê and neither did he ever tell me to do anything. He would lay the table himself and then say: "Brother, come and eat if you like." I would say to him: "Abba, I came to you to reap some benefit; why do you never tell me to do anything?" but the elder kept completely quiet. I went and told this to the elders. The elders came to him and said to him: "Abba, the brother came to your holiness to reap some benefit; why do you never tell him to do anything?" The elder said to them: "Am I the superior of a coenobion to order him around? For the time being I don't tell him [to do] anything. He will do what he sees me doing if he wants to." So from then on I began anticipating, doing whatever the elder was about to do. For his part, if he was doing anything, he used to do it in silence; this taught me to act in silence.' [Isaac of Kellia 2]

Yet some fathers could make really bizarre demands: witness the story of John Colobos and 'the tree of obedience' (see Chapter 2). It could be even worse than that:

> They used to say of Abba Silvanus that once when he was walking around with the elders at Scêtê he wanted to demonstrate the obedience of Mark, his disciple, and why he loved him. Seeing a small boar, he said to him:

'Do you see that little antelope, my son?' 'Yes, abba,' he said. 'And its horns, how plausible they are?' 'Yes, abba,' he said; the elders were astounded at his answer and were edified by his obedience. [Mark 2]

The Importance of the Cell

Where and how the new disciple was housed appear to have varied. It is certain that he would be allocated his own living space, maybe a separate room in his abba's cell, maybe a shack close by or one some considerable distance away. But wherever it was located and no matter what its nature, this was his cell and it was of greatest importance to the monk, presumably as the Dominical command required: 'When you pray, go into your room, close the door and pray to your Father, who is unseen. Then your Father, who sees what is done in secret, will reward you' [Mt 6.6].

Abba Antony emphasised the importance of the cell with a memorable simile:

> Just as fish die if they are on dry land for some time, so do monks who loiter outside their cells or waste time with worldlings release themselves from the tension of *hesychia*. So we should hasten back to the cell (like the fish to the sea) lest while loitering outside we forget to keep a watch on the inner [self].[2] [Antony 10 / 2.1]

Another saying pushes the same image even further: 'Just as a fish cannot live without water, so neither can a monk live wholly and exist for God without continual prayer, fasts and vigils' [G23].

When Abba Isaiah asked Abba Macarius what was the meaning of the familiar injunction to flee from men, the elder told him: 'It is to remain in your cell and to weep for your sins' [Macarius the Egyptian 27], because a monk's cell is his natural place of refuge. John Colobos put it very succinctly:

> I am like somebody sitting beneath a large tree who sees wild beasts and serpents coming at him. When he cannot withstand them, he runs up into the tree and is saved. So it is with me: I stay in my cell and I see the evil *logismoi* above me. And when I do not have the strength [to oppose] them, I flee to God in prayer and I am saved from the enemy. [John Colobos 12 / 11.40]

---

[2] Cf. Chaucer's Monk: 'He yaf nat of that text a pulled hen, / That seith that hunters beth nat hooly men, / Ne that a monk, whan he is recchelees, / Is likned til a fissh that is waterlees, / This is to seyn, a monk out of his cloystre' [*Canterbury Tales*, GP 178–182].

There were others who spoke of the cell in yet more lofty terms, e.g. those elders who said: 'When Moses entered into the cloud he was speaking with God: when he came out of the cloud, with folk. So it is with the monk: when he is in his cell, he is speaking with God, but when he comes out of his cell he is among demons' [L22].

There were, however, some dangerous *logismoi* that would tempt a monk to abandon his cell [394 / 10.171], the most powerful ones being *porneia* [Moses 1, 18.17] and *accidie* [12.21] (see Chapter 4 for these terms). But these could be dealt with, e.g.: 'If, while staying in his cell, a monk recall his sins, the Lord is his helper in all things and he will not suffer *accidie*' [L29]. There was this aassurance:

> A brother asked an elder: 'My *logismoi* are roaming around and I am afflicted,' but he said to him: 'Stay in your cell and they will come back to you. Just as when an ass is tethered, her colt runs hither and thither but, no matter where it goes, it comes back to its mother, so too do the *logismoi* of one who waits patiently upon God in his own cell return to him again, even though they might roam around a little.' [198 / 7.37]

There were other rewards for the one who stayed within. An unnamed elder said: 'If a person remain in his cell under the discipline of silence [*siôpê*], dedicating himself wholeheartedly to prayer and work, he can be saved in this age' [464 / 2.34 end]. Abba Sisoes said: 'Remain in your cell with vigilance and commit yourself to God with many tears and you will experience repose' [11.66]. Another elder said: 'Remaining in your cell, keep God in mind all the time and the fear of God will encircle you. Cast everything that is sinful and all evil out of your soul in order to find repose' [3.46].

'How should one remain in his cell?' a brother asked Abba Poemen. The elder replied:

> The visible components of staying in one's cell are: doing manual work, eating once a day, silence and meditation; but secretly to make progress in one's cell is to tolerate laying the blame on oneself in every place where you go and not to be neglectful of the times for *synaxeis* or for secret [prayers]. If a slack-time occur in manual work, go into the *synaxis* and discharge it with an untroubled mind. Finally, keep good company too and eschew bad company. [Poemen 168 / 10.93]

The prescription of Evagrius of Pontus is less humane, but then there is little indication that it was heeded, at least in the early days:

> While staying in the cell, collect your mind; remember the day of death; behold the subsequent decomposition of the body; consider the misfortune;

accept the pain; condemn the vanity of the world; be attentive to the reason-
ableness and zeal [of your spiritual discipline?] that you might be able ever
to remain in the same intended *hesychia* without weakening. Keep in mind
too the state of things in Hades and think what it is like for the souls who
are therein: in what most bitter silence, amidst what most horrid groaning,
in how great fear and agony, in what apprehension as they anticipate the
unrelenting torment or the eternal and internal weeping. But remember
too the day of resurrection and of [our] appearing before God.' [Evagrius
1 / 3.2]

The beneficial effects of staying in the cell are frequently affirmed.
Arsenius 'was aware that remaining patiently in one's cell is what brings a
monk into line' [Arsenius 11 / 7.34 and 195, anon.]. Abba Moses at Scêtê
told a brother that remaining in his cell would teach him everything
[Moses 6 / 2.19], while another elder said that the cell furnishes the monk
with a plethora of good things [116 / 21.35]. 'Stay in your cell and God will
give you relief,' a distressed brother was told [117], and Poemen was of the
opinion that one acquired the fear of God from remaining [in one's cell]
[Poemen 174].

'What am I to do, father,' a brother asked an elder, 'for I am accomplishing
nothing that becomes a monk? I am in disarray, eating, drinking and
sleeping, beset by disgraceful *logismoi* and in deep distress, flitting from
one task to another and from *logismoi* to *logismoi*.' The elder said: 'Stay in
your cell and do what you can do without getting upset. In my opinion, the
little that you accomplish here and now is comparable to the great deeds
which Abba Antony accomplished at the [Inner] Mountain. I believe that,
remaining in [your] cell in the name of God and keeping a watch on your
own conscience, you are yourself in the same situation as Abba Antony.'
[202 / 7.41]

Such a brother needed to hear that father who said: 'Let us make a diligent
effort to work a little at a time and we are being saved' [387 / 10.169], but
he must indeed remain in his cell. 'Go, stay in your cell; pledge your body
to the wall of the cell and do not come out of there. Let your *logismos* think
what it likes, but do not move the body from the cell,' another brother
was told [205 / 7.45], for 'A monk's cell is the furnace of Babylon in which
the Three Children found the Son of God [Dan 3] and the Pillar of Cloud
from which God spoke with Moses' [Ex 33.9; 206 / 7.46].

Remaining in one's cell was not simple:

A brother said to an elder: 'What am I to do, for my *logismoi* are afflicting
me, saying: "You can neither fast nor labour; at least go visit the sick, for
that is [a labour of] love."' Recognising the sowings of the demons, the

elder said to him: 'Eat, drink and sleep, only do not leave your cell, knowing that remaining patiently in the cell brings a monk up to what he should be.' When he had lasted three days of that he was in *accidie*; he found a few palm-fronds, split them and, again next day, began braiding them. When hunger assailed him, he said: 'Look, here are a few more palm-fronds: I will braid these and then eat.' Whilst he was working the palm-fronds he also said: 'I am going to read a little and then eat.' After he read, he said: 'I shall recite a few psalms and then eat without worrying.' With the help of God, he made progress, little by little, in this way, until he came up to what he should be and, gaining confidence against his *logismoi*, he overcame them. [195 / 7. 34; cf. Arsenius 11]

One needed to be taught *how* to remain in the cell, for 'What is the point in anyone taking up a trade without learning it?' [Poemen 128 / 10.56]. Abba Ammonas said: 'There is a person who spends a hundred years in his cell and does not learn how one should live in a cell' [Poemen 96]. Thus an unnamed elder 'informed [a brother] how one should stay in his cell' [291 / 14.23]. 'Abba John told a brother: "Do not offer a prayer at all; just reside in your cell"' [Paphnutius 5], and when a brother begged a saying of Abba Hierax, he replied: 'Remain in your cell. Eat if you are hungry, drink if you are thirsty; speak ill of nobody and you will be saved' [Hierax 1]. But as John Colobos said, it was not quite so simple as that:

> If a person have something of God in his soul, he can remain in his cell even though he have nothing of this world. And if a person have something of this world and nothing of God he too can remain in his cell having something of this world. But he who has nothing either of God or of this world cannot remain in his cell at all. [John Colobos 54]

'My son, if you want to receive benefit, remain in your cell, paying attention to yourself and to your handwork,' said Abba Serapion, 'for coming out does not procure you such benefit as staying [inside]' [Serapion 4 / 8.12].

The Nature of the Cell

Whenever a cave was available, a cave sufficed; otherwise a monk's dwelling is called a cell. The word can mean any kind of small residence, such as a greengrocer's shack [20.22] or the place where a shepherd and his wife live [20.2]. For all monks, male and female (with the exception of those who obliged themselves to endure the weather),[3] a cell was the single

---

[3] E.g. Macarius the Egyptian 2 / 20.4; Bessarion 12; 565 / 15.116; and yet another Macarius, 'the Younger', who 'stayed outdoors in the desert for three years' [*HL* 15.1].

material object necessary for their profession. As we have said, monks were to remain within their cells, all alone, at all times, other than hours of common worship, when consulting with one's elder or taking part in a conference [18.43]. The cell was a private, single-occupancy living-space, a rare luxury for most people in 'the world'. For the monk his cell was his workshop [20.14] and his smithy [15.118], the place where he spent most of his time and made his most serious efforts to achieve *hesychia* while accomplishing the work of God.

Physically the cell would consist of four walls providing protection against intruders and wild animals, with a roof to ward off the weather and the sun. (Some Syrian ascetics had cells without roofs.) Most cells had a door – Sisoes always kept his cell door shut [Sisoes 24 / 20.06] – that could be locked [Poemen 1 / 11.55; 341 / 16.24]. There would also be a window [Arsenius 2 / 18.2; Macarius the Egyptian, 7.14] with a shutter that could close out the light [230 / 10.152]. Some cells had their own yard [*aulê*, Gelasius 6 / 7.13; 20.11] or a garden, bounded by a wall with a gate in it. The construction would be of whatever materials were available, or it might be a ready-made retreat such as a disused sepulchre [*VA* 8.2], a hole in the ground [*BHG* 1449x] or a cave. To judge by the frequency with which the word *cave* occurs, a cave may have been the preferred retreat of some. And not all caves were single dwellings: one of the fathers named Apollo 'was in the mountain cave with five brothers' [*HME* 8.38]. There was certainly no shortage of caves, for a layer of limestone covers most of what is now Egypt; no stone is more prone to be perforated by caves.

While most monastic cells came to be close (eventually very close) to one another, the earliest monks and a few who came after them preferred isolated cells far removed from others. As already noted, at Nitria the cells were at a considerable distance from one another [*HME* 20.7]. Cells could be remote from water [27 / 19.21]. In rare cases monks had their cell doors walled up, receiving supplies and communicating with folk outside through a window, as Antony did at Pispir [*VA* 12.3–5].

Building the Cell

Ammonius made himself responsible for finding cells for new arrivals [*HME* 20.9], while Dorotheos prepared for their arrival: 'All day long, in the burning heat of the desert, he collected stones along the sea-coast and was always building with them, constructing cells which he would provide for those who were unable to build, completing one cell a year' [*HL* 2.2]. Sometimes cell-building was a cooperative effort:

[Abba Ôr] was so outstanding among many other fathers that, when several monks came to him, he called together those who were already there and made cells for [the new arrivals] in one day. While one brother contributed clay and one brought bricks, another one was drawing water while yet another hewed timber. And when the cells were completed he himself made provision for the needs of those who were arriving. [*HME* 2.11; cf. 361 / 18.31]

Others built their own cells: Pambo [*HL* 10.6], Macarius the Younger [*HL* 15.2] and two newly arrived young strangers – but not without help [Macarius the Egyptian 33 / 20.3]. A monk who dismissed his wife [*sic*] 'came and built himself a cell near the elder [Poemen]' [9.20].

A typical cell would be very sparsely furnished: there might not be anything more than a rush mat on which the monk would sit to do his handiwork, to eat and lie down to sleep. Evelyn White says that in monks' cells, 'There was a table for meals',[4] citing in evidence a phrase [Macarius the Egyptian 33 / 20.3 line 40] that often recurs [Sisoes 15, 8.24; Isaac of the Cells 2; Eucharistos, 20.2; 229 / 10.150; 464 / 4.94], usually translated as 'laid the table' or 'set the table'. This, however, does *not* imply the presence of a table as we know it, for such an object was unnecessary. There are still many people in the world today who manage perfectly well without a table: who sit down on the floor to eat food laid out before them. This is probably what the majority of the early monks had been used to, for they were simple folk, fellahin, by no means accustomed to a comfortable way of life [see The Roman 1 / 10.110]. Given the austere simplicity of their existence in all other things, it seems probable that the monks ate (as they probably worked and in some cases wrote and read) sitting on the ground. A monk who *stood* to eat is noted as exceptional [Helladius 2] and so is this one:

They used to say of Abba Pior that he used to eat walking around. When somebody enquired why he ate like that, he said: 'I do not want to treat food as work, but as an odd job.'[5] To somebody else who had asked the same question he replied: '[It is] so that my soul may experience no physical pleasure even when I am eating.' [Pior 2 / 4.42]

'When Bane was going to eat he would stand in front of a wall and eat his bread; and he used to work standing up. Moreover, when he was going to sleep, he would lean his chest against the wall which he had built for this purpose' [c8].

---

[4] H. G. Evelyn White, *Monasteries of the Wadi'n Natrnû*, Part II: *The History of the Monasteries of Nitria and Scetis*, New York 1932–1933, p. 215.
[5] There is a word-play here: *ergon – parergon*.

Otherwise, monks sat, but this does not mean that they sat on the bare ground. Some did *sleep* on the bare ground: 'For fasting and sleeping rough [*chameunia*] have also been prescribed for us on account of pleasures' [Syncletica 8 / 7.24; *VA* 7.7]. Thus Dioscorus: 'For sleeping, he never puts a reed mat or a fleece or anything like it beneath him but sleeps on the earth itself (as we have heard)' [c14]. Normally monks would sleep [Macarius the Egyptian 33] and sit on the ubiquitous rush mat which many monks were capable of making themselves from raw materials easily obtainable. Or they may have used what has been optimistically translated as 'cushions' [*embrimia*]: 'bundles of coarse papyrus stalks bound at intervals of a foot so as to form long slender fascines which were also used as seats for the brethren at the time of the office [Daniel 7 / 18.4 line 36] and on other occasions' [Cassian, *Conf* 1.23.4] (cf. 'If the cushion beneath me do not speak') [29 / 4.97].

The word *table* clearly does sometimes mean what we mean by it; witness the references to the altar as the Holy Table [48; Mark the Egyptian 1 / 9.6; 18.48], but 'to lay the table' may mean to set out the provisions on one of those 'cushions', for: 'The brothers spoke about an elder who had a disciple who, when he sat down to eat, placed his legs upon the table ... As they were sitting down, [the elder] immediately placed his two feet upon the table, and that brother said to him, "Abba, it is not proper to place your feet upon the table"' [s36]. Something considerably less elevated than a conventional table seems to be implied.

The cell might have a place where a small fire could be made to prepare food [Moses 5 / 13.4], but some monks made a point of never eating anything that had been cooked: 'Of things that grow [Theonas] [only] ate the ones that do not have to be cooked' [*HME* 6.4]. (This is he of whom 'It was said that he used to go out of his cell by night and mingle with the wild beasts, giving them to drink of what water he had to hand.') For utensils there would be some kind of dish and a water-jug; two monks are said to have possessed a knife [Agathon 7 / 6.5 and 25 / 17.7; Pistos 1 / 15.60]. A cell would contain some raw materials for handiwork (rushes, palm-fronds, etc.) and some finished products (baskets, rope, mats and the like). A certain corner of the cell might be set aside for prayer, but it was said of Moses the Ethiopian that 'for six years he stayed in his cell, standing in prayer all the nights long *in the middle of his cell*, not closing an eye' [*HL* 19.8]. Eventually some cells acquired an attached oratory, which would explain why Amoun of Nitria 'built himself a cell consisting of two domed chambers' [*HL* 8.5].

In recent years archaeologists have made considerable progress in excavating various monastic sites. In 2005 some monastic cells were discovered during renovations to the church of St Antony's Monastery on the Red Sea. These are thought to be part of the original foundation; they could be the oldest known examples of Christian monastic cells.

CHAPTER 4

Impediments to Progress

Logismos, -oi

One can be shipwrecked through *logismoi*: one can receive a crown through *logismoi*. [218 / 10.123]

The apothegms frequently speak of monks being assaulted by what they call *logismoi*, singular *logismos*. This word is best left untranslated, for there is no English word capable of embracing its entire range of meaning. *Logismos* denotes almost any activity of the mind and even the mind itself: thought, notion, idea, concept, emotion, etc. Some meanings of *logismos* are good, such as contemplating the Deity or recalling the teachings of the fathers; some are neutral, such as arranging the details of daily life; but on the many times *logismos* occurs in the apothegms it nearly always has a pejorative meaning. The word has sometimes been translated as 'black thought', which is adequate when, for instance, it describes thinking ill of a person or recalling the life one lived and the relatives one cherished before renouncing the world. But the word usually connotes a particular kind of black thought in the apothegms: more often than not it means more or less what we call temptation. Thus *logsimos* usually signifies a compulsion either to leave undone that which one ought to do or to do something one ought not to do. A *logismos* is not, however, a compulsion so severe that it cannot be resisted; it was precisely by resisting *logismoi* that a monk progressed, gaining strength with each success. Antony said: 'Nobody who has not been tempted will be able to enter the Kingdom of Heaven for, take away temptations and nobody is being saved' [Antony 5], and Evagrius echoes him: 'Take away temptations and nobody is being saved' [Evagrius 5]. A frequent example of a salutary *logismos* is the one that prompts a monk residing in his cell to get up and leave it, hence to abandon the endeavour: to resist is to progress [e.g. G39].

Porneia

These bad *logismoi* were thought to be the work of demons and devils, actively engaged in frustrating the monk's attempts to progress by leading the good life. The demons were believed to attack on many fronts: there is mention of a *logismos* of greed, of laziness, of unbelief, and even a *logismos* of blasphemy [Poemen 93 / 10.63; G45]. But it is the *logismos* of *porneia* (also referred to as the lust, or the passion of *porneia*) that occurs most frequently and which provides the most effective impediment to a monk's progress. No single English word is adequate to translate *porneia*, for it has the meaning of any and every illicit sexually or erotically associated activity in thought, word or deed. This means that *porneia* covers every conceivable such activity for the monk; hence, it was often a very serious problem, especially for the younger folk, e.g. 'A brother was embattled by *porneia* and the warfare was like fire burning in his heart, day and night' [163 / 5.15]. It was not a problem for men only:

> They recounted of Amma Sarah[1] that for thirteen years she continued to be fiercely embattled by the demon of *porneia* and never prayed for the battle to be concluded, but would only say: 'Oh God, give me strength!' The same spirit of *porneia* once attacked her more vehemently, suggesting the vanities of the world to her. But she, without diminishing her fear of God or her spiritual discipline, went up to her roof-top one day to pray. The spirit of *porneia* appeared to her in bodily form and said to her: 'Sarah, you have conquered me,' but she said to him: 'It is not I who have conquered you but Christ, my lord-and-master.' [Sarah 1 and 2 / 5.13 and 14]

Old age did not always bring relief. A dying anchorite said: 'Brothers, I am a virgin in the body, but in the soul until now I was being inhumanly driven into *porneia*. Here I am speaking to you and I am seeing the angels waiting to take my soul and Satan standing over there thrusting perverse *logismoi* of *porneia* at me' [63 / 5.49] and, with that, he breathed his last. There was no respite: it was a life-time struggle against *porneia*. Poemen warns: 'Just as the guardsman of the emperor stands by his side, always at the ready, so must the soul be at the ready against the demon of *porneia*' [Poemen 14 / 5.7].

---

[1] 'When Amma Sarah leapt over a small stream while she was walking in the way, a worldling saw her and laughed. Unaware that the grace of God had come upon her, she said to the worldling: "Be quiet: you are going to burst." She turned around and saw him with his intestines spilled out. Stricken with fear, she prayed, saying: "May Jesus, bring him back to life and I will never say such a thing again"' [L44].

Inevitably some fell prey to this *logismos*. Others thought they knew why: 'An elder was asked: "How does it come about that I am tempted to *porneia*?" and he replied: "Through much eating and sleeping"' [94 / 21.10]. Another elder averred: 'Laziness, relaxation, eating twice a day and sleep are in the habit of bringing upon us the demon not only of *porneia*, but also the [demon] of *accidie*, arrogance and of pride' [741].

Opinion was divided about whether one who had fallen into *porneia* could ever be reconciled and forgiven:

> A brother asked an elder: 'What shall I do about *porneia*, abba?' The elder said to him: 'It is up to you to take precautions to the best of your ability against this *logismos,* for despair of one's salvation comes about through this *logismos* to him who is worsted by it. Just as a ship encountering waves, tempest and storm runs into yet greater danger if it loses its rudder (likewise if the mast or something like that is broken), yet there are still high hopes of the vessel being saved; so the monk, if he lets himself go to the other passions, still hopes to overcome them by repentance. But if he is once shipwrecked by falling into the passion of *porneia*, he comes to despair [of his salvation] and his vessel goes to the bottom.' [393 / 5.34]

'*Porneia* is physical death,' one father said [Matoes 8 / 5.6], but not all fathers were of his mind; there are several cases of the fallen being restored, in one case a bishop [31]. 'Is there repentance, abba?' a brother who had gone and taken a wife asked. '"There is," [the elder] said and [the former brother] left all and followed him. He came into Scêtê and, from his experience, he became a tried and tested monk' [Paphnutius 4]. The following story has a similar message:

> A certain monk dwelt in the wilderness and conducted himself in an excellent way of life. He was famous among people in the way he drove away demons and healed the sick. Then by the work of Satan it happened that the passion of *porneia* was aroused against him, and because he was not humble enough to reveal his battle to the elders around him, in a few days he fell into *porneia* with a woman who had constantly been coming to him to receive help. But when he fell, he gave up hope for himself and rose up to go back to the world, being sad and distressed concerning his fall.

Wandering in the wilderness he encountered 'an older monk who dwelt in the cleft of a rock'. Relieved that the monk was not guilty of what *he* considered the worse sin of misappropriating monastic resources [*sic*], the older monk told him:

> 'Do you, my brother, take heart and return again to your cell, and pray to God while repenting, and [God] will restore you to your former status.' Then he returned to his place and shut himself in it and no longer allowed

himself to talk with anyone, except with that person who handed him food through the small window [in the cell]. He remained there until the end of his life, having attained the highest [degree] of perfection. [s31]

A number of apothegms suggest remedies against the *logismos* of *porneia*. 'Not since I became a monk have I taken my fill of bread, of water or of sleep. Concern on account of those things greatly disquieted me and did not permit me to experience the warfare [against *porneia*] of which you spoke,' an elder said [183]. 'Concerning the *logismoi* of *porneia*, an elder said: "We experience these because of our negligence, for if we were convinced that God dwells within us, we would admit no alien matter to our person"' [78 / 5.20]. Afflicted persons were urged to confide in an elder [164, 165]. One brother confessed to the entire community, stark naked, and 'On account of his humility, the battle was stilled' [64 and G7]. Others struggled on alone and some even succeeded. For example,

> A brother was enflamed by the demon of *porneia*. Four demons transformed into the appearance of beautiful women were around for twenty days, struggling with him to draw him into shameful intercourse. He bravely struggled on and was not overcome. When God perceived his valiant struggle, he granted him grace never to burn in the flesh again. [1 Cor 7.9; 188 / 5.41; cf. 170 / 5.24]

Accidie

Another major but rather different impediment to progress was *accidie*. Antony is reported to have said: 'He who stays in the desert in *hesychia* is released from fighting on three fronts: hearing, speaking and seeing. He has only one to contend with: *accidie*'[2] [Antony 11/ 2.2]. Antony knew what he was talking about: as we saw, 'Once when the holy Abba Antony was residing in the desert, he was overcome by *accidie* and a great darkening of *logismoi*' [Antony 1 / 7.1], and Macarius the Great used to say: 'When I was young, a prey to *accidie* in my cell …' [Macarius the Egyptian s1 and 37].

Accidie (from the Greek *a-kêdia*, 'without care') has been variously defined as mental and/or spiritual sloth, apathy, dejection, indifference, listlessness, carelessness and melancholia. The word can mean little more than downhearted-ness [VA 17.4, 19.1], but with the monks it usually refers to something far more severe: a debilitating condition; one to which those living on their own were particularly susceptible. Dorothy Sayers describes

[2] Some manuscripts read *heart* for *accidie* here (*kardias / akêdias*).

sloth (*accidie*) as 'a sin that believes in nothing, cares for nothing, seeks to know nothing, interferes with nothing, enjoys nothing, hates nothing, finds purpose in nothing, lives for nothing, and remains alive because there is nothing for which it will die'. In the apothegms, however, *accidie* is never treated as a sin nor is it ever designated a *logismos* in the sense of a temptation, for it is not an incitement to do or not do something: it is rather a debilitating condition that descends on a person willy-nilly. It is a condition not unlike what would now be called a severe depression, possibly an equally intractable condition.

Just as depression can be accompanied and complicated by physical symptoms, so too can *accidie*. Thus Amma Theodora, of whom ten apothegms are known and nothing else, says:

> Be aware that if one proposes to take up *hesychia,* the Evil One comes right away, weighing down the soul by attacks of *accidie* and discouragement and with *logismoi.* He weighs down the body too with illnesses and debility by enfeebling the knees and all the members, draining the energy of soul and body so that I am sick and cannot offer the *synaxis.* [Theodora 3]

For Evagrius of Pontus the demon of *accidie* is the most dangerous of eight *logismoi,* 'the one that causes the most serious trouble of all' [*Praktikos* 14]. For John Cassian it is 'the destruction that wastes at noonday [Ps 90/91.6] like some foul darkness' [*Inst* 10.1].

> Whenever [*accidie*] begins in any degree to overcome a person, it either makes him stay in his cell idle and lazy, without making any spiritual progress, or it drives him out from thence and makes him restless and a wanderer, and indolent in the matter of all kinds of work, and it makes him continually go around the cells of the brethren and the monasteries, with an eye to nothing but this: where or with what excuse he can presently procure some refreshment. [*Inst* 10.6]

There were, however, those who believed *accidie* could be avoided or escaped. Cassian seems to say that plentiful hard work will suffice [*Inst* 10.9ff.]. 'You have one battle: against *accidie* and God is able to suppress it if you continually fall down before him in humility and with a broken heart, beseeching his assistance, for he knows your frailty in all things and he will not permit you to be tempted beyond what you can stand' is one piece of anonymous advice [G39]. Here is another: 'If, while staying in his cell, a monk recall his sins, the Lord is his helper in all things and he will not suffer *accidie*' [L29].

The idea that *accidie* could be repelled may explain why it eventually figured as one of 'the seven deadly sins' in the west; why, according to

The Rule of Saint Benedict, he who was afflicted with it should first be reproved and then punished, and why Theodore of Studium (759–826) treated it as a vice. The Roman Catholic Catechism still describes sloth/ *accidie* as 'a culpable lack of physical or spiritual effort that can actually refuse the joy that comes from God'. 'The slothful person is lukewarm towards, perhaps even repelled by, divine goodness and spiritual practices' [*Catechism* 1866, 2094, 2733].

The Desert Fathers were wise enough not to regard *accidie* as a sin, but they certainly were in dread of it, for there was no telling where or when it might strike. According to Poemen: '*accidie* is present at every beginning and there is no passion worse than this. But if a person recognise it for what it is, he experiences repose' [Poemen 149 / 10.87]. The wise Syncletica calls *accidie* a destructive sorrow, i.e. as opposed to a beneficial sorrow; an affliction from the Evil One. 'It is necessary to scare this spirit away by prayer and psalm-singing,' she says [Syncletica s10 / 10.102]. And among the reported cases of *accidie* experienced by the monks [e.g. *HL* 5.3, 16.2], there is at least one splendid story of a monk who overcame it:

> There was a brother in the desert, practising *hesychia* in his own cell. He was being severely afflicted by *accidie*, [inciting him] to go out of the cell. He would say to himself: 'Soul, do not grow weary from remaining in your cell. Even if you are doing nothing, this suffices: you are offending or afflicting nobody nor are you being afflicted by anyone. Just think from how many evils the Lord has delivered you through practising *hesychia* and praying to him without distraction. You speak no idle words; you do not hear what is inappropriate nor do you see harmful things. You have one battle: against *accidie*. God is capable of depleting that too as I acquire humility; for he knows my weakness in all things and for that reason he permits my soul to be tried.' As he turned these things over in his mind, great consolation came to him through unceasing prayer. This brother had that teaching from the holy fathers who had grown old in the desert. [12.21][3]

Predictably, the apothegms only speak of those who won the fight against the terrible foes of *logismoi*, *porneia* and *accidie*. As with emigrants to a new land, one only hears of those who succeeded while nothing is said of the ones who failed and gave up the struggle, and hardly any attempt is made to number them. So, similarly, we know virtually nothing of those who abandoned the world only to return to it, defeated by the demands of the desert.

---

[3] See also Heraclius 14.30; Arsenius 11, 195, 7.34; Zeno 8; Macarius the Egyptian s1 (cf. Macarius the Egyptian 37); Heracleides 1, 14. 30; *HL* 21.1. The noun *accidie* only occurs once in VA [36.2] the related verb three times. *Accidie* is never mentioned in *HME*.

CHAPTER 5

The Object of the Exercise

We have it within ourselves to be saved, if we so desire. [226 / 10.148]

Silence

John Cassian says:

> The aim of every monk and the perfection of his heart tends to continual
> and unbroken perseverance in prayer, and, as far as it is allowed to human
> frailty, strives to acquire an immovable tranquillity of mind and a perpetual
> purity, for the sake of which we seek unweariedly and constantly to practise
> all bodily labours as well as contrition of spirit. [*Conf* 1.2]

We have established that a monk who has withdrawn from society and
placed himself under unquestioning obedience to an elder constantly prays
to be 'saved' from ever failing in his endeavour by returning to the wicked
world. What does he/she hope to achieve by maintaining that degree of
isolation, living in solitary confinement (with hard labour) five or six
days a week? Judging by what is said in a number of apothegms (some
of which have already been cited above), the answer appears to be: repose
[*anapausis*]. This is certainly not repose in the sense in which the word is
usually understood. 'Let us hate all physical repose so that our soul can be
saved,' says Antony [Antony 33, 3.1] and Isaiah of Scêtê warns: 'Hate everything in the world and repose of the body, for these made you an enemy
of God. As a man who has an enemy fights with him, so we ought also to
fight against the body to allow it no repose' [1.10]. 'Little sons, we ought to
be averse to all kinds of repose in this present life,' says another elder [LI].
The repose the monk hoped to attain is that which Cassian calls 'immov-
able tranquillity of mind'.

It is not, however, always clear whether the repose one hoped to attain
is meant to be in this world or in the next. There are sayings that speak of
it somewhat ambiguously. We have already heard Alonios saying: 'Unless

48

a man say in his heart: "I alone and God are in the world," he will not experience repose' [Alonios 1, 11.13; see also 3.46, 14.10, 21.50, 21.60]. Sisoes' instruction is similarly ambivalent: 'Remain in your cell with vigilance and commit yourself to God with many tears and you will have repose' [11.66], but Poemen, in reply to one asking how to become a monk, says: 'If you want to find repose here and in the age to come, say in every situation: "I, who am I?" and do not pass judgement on anybody' [Joseph of Panepho 2 / 9.8]. A venerable elder confirms: 'Many are they who opt for repose in this age before the Lord grants them repose' [Theodore of Phermê 16 / 10.35].

How then might one achieve repose 'in this age'? The two necessary preliminaries to repose appear to be, first, silence, then *hesychia*. Silence was (and remains) a crucial element of the monastic life: 'Silence at the appropriate time is a good thing, being nothing other than the mother of wisest thoughts,' said Diadochos of Photice [2.12]. 'Love silence more than speaking, because silence concentrates the mind, but speaking scatters and destroys' [A12], counselled another Isaiah.

There are several anonymous sayings that discern silence as a path to salvation, e.g. 'If you wish to be saved, pursue poverty and silence, for on these two virtues depends the entire monastic life' [596.7]. 'Flee from men and remain silent – and you shall be saved' [132D / 20.13]. Silence in itself is also a great prophylactic: 'He who loves silence will not be pierced by the arrows of the Enemy' [E191]. 'Practise silence; be anxious about nothing; at lying down and getting up, apply yourself to your meditation with fear of God and you will not fear from the assaults of the godless' [274 / 11.105]. When combined with other practices, silence can also confer goodness in its own right: ' "Taking no thought" [Mt 6.25–34], keeping silent and silent meditation bring forth purity' [127 / 5.29].

Monastic silence does not, however, simply mean avoiding any disturbance of the air-waves. The following apothegm may refer to the marsh at Scêtê:

> Abba Arsenius once visited a place where there were reeds and they were moved by the wind. The elder said to the brothers: 'What is that disturbance?' and they said to him: 'It is the reeds.' The elder said to them: 'Naturally, if somebody is living in *hesychia* but hears the sound of a sparrow, his heart does not have the same *hesychia*; how much more so you who have the disturbance of these reeds!' [Arsenius 25 / 2.8]

If Arsenius is telling the brother to move away from the marsh to avoid the sound of the wind in the reeds, there was another way of dealing with extraneous noise:

The brothers of Abba Poemen said to him: 'Let us go away from this place for the monasteries of this place are disturbing us and we are losing our souls. Here too the children's crying prevents us from practising *hesychia*.' Abba Poemen said to them: 'You want to get away from here because of the angels' voices?' [Poemen 155]

That is not the only time there is mention of children disturbing the peace in the desert:

Certain brothers visiting a holy elder living in a desert place found some children outside the monastery minding [animals] and making inappropriate remarks. After [the brothers] had revealed their *logismoi* to him and benefited from his knowledge, they said to him: 'Abba, how do you tolerate these children and do not tell them not to be boisterous?' The elder said: 'There are indeed some days when I would like to tell them [that] but I restrain myself, saying: "If I do not stand this little [disturbance], how am I to withstand severe temptation if it comes upon me?" For that reason, I say nothing to them so I can get used to putting up with things to come.' [338 / 16.23; cf. 67]

Loose Talk

Silence did not mean a total embargo on speech for monks, but it did mean a severe limitation of speaking. A certain limitation was something the monk ought to impose on himself; some went to extreme lengths. 'They used to say of Abba Agathon that he kept a stone in his mouth for three years until he had learnt to keep silence' [Agathon 15 / 4.7]. The same Agathon (having removed the stone) told a brother who came to ask how he was to live with other brothers:

'All the days of your life remain a stranger to them, just as you were the first day you came to them, so there be no loose talk with them.' Abba Macarius said to him: 'Is loose talk so dangerous?' Then Abba Agathon said: 'There is no passion more dangerous, for it is the begetter of all the passions. Loose talk is like a great heat wave: when it happens, everybody flees from the face of it and it destroys the fruit of the trees. One who is fighting the good fight should not indulge in loose talk, even if he be alone in his cell.' [Agathon 1 / 10.11]

Another elder said: 'Loose talk and laughter are like a consuming fire in a reed-bed' [118 / 21.37]. Loose talk, familiar discourse, unnecessary chatter and most especially anything even slightly malicious – all these are covered by one word: *parrhêsia*. But not all discourse was loose talk: 'A brother asked Abba Poemen: "Is it better to speak or to remain silent?" The elder said to him: "He who speaks in a godly manner does well; he who remains silent in the same way, likewise" ' [Poemen 147]. The important thing was to be able to recognise the difference: 'Get control of your tongue and your belly,' said Antony [Antony 6 / 1.2].

Control of the tongue has many additional advantages [Jas 1.26; 3.5–8], such as preventing one from lying and from slandering. Sisoes used to pray: 'Lord Jesus Christ, protect me from my tongue, for every day even until now I fall because of it and commit sin' [Sisoes 5 / 4.47]. There can be no hope of repose without mastery of the tongue:

> Abba Joseph says to Abba Nisterôs: 'What am I to do about my tongue for I cannot control it?' The elder said to him: 'So when you speak, do you experience repose?' 'No,' he said to him, and the elder said: 'If you do not experience repose, why do you speak? Better to keep quiet; and if a conversation is taking place, hear a great deal rather than speak.' [Nisterôs 3]

Poemen said: 'Whatever trouble comes upon you, victory over it is to remain silent' [Poemen 37 / 16.12], and one whose name is not known suggests why: 'In my opinion it is good to keep silent, for *that* is humility' [318 / 15.96]. 'Keep silent and do not measure yourself' is a maxim mentioned twice [Bessarion 10; Poemen 79]. 'A brother asked Abba Sisoes: "What am I to do?" He said to him: "What you are looking for is an intense silence and humility, for it is written: 'Blessed are they who remain in him' [Is 30.18]. In this way you will be able to stand fast"' [Sisoes 42].

As well as being linked with humility, silence is often shown as being of equal importance with work and prayer: 'As long as a man stay in his cell, devoting himself wholeheartedly and in silence to prayer and work, he can be saved' [464 / 2.34]. But in one rare passage, silence is portrayed as a lesser virtue:

> A brother asked an elder: 'What is humility?' and the elder said: 'It is when you do good to those who do bad things.' The brother said: 'If one cannot measure up to that standard, what should he do?' 'Let him run away and elect to remain silent,' said the elder. [305A / 15.81]

Hesychia

Hesychia may well be the most difficult word in the monastic vocabulary to define; that is why it is left untranslated. The word has already appeared above in its primary meaning, no more than *silence*. But in its monastic context it quickly came to mean more than, and probably something quite different from, mere absence of speaking. 'Keep yourselves in silence and *hesychia,*' an elder instructs two philosophers [720], indicating that these are separate conditions.

What can be deduced from the apothegms is that *hesychia* was perceived to be a state in which one lived or resided (this is the most common use of the word). One might occasionally sail [Arsenius 38] or go one's way [Macarius the Egyptian 18 / 16.8] in *hesychia,* but it is usually characterised as something one practised or maintained. Less often *hesychia* is said to be pursued in order to be attained, or simply said to be a state in which one *is.*

Certain benefits are credited to *hesychia.* In one elder's eyes it enjoys a particularly elevated status: 'God has selected *hesychia* before all the virtues, for it is written: "To whom shall I look, other than to him who is lowly and in *hesychia* and who trembles at my words?"' [Is 66.2; 506]. As for its benefits: '*hesychia* produces grief for sin, baptises the man and makes him sinless' [760], for 'The monk who loves *hesychia* remains unwounded by the darts of the Enemy' [Nil 9].

Discreet kinds of *hesychia* are mentioned, such as the *hesychia* of the night [Paul the Barber 2 / 11.64] and the *hesychia* of the Holy Eucharist/ *synaxis* [Isaac of Thebes 2 / 11.47], but it is in certain almost casual remarks that its true nature is glimpsed, e.g. 'When this elder saw something and his *logismos* wanted to find fault, he would say to himself: "Agathon, do you not do it," and thus his *logismos* was in *hesychia*' [Agathon 18] and 'My ears were full of disputation so I walked around to cleanse them and so entered my cell in *hesychia* of mind' [John Colobus 25].

Remarks like these indicate that *hesychia* is indeed a state of mind: a state of mind (it can be detected elsewhere) peculiarly associated with aloneness: e.g. the father who 'secluded himself in *hesychia* at a cell outside the lavra' [Phocas 1]. 'Two brothers once agreed together and became monks; having achieved that, they thought it best to build two cells at some distance apart and each one withdrew on his own for *hesychia*' [622], presumably because they could not practise *hesychia* while living together. Each needed a place of his own, i.e. somewhere for the mature: not at all the right thing for juniors. This explains why 'Our fathers would not tolerate young men staying in cells or places of *hesychia,* but in coenobia' [741].

It can now be appreciated that it is possible to learn a good deal *about hesychia* from the apothegms without being able to discover what *hesychia* really is. The following passage comes as near as any apothegm does to providing an answer:

> A brother asked Abba Rufus: 'What is *hesychia* and what is its benefit?' The elder said to him: '*Hesychia* is remaining in a cell with fear and consciousness

of God, refraining from rancour and arrogance. That kind of *hesychia* is the mother of all virtues and protects the monk from the fiery darts of the Enemy, not allowing him to be wounded by them.' [Rufus 1 / 2.35]

This is from a very long apothegm concerning several monastic virtues. Later on, it returns to the same subject: 'O, *hesychia*, that importunes God, a weapon of the young that maintains a state of mind for which one need not repent and which preserves untroubled those who are desirous of remaining in their own cells.' What then is this 'state of mind for which one need not repent'? Poemen supplies a pointer when he says:

> There is a person who seems to keep silent, while his heart is passing judgement on others: such a person is speaking all the time. There is another person who is speaking from dawn to dusk yet maintains silence: I mean, he says nothing that is not beneficial. [Poemen 27 / 10.75]

A person may keep his mouth completely shut (and live in utter silence) but still have the inner man seething with *logismoi*. Not infrequently in the apothegms an elder is asked what a brother is to do about his *logismoi*, usually meaning how is he to handle (i.e. escape from) this or that temptation. But the question can just as well mean how is he to still the churning of his mind, and this provokes a variety of responses. Those for whom any of those responses worked, i.e. those who succeeded in mastering their own thoughts, are the ones who can be said to have achieved *hesychia*.

Repose

Now *hesychia* is the precursor of repose. Thus an apothegm about the two brothers noted above:

> Abba Paul and Timothy his brother were barbers at Scêtê and they were importuned by the brothers. Timothy said to his brother: 'What do we want with this profession? Throughout the whole day we are not allowed to practise *hesychia*.' In response Abba Paul said to him: 'The *hesychia* of the night is enough for us if our mind is keeping watch.' [Paul the Barber 2 / 11.64]

Paul and Timothy had not found it easy living together, but once they had agreed to put up with each other and had established at least a degree of *hesychia*, 'they experienced repose the rest of their days' [Paul the Barber 1, 16.10].

> Abba Moses said to Abba Macarius at Scêtê: 'I want to live in *hesychia* but the brothers do not let me.' Abba Macarius said to him: 'I see that your

nature is simple and you cannot turn a brother away. Go into the inner desert, to Petra and live there in *hesychia*.' He did so and experienced repose. [Macarius the Egyptian 22]

Repose appears to have been the reward those who had renounced the world hoped to attain in this world. John Colobos told of an elder who, on becoming famous, said: 'My reputation will be greatly enhanced and I will *get no repose* from that' [John Colobos 38]. A brother told Abba Simon: 'If I go out of my cell and find a brother distracted and I become distracted with him; and if I find him laughing and I laugh with him too, then when I enter my cell I am not permitted to experience repose' [Poemen 137]. Laughter was dangerously distracting for monks: 'Somebody saw a young monk laughing and said to him: "Do not laugh, brother, for you are driving the fear of God away from you"' [54 / 3.51].

It is a given that for those who follow the fathers' precepts, repose can be experienced (at least partially) in this world as well as in the next. Thus one anonymous elder says: 'Even if the saints toiled here below, they were already receiving a portion of repose' [235 / 10.161]. It is stated categorically of Abba Megethius that when he heeded his elders 'he experienced repose' [Megethius 2b / 14.10], while Joseph of Panepho instructed a brother: 'Stay wherever you see your soul experiencing repose and not being damaged' [Joseph of Panepho 8].

Was it then in order to attain repose that all those men and some women withdrew into the desert? There are a few indications that in certain cases it was. An unnamed 'great elder' said to a troubled neophyte: 'So it is not that you might follow the will of the elder [that you became a monk], but that he should follow your will and that in this way you would attain repose?' [245 / 10.174]. A saying of Theodore of Phermê states the matter more clearly:

A brother living in solitude at Kellia was troubled; he went to Abba Theodore of Phermê telling him his own condition and *he* said to him: 'Go and humble your *logismos*; be submissive and live with others.' He came back to the elder and said to him: 'I find no repose with other people either.' The elder said to him: 'If you find no repose either alone or with others, why did you come out to be a monk?' [Theodore of Phermê 2 / 7.9]

That brother certainly appears to have come out into the desert expecting to experience repose; but the same elder has a stern and salutary warning for him: 'Tell me now: how many years have you worn the habit?' 'Eight years,' he said and the elder replied: 'Right; well, I have worn the habit for seventy years without finding repose for one day and you want to have

repose in eight years?' [Theodore of Phermê 2 / 7.9]. Theodore was one
of the more significant monks, first at Scêtê until the devastation of 407,
then at Phermê, 11 kilometres south-east of Kellia, a community of five
hundred monks according to Palladius [*HL* 20.1]. Famous for his rejection of all distinction, his advice was greatly sought after. That a monk of
his calibre claims not to have known a day's repose in seventy years might
suggest that he is playing on the *polyvalence* of the word *repose* or that he
was reproving the brother for expecting to find a repose associated with the
body rather than the spirit. On the other hand, he may have been warning
that the fulfilment of the promise 'Come unto me ...' [Mt 11.28–29] lay
in the confident expectation of repose rather than in the actual realisation
of it. And yet:

> [Abba Mark] also said: '*Hesychia* is good for this reason: because it does
> not see that which is harmful and the mind does not absorb what it did
> not see. That which is not lodged in the mind does not stir a memory
> through imagination; that which does not stir the memory does not excite
> the passion and when the passion is not excited, one experiences *profound
> calm and great peace within*.' [2.22, γαλήνην ἔχει βαθείαν καὶ πολλὴν εἰρήνην
> τὰ ἔνδον; cf. Mk 4.39, etc.]

CHAPTER 6

Prayer

If it is only when a monk stands up for prayer that he prays, such a one is not praying at all. [104 / 21.23]

Continuous Prayer

'Pray without ceasing' or 'uninterruptedly', says Paul to the people of Thessaly [1 Thess. 5.17]; it was an injunction that the Desert Fathers took seriously to heart from the very beginning. Antony 'prayed continuously, for he learnt that one should pray alone *without ceasing*' [VA 3.7] – the same word used by Paul. 'Prayer is the monk's mirror,' they said [96 / 21.12], and 'If you love the salvation of your soul, pray all the time, as it is written, with fear and trembling; with a vigilant heart, in full knowledge that you have wicked enemies seeking their opportunity to take you captive' [E192]. 'Three things are of capital importance [for the monk],' says Poemen: 'that he fear the Lord, that he do good to his neighbour and that he "pray without ceasing"' [Poemen 160, 11.61]. The same injunction recurs again and again, e.g.: 'Man needs to fear the judgement of God, to hate sin and love virtue, and to intercede continuously with God' [123 / 21.42]; 'Hard labour, humility and ceaseless prayer [allow one to] acquire Jesus' [11.129]; 'Flee vain glory and pray without ceasing,' says Antony; 'Sing psalms before and after sleeping and learn by heart the precepts of the Scriptures and call to mind the deeds of the saints' [VA 55.3].

Prayer, however, was no easy matter; thus Agathon:

> Forgive me; I reckon there is no exertion like praying to God for, when a man wishes to pray, the enemies always want to interrupt him; for they know that he cannot be impeded in any other way but [by interrupting] his prayer to God. One experiences some repose in every activity he practises and perseveres in it. But to pray: that requires struggle until the last breath. [Agathon 9 / 12.2]

The Little and the Great Synaxis

The earliest monks may have 'prayed without ceasing' to the extent that they made no distinction between hours of prayer and other times. Abba Isidore, a first-generation monk at Scêtê, said that when he was young there were no limits to the act of worship [*synaxis*]; 'Night and day were *synaxis* for me' [Isidore 4].

Synaxis is the usual word for a religious service (roughly equivalent to the French word *culte*), but it has two different aspects: congregational and private. In its first aspect, the literal meaning of *synaxis* applies, 'assembly', and in this sense it denotes the worship of a *con-gregation* (gathering together), usually a weekly event for monks (see below p. 107).

It is the private acts of worship of individual monks in their cells or 'where two or three are gathered together' [Mt 18.20] that are most frequently mentioned in the apothegms. In an apothegm already noted [Antony 1 / 7.1], the angel seems to be telling Antony to take frequent 'prayer breaks' from the monotony of rope-making, but that is not the only way his words could be understood. There was a father living at Enaton, a significant monastic community located at the ninth mile-post to the west of Alexandria. One day he was visited by some Messalians, also known as Euchites, meaning 'they who pray'. The Messalians were a mendicant, pietistic sect who 'prayed without ceasing' to the exclusion of work. After teasing them about how they prayed while sleeping, eating, etc., the monk said to them:

> Look, I am going to show you how I 'pray without ceasing' while working with my hands. After steeping some reeds [i.e. to soften them for working] I sit down with God and, while braiding them into rope, I say: 'Have mercy upon me O God after thy great goodness; according to the multitude of thy mercies do away mine offences' [Ps 50/51.1]. And he said to them: 'Is that not praying?' 'Yes,' they said, and the elder continued: 'When I pass the whole day working and praying, I earn more or less sixteen pence; I put two pennies by the door and eat with the rest. He who takes the two pence prays for me while I am eating and sleeping and in this way, by the grace of God, he fulfils for me the command to "pray without ceasing."' [Lucius 1 / 12.10]

His mode of prayer when waking would have won the entire approval of Macarius the Egyptian, for he says there is no need of 'vain repetitions' [Mt 6.7] when one prays. 'One should frequently stretch out his hands and say: "Lord, have mercy on me the way you want to and the way you know how," and if the [devil's] assault continues: "Help me Lord!" For he knows what is right for us and he will be merciful' [Macarius the Egyptian 19 / 12.21].

Scripture and Apothegms

Macarius' mention of 'vain repetitions' may indicate his awareness that some people prayed by simply repeating the same verse over and over again, as in the case of Marcellinus of the Thebaid noted below. There are other examples, e.g. 'Abba Ammonas said: "I and Abba Betimes visited Abba Achilles and we heard him meditating this phrase: *Fear not Joseph to go down to Egypt* [Gen 46.3]; and he went on meditating this phrase for a long time"' [Achilles 5]. There were others who employed the same technique but repeated sayings of the fathers rather than scriptural verses. This is understandable for, in most cases, as we saw, those sayings had been uttered in response to the request: 'Tell me a saying showing how I might be saved.' So naturally such sayings were highly revered; had they not been we might not have them now. Indeed a number of sayings survive which raise the possibility that apothegms may have been revered as highly as (if not higher than) verses of Holy Scripture, e.g.: 'A brother said to me: "My father Abba Soy of the Mount Diolcus told me, 'If [bad] thoughts come into the heart of a brother, he will not be able to hold [them] back completely from his heart, unless he invoke words from the Scripture or from the sayings of the elders'"' [E77]. Poemen said:

> Take care that, from now on, you do not dare to tell me that I might speak to the brothers with [the words of] Scripture, even though you would talk to them with the sayings of the elders, or I will destroy my dwelling place in order to build a dwelling place for my brother. [E2]

If, however, that saying is a little confusing (the text may be corrupt), this one leaves little doubt that sayings are to take precedence over Scripture:

> Abba Amoun said to [Abba Poemen]: 'So if a necessity arises to speak with my neighbour, do you want me to speak of the Scriptures or of the sayings of the elders?' Said the elder, 'If you cannot keep silent, it is better to speak of the sayings of the elders and not of the Scriptures, for *there* is no small danger.' [Amoun 2 / 11.56]

This may have prompted an unknown sage to comment: 'To speak of the faith and to read doctrine dries up a man's grief for sin and obliterates it, whereas the lives and sayings of the elders enlighten the soul' [553].

It may be possible to detect in the Ethiopic Sayings a tendency in prayer which would eventually lead to the so-called 'Jesus prayer': the constant repetition of a phrase that is neither scriptural nor (so far as we know) apothegmatic:

> A brother said to me: 'God's patient expectation [*lacuna*] also his heart is [directed] to the Lord, while he shouts, saying: "Jesus, have mercy on me! Jesus, help me! I bless you, my living Godhead, all the time!", and little by little he raises his eyes while uttering these three phrases to God in his heart.' [E26]

Abba Paul the Coenobite said: 'When you live in a community, work, learn and, little by little, raise your eyes towards heaven, saying to God in your heart: "Jesus, show grace and have mercy on me. Jesus, help me. I bless you, my Lord!"' [E42; cf. E43]. But then Macarius the Egyptian is said to have heard a brother praying: 'Lord, even if your ears do not ring with my crying to you, have mercy on me concerning my sins; for I myself do not grow weary pleading with you' [16].

Continuous and Occasional Prayer

The emergence of two complementary prayer-practices can be observed: of having a prayer for ever in one's mouth (or mind) no matter what the task in hand, and of stopping work at certain moments of the day to make a deliberate act of worship, as the angel directed Antony.

> If you are employed at handwork in your cell and the time for your prayer arrives, do not say: 'I will just finish the few fronds or the small basket then I will get up,' but stand up every hour and render God the prayer owing him, since [otherwise] you will gradually get used to being negligent of prayer and of your worship. Your soul will become destitute of any task, spiritual or corporal, for it is early in the morning that your eagerness is apparent. [592/47]

'Stop work promptly to perform your *synaxis*,' says Arsenius, 'and drink your water [i.e. break your fast] or your body will soon fall sick' [Arsenius 24]. As a monk living in a remote cell would have no way of knowing the time of day (other than when it was noon), one might assume 'the time for prayer' was signalled in some way, e.g. by a *semantron*, clear evidence of a degree of communality.

Just how many times in a day one was to take a 'prayer break' we cannot say; indeed, John Cassian comments on the astonishing variety of prayer-practices he observed in Egypt [*Inst* 2.2–3]. In a somewhat enigmatic saying Poemen warns the brethren: 'Be not negligent of the times for *synaxeis* [plural of *synaxis*] nor of [the times for] secret prayers' [Poimen

168 / 10.93], meaning (presumably) that those must not replace these. Isaiah of Scêtê says one should spend half the night on the *synaxis* and the other half of it sleeping: 'Spend two hours before going to bed praying and psalm-singing then lay yourself down to rest. When the Lord awakens you, celebrate your [dawn] *synaxis* zealously' [*Asceticon* 4.45–46]. The night *synaxis* could last until dawn [229 / 10.150] and:

> They said of someone who lived at Kellia that he had this rule: four hours of the night he slept, four hours he stood for the *synaxis* and four hours he worked. In the day he worked again until the sixth hour; he read [*sic*] from the sixth to the ninth while cutting palm leaves then from the ninth hour he busied himself with food. He thought of his cell as *parergion* [a subsidiary task, meaning the housekeeping?]. This is how he passed the day. [20.14]

'And if you happen to sleep in until dawn,' says an unnamed father, 'get up, shut the windows and doors and perform your *synaxis*' [230 / 10.152]. There should be a self-examination both in the evening and at dawn [264 / 11.91] and on rising from sleep one should say: 'Body, work to feed yourself; soul, be vigilant in order to inherit the Kingdom of Heaven' [269 / 11.99].

'Casting' One's Prayer

Just as 'your little *synaxis*' is the most frequent term for the monk's (or some monks') private act of worship, *ballô*, meaning to cast or throw, is the verb most frequently associated with it. This may indicate the frequent prostrations which punctuated the monks' devotions, for one normally stood to pray. 'When you are standing in your cell to offer your *synaxis* ... hold yourself upright in the fear of God. Do not lean against the wall and do not relieve your feet by putting your weight on the one to rest the other like silly men' stipulates Isaiah of Scêtê [*Asceticon* 3.58]. There is a story of a monk who had fallen sick and was too weak to 'cast' his *synaxis*, because he was prostrate, therefore he could not perform the prostrations required. The point of the story is that he forced himself to stand and, when the *synaxis* was over, the sickness had left him [Theodora 3].

The regular prayer of monks is already referred to sometimes by the term which Benedict would use: the 'work of God' [*opus Dei*]:[1]

> A brother put this question to an elder: 'Why is it that when I perform my little *synaxis* I do it negligently?' The elder replied: 'This is how one's

---

[1] 'The work of God' is found occasionally elsewhere to denote the entire monastic endeavour [Antony 13 / 10.3; John Colobos 29; Sisoes 37; John the Eunuch 1; 241 / 10.168].

love for God shows itself: it is when you perform the work of God with enthusiasm, sorrow for sin and undistracted thoughts.' [395 / 10.186; see also 399 / 11.86, 401 / 11.121]

Psalms

Marcellus of Monidia said:

> Believe me, children, there is nothing which so troubles, incites, irritates, wounds, destroys, distresses and excites the demons and the supremely evil Satan himself against us, so much as the constant study of the psalms. The entire holy Scripture is beneficial to us and not a little offensive to the demons, but none of it distresses them more than the Psalter. [*PS* 152]

The 'little *synaxis*' apparently consisted almost completely of psalms. John Cassian says: 'The Egyptian monks recited psalms continuously and spontaneously throughout the course of the whole day, in tandem with their work ... taking up the whole day in affairs that we [in Gaul] celebrate at fixed times' [*Inst* 3.2]. There is little doubt that many of the Desert Fathers had the Psalter by heart [222 / 10.135] and that their *synaxis* was also known as 'the rule of psalm-singing' [18.48]. 'It is also clear' (writes Dom Lucien Regnault),

> that the practice of praying morning and evening was in existence for a long time throughout Christendom, but it was only in the fourth century that the practice of offering *twelve psalms, twice a day*, became more or less universal. Among the anchorites the morning *synaxis* was offered in the second part of the night, the evening service at the going down of the sun. When two or three monks were together at the time for the *synaxis* each one in turn would stand to sing a portion of the twelve psalms while the others sat, joining silently in the prayer [which followed each psalm]. [*Vie*, p. 120]

There were, however, occasions, exceptional no doubt, when the service was considerably longer:

> Another elder visited one of the elders; he cooked a few lentils and said to the visitor: 'Let us offer the little *synaxis*.' He recited the entire Psalter then the other one repeated from memory the two greater prophets [presumably Isaiah (66 chapters) and Jeremiah (52 chapters)]. The visiting elder departed when dawn broke; they forgot about the food. [150 / 4.70]

A father at Kellia had fourteen books of the Bible by heart [227 / 10.149]. Palladius tells of some monks who (as they travelled) recited fifteen psalms, then the great psalm (118/119), then the Epistle to the Hebrews, Isaiah, a part of Jeremiah, Luke's Gospel and Proverbs; but then there was Serapion

Sindonios who had the entire Bible by heart [*HL* 26.3, 37.1]. Another father of the same name, when visiting a prostitute, 'began the *synaxis* and, starting the Psalter, he offered a prayer … for her at each psalm, that she might repent and be saved. The woman fell down when he had finished the psalms. The elder began the Apostle and read a great deal of it and thus he completed the *synaxis*' [Serapion 1 / 17.34].

Prayer and psalms were very closely linked in the thinking of the Desert Fathers. 'If God were to hold against us our lack of attention in prayers and psalm-singing we could not be saved,' said one of them [Theodore of Enaton 3 / 11.35]. In fact, psalms often *were* the monks' prayers: ' "Why did the elder oblige me to say no prayers?" a brother asked himself, so he stood up and sang [*sic*] several psalms' [Heraclius 1 / 14.30].

Psalms were often sung, rather than recited or repeated mentally. The word commonly used, *psalmôidia*, means exactly 'psalm-singing' and occasionally it is indicated explicitly that this is no mere convention, e.g. 'The younger brother *sang* five psalms' [Macarius the Egyptian 33 / 20.3]; 'When we fall sick, let us not be sorrowful because … we are unable to stand or to sing out loud,' counsels Syncletica [Syncletica 8 / 7.24]. When demons wish to be taken for Christians, they pretend to 'sing the psalms *with a tune* and repeat passages taken from the Scriptures' [*VA* 25.1, 39.5].

Meditation

There is another element of the monks' prayer which must be taken into consideration: what the translators often call 'meditating on the Scriptures'. Given the usual meaning of *meditate* today, this is quite misleading. For one thing, the monks' meditation was rarely silent while for another it required very little intellectual activity. A more accurate translation would be 'reciting out loud biblical texts which have been memorised'. John Colobus used to give himself to prayer, meditation and psalmody after an absence from his cell 'until his mind was restored to its former state' [John Colobos 35]. This activity is frequently cited as an essential element of the monastic life. Manual work, eating once a day, keeping silence and meditation is Poemen's prescription for the 'visible' aspects of life in the cell [Poemen 168 / 10.93]; manual labour, meditation and prayer is the prescription of Isaiah of Scêtê [*Asceticon* 9.20]; also 'Do not neglect your meditation and ceaseless prayer' [*Asceticon* 1.4]. A brother in trouble says: 'I do a little fasting, praying, meditation and *hesychia*, purifying my thoughts so far as I can,' while an unnamed father says the monk's life consists of manual labour, obedience, meditation, not judging another and never grumbling [Joseph of Panepho 7 / 12.9; 225 / 1.32]. 'Do not be anxious about anything. Keep silent, be careful for nothing [Phil 4.6], give yourself to your meditation, sleeping and waking in the fear of God and you will not fear the attacks of the godless,' a young monk is advised [274 / 11.105]. If a monk succumbs to temptation and repents, he has several aids at his disposal: meditation, psalmody and manual labour, 'which are the foundations' (presumably of the monastic life) [168 / 5.22]. It is probably no coincidence that prayer is only once mentioned in the above quotations, but rather an indication that prayer is engrossed in meditation. This is somewhat confirmed by the occasional mention of meditation together with psalms or psalmody, e.g. a young monk 'wishing to pray' stands up and repeats several psalms [Heraclius 1 / 14.30].

Meditating on (i.e. reciting) psalms is a great prophylactic: 'Constrain yourself to the meditation of the psalms for this protects you from being captured by the Enemy,' says Isaiah of Scêtê [Isaiah 9 / 5.53]. 'Once I [anon] saw a brother doing meditation in his cell when a demon came and stood outside the cell. As long as the brother continued his meditation [the demon] was unable to enter but once the brother desisted, in he went' [366 / 18.38].

Saying and Singing

Meditation and psalmody may have resembled each other in another important way, for meditation, far from being the silent practice of today, may have involved singing. 'Let there be a spiritual song [Ep. 5.19] in your mouth,' says Hyperechios, 'and let meditation assuage the force of the temptations you encounter. A good example of this is a heavy-laden traveller who dissipates the discomfort of his journey with a song' [Hyperechios / 7.27]. Just as *psalmody* means psalm-*singing*, it is very likely that a monk 'meditated' the passages of Scripture he had by heart by chanting or singing them out loud, possibly in a sort of *cantilena*, the way the suras of the Qur'an are recited to this day and the lessons in the mass used to be. Hence, despite frequent insistence on *silence* being maintained by monks ('you will experience repose anywhere, if you remain silent') [L48], this must be understood to mean something other than the absence of sound. John Colobos 'would spend a long time in silence; in prayers, readings of and meditations on the Holy Scriptures' [L60]. The practice of spacing out monks' cells at Kellia and elsewhere so they were not within hearing distance of each other [*HME* 20.7] would not have been necessary if the occupants had prayed and meditated in silence. But they did not, for Palladius says: 'If you stop about the ninth hour [at Nitria, *c.* 394] you hear the psalm-singing coming from each monastic dwelling' [*HL* 7.2–5]. Athanasius wrote even earlier: 'In the mountains the monastic dwellings were like tents filled with divine choirs singing psalms, reading the Scriptures, fasting, praying' [*VA* 44.2].

Singing may have 'dissipated the discomfort of the journey with a song', but singing did not meet with universal approval:

> A brother questioned Abba Silvanus: 'What am I to do, abba? How am I to acquire sorrow for sin? I am severely afflicted by *accidie*, by sleep and by lethargy. When I rise from sleeping I make very heavy weather of the psalm-singing. I cannot shake off my languor, nor can I recite a psalm without a tune.' The elder replied: 'My child, in the first place, to recite the psalms with a tune smacks of pride, for it puts you in mind that you are singing while your brother is not. Secondly, it hardens your heart, insulating it against sorrow for sin. So, if you want to acquire sorrow for sin, leave singing aside. When you are standing in prayer, let your mind study the meaning of the verse. Consider that you are standing in the presence of the God who "searches the very hearts and reins [kidneys]" [Ps 7.10, 7.11 *LXX*] … Think of the great fathers, how simple they were. They knew nothing of tunes and tropes, except for a few psalms; and they were brilliant luminaries in the world … They even raised the dead and performed mighty works, not with singing and troping and tunes, but in prayer, with a broken and contrite heart and with fasting … As for singing, it has brought many down to the lowest most parts of the earth; not only worldlings but even priests have been feminised by singing and have been lured into *porneia* among other wicked desires.' [726]

'You are singing while your brother is not'; but he might be singing in his heart. It is reported of Macarius of Alexandria that 'He would stand *in silence*, prayer in his mouth, palm-leaves in his hands' [*HL* 18.15]. Also:

> Some of the fathers said of Abba Marcellinus of the Thebaid that, according to his disciple, when he was setting out for worship on Sunday, he would always provide himself with a passage from the Scriptures for the journey. This he would recite by heart until he arrived at church. Although he meditated in this way his lips did not move, so no one could hear him. [567 / 18.19]

These are not the only times secret (or silent) meditation is mentioned. The practice is referred to often enough to suggest that it was not altogether exceptional, e.g. the elder who said: '"Taking no thought" [Mt 6.25–34], keeping silent and secret meditation produce purity' [127 / 5.29]. Another told a brother: 'Subdue your body with numerous prostrations and vigils in silent meditation' [741], while a certain Palladius (not the author of *HL*) warned somebody: 'Tame your body by much repentance and watching and other labours; in secret meditation too' [G25; cf. Zeno 8; Eulogius 1 / 8.4; Poemen 168 / 10.9].

No matter how one meditated (secretly or audibly, saying or singing), one uttered (or thought) *words*, in one language or another. Apparently not everybody who meditated understood the meaning of the words he/she was using. This is revealed by the confession of a brother who came to his elder and said: 'Look, abba, I meditate but there is no sorrow for sin my heart, for I do not know what the phrase means.' It was probably not by any means the first time the elder had heard this complaint, for he well knew how to deal with it:

> 'Just keep on meditating,' he said; 'I have heard that Abba Poemen and many of the fathers had this saying: "The snake-charmer does not know the meaning of the words he speaks, but, when it hears them, the serpent knows the meaning of the phrase and is obedient." That is how it is with us; even if we do not know the meaning of what we are saying, the demons hear and retreat in fear.' [184/ 5.37]

There is no record elsewhere of Poemen or any of the fathers having ever said any such thing.

CHAPTER 7

Discretion

The fear of God and discretion prevail over every stain. [E7]

When Discretion Is Appropriate

It is generally believed that the Desert Fathers bequeathed a somewhat excessive form of spiritual discipline and that it was *The Rule of Saint Benedict* that introduced a note of moderation into the monastic life. In fact, at least some of those early monks showed a considerable amount of discretion in their teaching if not in their behaviour. Thus Palladius:

> First I will tell of [Macarius] the Egyptian who lived a total of ninety years, spending sixty of them in the desert, where he went as a young man of thirty. He was thought worthy of such discretion that he was called 'young elder'; on that account he made rapid progress. [*HL* 17.2]

But as no doubt Macarius was well aware, there are certain aspects of the monastic life where discretion is *not* appropriate, that is, when monks are responding to the *absolute* commands of Jesus, such as: 'If you would be perfect, etc.' and the rest of the sayings which are said to have inspired Antony [Mt 5.48, 19.21; Lk 12.33; cf. Mk 10.21]. There could be no partial renunciation, no conditional following [17]. No less demanding than the forbidding of property is the exclusion of relatives [Lk 14.26; see note 20 XX; cf. Mt 10.37–38]. This requirement too is absolute: it leaves no room for compromise.

The same, however, is not the case with some other of Jesus' commandments. He says that he came 'not to dissolve, but to fulfil, the law and the prophets' [Mt 5.48]. This is usually taken to mean to replace the multiple regulations of the Mosaic Law by certain general principles. In theory at least, the precise directives of the law required little more of the person than obedience, although, as Jesus points out, in fact one's judgement sometimes had to be brought into play, e.g.: 'Which of you shall have an ass or an ox fallen into a well and will not straightway draw him up on the Sabbath day?' [Lk 13.15 and esp. 14.5]. That is a relatively easy matter: whether or not to obey the fourth commandment to 'remember the Sabbath day to keep it holy' [Ex 20.9]. But Jesus utters commandments that require a far more demanding application of one's judgement, e.g. to love one's neighbour as oneself [Mt 22.39; Lk 10.27]; the so-called Golden Rule, 'Do unto others, etc.' [Mt 7.12; Lk 6.31]; 'Love your enemies' [Mt 5.44; Lk 6.27]; and the New Commandment, *viz.* 'That you love one another' [Jo 13.34]. Even where Jesus' directives regard specific topics, such as almsgiving, fasting, forgiveness, humility, judging and so forth, they are rarely explicit in the way the regulations of the Mosaic Law were often explicit. These directives frequently require one to engage one's intelligence and to make moral judgements, sometimes very fine moral judgements.

The Gospels give little guidance as to *how* such judgements are to be made when discretion is called for, and Paul not much more (but his 'Let your magnanimity [*epieikes*] be manifest to all' [Phil. 4.5] should not be overlooked). Only once is the word *discretion* [*diakrisis* in Greek, meaning discernment or discrimination] to be found in the Christian Scriptures in the sense of discerning good and evil [Heb 5.14]. (It has a different significance at Rom 14.1 and 1 Cor 12.10.)

The Aristotelian Mean

The Greeks had long experimented with the idea of virtue as a mean between two extremes – as an avoiding of excess and of all things being done in due proportion. This kind of thinking, however, is rarely found in early Christian thought – until the advent of Christian monasticism, that is. It finds classic expression in the *Instructions* of Dorotheos of Gaza:

> The virtues are a mean. This is the Royal Road [see below] of which that holy elder spoke: 'Travel the Royal Road [Nu 20.17, 21.22], count the mile-posts and you will not be discouraged' [Benjamin 5 / 7.5]. As I said, the virtues are a mean, between too much and too little; that is why it is written: 'Diverge neither to the right nor to the left but travel the Royal Road.' [cf. Prov 4.27; *Instructions* 106]

Clearly this definition of virtue bears a striking similarity to Aristotle's [*Nichomachean Ethics* 2.7.2]. Although it is never so fully expressed in the apothegms as it is here, there are hints of it there, e.g.:

> Let us guard against asking of God for more than we can handle and
> agreeing to do what we are in fact incapable of delivering. For it is better to
> travel the Royal Road by which (deviating neither to right nor to left) we
> will be able to be saved from this present wicked age, having humility in all
> things. [620]

'Deviating neither to right nor to left' requires a good deal of discretion; it is precisely in the tales and sayings of the fathers that the word
discretion begins to appear in the sense indicated – not only to appear,
but to be accorded a status of the greatest importance. One father
says: 'Discretion is greater than all the virtues' [106 / 21.25] and when 'An
elder was asked: "What is the monk's task?" "Discretion," he replied' [93 /
21.9]. Poemen said: 'The fear of God and discretion prevail over every stain'
[E7] and an elder at Scêtê opined: 'It is either [the fear of] God or discretion; but fear of God and discretion are really brothers' [E7]. 'Gain discretion,' said Silvanus; 'know yourself' [L93]. The message seems to have
been heard at Nitria, for when Evagrius went to Egypt in 385 and saw the
way of life of the fathers who were there, he was astonished. He asked a
great elder: 'Why is there not such spiritual discipline and discretion in the
nation of the Greeks?' [A39] It is well, for works without discretion are virtually worthless according to this saying first found in an eleventh-century
source, but probably from much earlier:

> Discretion is the greatest among the virtues and the man of faith must do
> what he does with [discretion] for those things which are brought about
> without discretion or aimlessly reap no benefit even though they be good;
> and sometimes they even do damage. [*Synag* 3:372; Hypothesis III.31]

In the form in which the 'Systematic' collection of sayings has survived
[*APsys*], the longest of its twenty-one sections is the tenth, the section
'Concerning Discretion'. The first of the 194 entries in that section begins
with a saying of Antony the Great which effectively says the same thing as
the one just considered: 'There are some who wore their bodies away with
spiritual discipline but became far from God because they did not have discretion' [Antony 8 / 10.1]. Palladius makes a similar point at greater length:

> For many of the brothers by giving themselves airs for their labours and
> almsgivings and boasting about their celibacy and virginity gained con-
> fidence through meditation upon the divine oracles and their zealous
> pursuits and failed to attain *apatheia* through lack of *discretion*, having
> fallen ill from certain meddling under the pretence of piety: whence there
> arises officiousness and evil-doing which distract from the doing of good
> deeds which is the mother of the cultivation of one's personal spiritual life.
> [*HL* Prologue 8]

That is clear enough, but the person who wishes to learn more about discretion and how it is to be acquired is doomed to be somewhat disappointed by section ten. For in spite of its title, it does not have much to say about the nature of discretion. The noun only occurs five more times, the verb only three. Thus, on hearing how Abba Agathon willingly accepted all kinds of slander *except* the charge that he was a heretic, 'they were amazed at his discretion and went their way enlightened' [Agathon 5 / 10.12]. This is echoed elsewhere: 'Abba Agathon took care of his own needs and was prominent for his discretion in all things, as much in his handiwork as in his clothing. He wore clothes that seemed neither to be too good nor too bad to anybody' [L10]. When John Colobos was charged with presumption for accepting the water-bottle from a priest, he replied: 'I accepted in order to get a reward for him and so he would not be distressed that nobody accepted from him.' 'They were astonished when he said this and much enlightened by his discretion', the passage concludes [John Colobos 7 / 10.37]. Abba Poemen states the matter very succinctly: 'There is a person carrying an axe who chops away the whole day long and does not succeed in getting the tree down. There is another person, experienced in felling, who brings the tree down with a few cuts and he used to say: "The axe is discretion"' [Poemen 52 / 10.88; cf. L38].

But not all fathers had axes. A brother asked an elder whether one has salvation if such-and-such a *logismos* comes to him. 'Having no experience in discretion, that [elder] replied: "He has lost his soul" … [The brother went to] report his *logismoi* to Abba Silvanus, for he was one of great discretion [who] poulticed his soul [with texts] from the sacred Scriptures [indicating] that there is repentance for those who consciously turn to God … I have told these things so we might see that there is danger in speaking of either our *logismoi* or our actions to indiscreet/undiscerning persons' [217 / 10.100].

Proportion and Measure

While it is clear from these apothegms that discretion is admirable, useful and essential in a confessor, almost nothing is said about what discretion *is*. There has, however, survived one saying that does shed a little light on this matter for it poses the very question one would like to see answered: 'There is an intensified spiritual discipline that is of the Enemy and his disciples practise it. How then are we to discriminate the godly and royal spiritual discipline from that which is tyrannical and demoniacal?', i.e. how is one to exercise discretion? 'Is it not clear from due proportion? … For lack of

proportion is destructive everywhere' [Syncletica 15]. Due proportion/lack
of proportion: that which is within the limit [*metron*] and that which is
beyond it, in either sense – of falling short of or of going too far. These
are what discretion is to discern and avoid, for there is danger in both.
For example, 'One can suffer damage from disproportionate [*a-metria*]
weeping' [135 / 3.38]. Syncletica goes further: '[The Enemy] will project a
totally unreasonable sorrow that has been called *accidie* by many people'
[Syncletica s10 / 10.103].

Evagrius Ponticus stresses that there is a proper *time* as well as proportion for every practice:

> Reading, watching and prayer stabilise a wandering mind; hunger, labour
> and isolation quench burning desire; psalm-singing, long-suffering and
> mercy put anger to rest, if these things are activated at the appropriate times
> and in due proportion [*metron*]. For that which is disproportionate or not
> in due season is short-lasting and harmful rather than beneficial. [*Practicus*
> 15 / 10.25]

The word *metron* [lit. 'measure'] is employed in two spiritual senses in
the apothegms. On the one hand, it is used to denote a person's actual
stature, meaning the point to which he has advanced in his spiritual progress, e.g. 'Until a man attain the *stature* of Moses and become almost
a son of God, he gets no help from the world' [538]. 'Macarius, you
have not yet attained the *stature* of those two women of this city' [489 /
20.21]. The monk is repeatedly warned *not* to attempt to measure himself
or to assess his own stature. 'A brother living with brothers asked Abba
Bessarion: "What am I to do?" Said the elder to him: "Maintain silence
and do not measure yourself"' [Bessarion 10; see Poemen 36, 73]. 'The task
of humility is this: silence and not to measure oneself in anything' [15.26].
[See also Macarius the Egyptian 1.16; John Colobos 34 / 1.13.] But such
warnings notwithstanding, the question frequently asked is 'have I arrived
at the stature [*metron*] of ...?' (or it is said, 'you have not yet arrived at
the stature of ...') [e.g. 67 / 20.22; 489 / 20.21; Eucharistus 1 / 20.2; 646 /
10.164; Carion 1 / 15.17; Sisoes 9 / 15.62].

On the other hand, *metron* can mean both a person's potential and his
capability, hence the *limit* beyond which he is incapable of proceeding:

> Abba Orsisios said: 'Unbaked brick set in a foundation near to a river does
> not last one day: but it lasts like stone if it is baked. Likewise, a person with
> a carnal mentality and not purged by the fire of the word of God like Joseph
> [Ps 104.19 *LXX*] falls apart when he proceeds to govern. For there are many
> temptations for such people. A person aware of his own limitations [*metra*]
> does well to flee from the burden of authority; but they who are firm in

the faith are immoveable … As for ourselves, knowing our own limitations [*metra*], let us fight the good fight for in that way we are only just able to escape the judgement of God.' [Orsisios 1 / 15.69]

An elder said: 'This is why we make no progress: we do not understand our own limits [*metra*]' [297 / 7.30].

> A brother asked an elder: 'What is humble mindedness?' 'It is to do good to those who wrong you,' the elder said. 'And if one cannot measure up to that stature [*metron*] what should he do?' the brother asked. 'Let him run away and elect to remain silent,' the elder said. [305A / 15.81]

It is clear that the monk needs to be aware both of his own limits and of his potential: 'An elder said: "This is why we make no progress: we did not understand our own limits [*metra*]; we do not persevere in the work we undertake and we seek to acquire virtue effortlessly"' [297 / 7.30].

It is perhaps even more important that one who is directing others is aware of (and respects) *their* limits. This is the point of the following well-known story about Antony:

> There was somebody in the desert hunting wild beasts and he saw Abba Antony taking his ease with the brothers. He was offended, so the elder wanted to convince him that the brothers needed to relax from time to time. He said to him: 'Put an arrow to your bow and draw it.' He did so. He said to him again: 'Draw,' and he drew. Again he said: 'Draw.' The hunter said to him: 'If I draw too much [beyond *metron*] my bow will break.' Said Abba Antony to him: 'So it is too with the work of God. If we draw on the brothers beyond measure, they will soon collapse; so they must relax from time to time.' [Antony 13 / 10.3]

It was no easy matter to identify one's own or (*a fortiori*) another's limitations. Fine distinctions were to be made, distinctions of which only a subtle discretion would be capable.

Cassian on Discretion

While there is little to be learned from the apothegms about what precisely the fathers meant by discretion, there is one father who has a good deal to say about it: John Cassian. The second book of *Conferences* is entirely concerned with discretion, the topic having already been broached at the end of the previous book. There Abba Moses of Scêtê engages in a dialogue with Germanus (the friend of John) and one or more unnamed companions. Having spoken at length of the goal of the monk, Moses goes on to say:

Tomorrow I want to tell you a little more about the excellence and grace
of discretion which among all the virtues holds the supreme and first place
and to demonstrate its excellence and usefulness, not only by day-to-day
examples, but also by the ancient opinions and sayings of our fathers. [*Conf*
1.23.1]

Next day Moses starts out by asserting that discretion 'is not some small
virtue nor one that can be attained by human effort along the way, unless it
be conferred by divine generosity' [2.1.3]. 'So you see,' he says a little later,
'the gift of discretion is nothing earthly or of small account but the highest
award of divine grace' [2.1.4]. (Palladius says discretion is a *charisma* [*HL*
24.1].)

In accordance with his promise to illustrate his message with examples
from the past, Moses goes on to recall how, as a young man, he once heard
Antony discussing the following question at great length: 'What virtue,
what observance could always keep the monk protected from the snares
and deceptions of the devil and bring him in a straight line and with a sure
pace to the summit of perfection?' [2.2.1–2] Antony's response echoes his
apothegm quoted above [Antony 8 / 10.2]: that some, having led lives of
impeccable and severe asceticism, came to a bad end, their lack of discretion having barred them from persevering to the end [2.2.3]:

> One can see no other reason for their fall other than that they did not have
> the opportunity of being instructed by those of old time and were not able
> to acquire that virtue [*sc.* discretion] which, keeping itself distant from the
> two opposing extremes, teaches the monk always to proceed along the Royal
> Road, permitting one neither to diverge to the right (to exceed the limit of
> just self-control by excessive fervour and inappropriate self-advancement)
> nor to the left (to relaxation and vice under the pretext of ruling the body
> correctly in a slackness of spirit). [2.2.4]

The Royal Road [*hê hodos basilikê*]

Prompted by many psalms, the ascetic endeavour is frequently referred
to as 'the way': 'the way of God' [248 / 10.115], the 'true way' [Poemen 8 /
10.54], 'the straight and narrow way' of Mt 7.14 [Ammonas 1 / 249 / 10.116]
and rather magnificently as 'the Royal Road'. (Syncletica may be making an
oblique reference to this last with her 'godly and royal spiritual discipline',
above.) The Royal Road is a reference to a passage in Numbers: requesting
permission to lead the Israelites through the land of Edom, Moses assures
its king: 'We will go along the Royal Road; we will not turn aside to the
right side nor to the left until we have passed your borders' [Num 20.17,

21.22; cf. Prov 4.27]. The idea appealed to the desert-dwellers. John Cassian has already been cited; also 'Travel the Royal Road; count ["do not count" in some mss] the mile-posts and be not discouraged' [Benjamin 5 / 7.5]. The image recurs occasionally. When Abba Poemen advocated a moderate degree of fasting, Abba Joseph commented: 'They gave us this way because it is royal and light,' an allusion to Mt 11.30 [Poemen 31 /10.61]. And at the conclusion of what may well be the most enigmatic item in the entire apothegmatic canon,[1] the writer concludes: 'Let us guard against asking of God for more than we can handle and agreeing to do what we are in fact incapable of delivering. For it is better to travel the Royal Road by which (deviating neither to right nor to left) we will be able to be saved from this present wicked age, having humility in all things' [620].

Basil says in the chapter of *Monastic Constitutions* entitled: 'That one must adjust abstinence to the strength of the body', 'It is appropriate for the ascetic to be detached from all conceit and to travel the truly middle and Royal Road, not at all inclining to either [side]: neither embracing relaxation nor disabling the body by excessive abstinence' [4.2; *PG* 31:345D]. He makes a similar reference to Num 20.17, 21.22 in the Homily *On Caring for One's Self*: 'If you are a traveller, pay heed to yourself like the one who prayed: "Direct my steps" [Ps 118/119.113] lest you turn aside from the way and incline to left or to right: travel the Royal Road' [c.4; *PG* 31:206C].

John Cassian avers that it is by discretion that one discerns the Royal Road and by discretion that 'we will not turn aside to the right hand nor to the left until we have passed thy border'. He makes Abba Moses assert that 'the lamp of the body' in the Gospel [Mt 6.2–23; Lk 11.34–36] is discretion [*Conf* 2.2.5] and to give various examples, in the course of which he says: 'For the parent, the guardian and the moderator of all the virtues is discretion' [*Conf* 2.4.4]. Three striking examples of the use of discretion follow, ending with the statement: 'So you see how dangerous it is not to have discretion' [*Conf* 2.8, end].

Acquiring Discretion

Germanus now asks a very pertinent question: 'It is abundantly clear from these recent examples and the pronouncements of those of old time that discretion is the source and in a way the root of all virtues. We want to be taught in what way one should acquire [discretion] or how it is possible to

---

[1] *BHG* 1450x, *de monacho superbo*, ed. J. Wortley, *AB* 100 (1982), 351–363.

know whether things are true and godly or false and devilish' [*Conf* 2.9.1].
Moses responds:

> True discretion is not acquired other than by true humility. The first evi-
> dence of this humility is if everything, not only that which is to be done
> but also what is contemplated, be submitted to the judgement of the elders,
> so that one trust nothing to one's own judgement but acquiesce in their
> decisions in all things and learn from their tradition what he ought to judge
> to be right and wrong. [*Conf* 2.10.1]

'Therefore the footsteps of the elders should always be followed with closest
attention and everything that arises in our hearts be brought without the
veil of shame' [*Conf* 2.11.8]. This is followed by a warning which found its
way into *APsys* as an apothegm:

> Abba Cassian said: 'Abba Moses used to tell us: "It is good not to hide the
> *logismoi* but to declare them to spiritual and discerning elders; not to those
> who have only gone white with time, for many are they who, considering [a
> father's] age, confess their own *logismoi* and, instead of healing, fall into des-
> pair on account of the inexperience of the one hearing [the confession]."'
> [5.4, citing *Conf* 2.13]

This point is made at some length (seventy-four lines), leaving no doubt
that, for John, discretion is in fact a habit of following in the footsteps
of those who have gone before, not of exercising one's own judgement.
'For in this way,' he says, 'we can easily attain true discretion. Walking
in the footsteps of the ancients, let us not presume either to do anything
novel or to conclude anything by our own judgement' [*Conf* 2.11.6]. Thus
John seems to be saying that, while on the one hand we can 'easily attain'
discretion, on the other hand, we must always have recourse to the counsel
of the fathers to guide us rather than exercise a grace granted to the individual. 'For by no other vice does the devil lead and draw the monk to
a sudden death as when he persuades him to neglect the counsels of the
elders and to trust in his own judgement and his own understanding'
[*Conf* 2.11.7]. This, however, is not really consonant with a scriptural text
(cited above, and which John has himself previously quoted) that seems to
say that discretion can grow in a person through experience: 'Solid food is
for full grown men who by reason of use [or "trained by experience"] have
their senses exercised to discern good and evil' [Heb 5.14; *Conf* 2.4.3]. And
in fact, elsewhere John concedes that this can be so for those well advanced
in spiritual discipline:

> There is an old and admirable saying of blessed Antony [*non inveni*] that
> if after living in a coenobium a monk seek to attain a higher [degree of]

perfection, having acquired the gift of discretion, he is then capable of relying on his own judgement and, attaining the summit of withdrawal-ness [*ad arcem anachoreseos pervenire*] he does not in the least have to ask of one person, even the greatest, about any of all the virtues. [*Inst.* 5.4.1]

A little later he characterises those who have attained 'the summit of withdrawal-ness':

[After] dwelling for a long time in coenobia, having been carefully and thoroughly instructed in the rule of patience and discretion, having mastered the virtues of both humility and poverty and having totally destroyed every vice, [these] penetrate the deep recesses of the desert in order to engage in terrible combat with the demons. [*Inst.* 5.36.1]

The dictum: 'Every effort should be made through the virtue of humility for the grace of discretion to be acquired which can keep us undamaged from either extreme' [*Conf* 2.16.1] leads into the final section in which the practice of fasting is used to illustrate the nature of discretion. It is well known that some people need more food and drink, also more sleep, than others, just as some people can work harder and longer than others. Likewise, for certain activities there is a right time for some people that would be wrong for others. To deviate from the right path, either by (for instance) drinking too much or too little, is equally harmful and, in the end, produces an equally noxious result. One who fasts too much will suffer malnutrition, he who eats too much will be in danger of losing his soul – and so forth. Discretion is what teaches a person how to identify and enables him/her to walk the tightrope between too much and too little.

Universal Need of Discretion

While the various sections of *APsys* do not by any means consist only of items clearly related to the stated topic of the section, they do for the most part contain a significant number of items clearly pertinent to that topic. Section ten appears to be an exception: it is difficult to tell what it is all about. There is, however, some indication of why this is so:

An elder said: 'This is the life of the monk: work, obedience, meditation, not judging, not back-biting, not grumbling, for it is written: "O you that love the Lord, see that you hate the thing that is evil"' [Ps 96/97.10]. The life of a monk is to have nothing to do with that which is unjust, not to see evil things with one's eyes, not to get involved in or to hear alien matters, not to use one's hands to snatch but rather to give; not to have overweening pride in his heart nor wicked thoughts in his mind nor a full belly, but rather to

act with discretion in all things: in these [the life of] the monk consists.'
[225 / 1.32]

Here is the root of the matter. In one way, discretion can be seen as a virtue
much like any other, but discretion has this distinction: that it is universally applicable. The monk must 'do *everything* with discretion', for it is
required at all times and in every situation. Discretion can be compared
with history: on the one hand, history is a discreet discipline, but on the
other hand, it is universal in that there is a history of everything. So it is by
no means inappropriate that a section on discretion should be the longest
of all, for it is in the exercise of discretion that the forbearance and restraint
characteristic of eremitic monachism are truly revealed. And they are never
more in evidence than when the demands on the capacity of the individual
are being adjusted, e.g.:

> [Somebody asked]: 'Three *logismoi* perplex me: whether to dwell in the
> desert, to go to a foreign land where nobody knows me or to shut myself
> up in a cell, meeting nobody and eating every second day.' Abba Ammonas
> said to him: 'It will not do you any good to do any one of the three. Do you
> rather remain in your cell, eat a little each day and always have in your heart
> what the Publican said [cf. Lk 18.13, "God be merciful to me a sinner"] –
> then you can be saved.' [Ammonas 4 / 10.20]

The ability of the discreet elder to adjust the 'normal' rules to the needs
of the individual (and indeed to go to the heart of the supposed 'rules') is
well illustrated by the following saying:

> Abba Longinus asked Abba Lucian about three *logismoi*: 'I want to live
> in a strange land.' The elder said to him: 'Unless you hold your tongue
> wherever you go, you are no stranger. So hold your tongue here and you
> are a stranger.' He also said: 'I want to fast every other day.' Abba Lucian
> said to him: 'The prophet Isaiah said: "If you bend you neck like a bul-
> rush, not even so will he call it an acceptable fast" [Is 58.5]. Do you rather
> abstain from evil *logismoi*.' A third time he spoke to him: 'I want to get
> away from people,' but he said to him: 'Unless you first get it right with
> people, you will not be able to get it right living alone either.' [Longinus
> 1 / 10.45]

Discretion can cut through appearances to the reality behind them: 'Our
mouth stinks from fasting; we have learnt the Scriptures by heart; we have
perfected [our knowledge of the psalms of] David and yet we do not
possess what God is looking for, i.e. fear, love and humility' [222 / 10.135].
These and several other items like them appear to be saying that, while one
can err to one side or the other, by attempting to do more or achieving less

than one is capable of, one can also err in failing to perform in the right spirit, like not being in love and charity with one's neighbour, e.g.:

> A brother asked Abba Joseph: 'What am I to do for I can neither endure distress nor work to provide charity?' The elder said to him: 'If you can do neither of these things, keep your conscience clear with respect to your neighbour and refrain from all evil; then you will be saved, for God seeks the sinless soul.' [Joseph of Panepho 4 / 10.40]

This is illustrated in an anonymous tale of a monk in the Thebaid who led a life of utter spiritual discipline, pursuing all the disciplines, eating a meal on Sundays only. The devil gave him to think that he excelled in fasting and ought now to be able to perform miracles – but God intervened. The monk resolved to go to some experienced elder to receive divine guidance on how he might be saved. The elder sent him to buy a quantity of bread and wine, then to sit quietly in his cell consuming it. He obeyed, praying fervently; gradually he began to understand why it came about that he was living indiscriminately and as he pleased. Returning to the elder in due course, he received this sage advice:

> My son, God, the lover of mankind, watched over you and did not let the adversary get the better of you. For [the adversary] is ever accustomed to lead astray those directed towards virtue with fine-sounding words and to bring them to the presumptuous state of mind. He also coerces them and leads them on to undertake high degrees of righteous activity in order to bring them down in this way. There is no sinful passion so abominable in the sight of God as pride: no righteous activity more honourable with him than that of humility. See both the examples of the Pharisee and the Publican [Lk 18.9–14]; the extremes of both sides are so precarious, for one of the elders said: 'Excess is of the demons.'[2] Follow then the Royal Road (as the Scripture says,) deviating neither to left nor to right. Use moderation in feeding, eating moderately in the evening. But if need arise, do not scruple to break the time-limit; for suffering, or any other reason, you should set aside the appointed hour. And if it happens that you are eating again in the day [i.e. twice a day] do not scruple, for we are 'not under law but under grace.' [Rom 6.14; 641]

That appears to be the one and only time Paul's famous dictum is cited by the Desert Fathers. This is unfortunate because that dictum indicates why and by what title each Christian (monk or worldling) is obliged to exercise discretion in every aspect of his/her living.

---

[2] Cf. 'All excesses [*hypermetra*] are of the demons' [Poemen 129]. But somebody opined: 'to humble oneself in one's deeds is good even when carried to excess, for it edifies the beholders' [486A].

CHAPTER 8

Work

That is a double disgrace if I both accept without needing and also take pride in giving away what belongs to another. [258 / 6.21]

The Importance of Work

It was a cardinal rule that the monk should not have idle hands: he must work and be self-supporting. Even so, the universality of this obligation was sometimes questioned:

> There was a monk who did not work at all, praying without ceasing. When evening came he would go into his cell and, finding his bread there, would eat. Another monk came visiting him bearing palm fronds; he obliged the elder to work the palm fronds. When evening came, he went in to eat as usual and found nothing. He went to sleep grieving and this message was revealed to him: 'When you were passing your time with me, I nourished you. But since you have begun working, you are to look to the labour of your hands to find your food.' [440]

Abba Serinos spelled it out when he said: 'I have spent the time harvesting, sewing, braiding; and in all these [activities] I would not have been able to be fed if the hand of God had not fed me' [Serinos 2]. For work was not only an obligation for the monk: it was a truly *salutary* obligation. When one monk asked an elder the familiar question: 'What should I do that I might be saved?', the elder answered: 'The work of your hands together with *synaxis* will deliver you' [E188]. Another elder was braiding rope when he was asked the same question. Without even looking up from his work, he replied: 'Look, you can see' [91 / 21.6].

But the work one undertook must not be merely a personal whim: 'Abba Poemen said: "For all the works that you do, take counsel, because it is written [*ubi?*]: 'Work without advice is stupidity'"' [E190]. Tasks must also be undertaken with an awareness of their significance: 'Blessed are they whose labours were executed with understanding, for they reposed themselves from every burden' [7.7].

The immediate object of a monk's labour was to make himself totally self-supporting, i.e. independent of any gifts or income. Thus, when Abba Pambo lay dying, he could say: 'From the time I came to this place in the desert [Nitria], built my cell and dwelt in it, I do not recall eating bread except what came from my hands' [Pambo 8 /1.25; *HL* 10.6]. It was said of Abba Agathon that he 'was wise in thought, resolute in body and self-sufficient in all things: handiwork, food and clothing' [Agathon 10 / 10.14].

The monk was not only required to support himself; he must also be capable of relieving those in need and of offering hospitality to any visitors who came his way. Thus Poemen: 'Apply yourself to handiwork as much as you are able, in order to perform deeds of mercy with it, for it is written, "Almsgiving and faith purge sins"' [Prov 15.27a; Poemen 69 / 13.7]. Another elder alleged: 'I have never yearned for work that is beneficial to me but disadvantageous to my brother, for I live in hope that my brother's advantage will bear fruit for me' [353 / 17.28]. One octogenarian elder could say: 'From the day I was initiated and born again by water and the Spirit until today I never ate another's bread without paying for it by my own labours [cf. 2 Th 3.8] and I have given to the lepers two hundred pieces of gold, earned by the work of my hands' [517]. That is a very large sum; it may indicate the underlying danger that work become *too* important, displacing prayer as the activity of primary importance. John the Eunuch regretted: 'When I was at Scêtê, the works of the soul were our work; we regarded handiwork as secondary work. But now the work of the soul has become secondary work and the [former] secondary work the [main] work' [Theodore of Phermê 10 / 10.33]. 'The love of [manual] work is the fall of the soul,' some elder said, 'but its establishment is stillness in God' [s61].

Work and Trade

Doubtless there were some monks who so far secluded themselves that they were able to find or grow enough provisions to supply their needs without any contact whatsoever with the world or with other monks. But most of the monks we know of were commercially engaged with 'the world' to a certain extent, exchanging finished goods for raw materials and the necessities of life. This exchange could be affected through the intermediary of a monastic agent (steward), by contact with a travelling merchant or by personal visits to the local market.

For the monks truly living in the desert there were raw materials at their immediate disposal, primarily reeds and palm-fronds. These could be transformed into a variety of useful (therefore marketable) commodities [Macarius of Alexandria 1]. The commodity most often mentioned is rope, handmade by braiding vegetable matter. Abba Achilles told some visitors from Kellia: 'From evening until now I have braided twenty fathoms and I don't really need them. But maybe God will be angry and accuse me, saying: "Why did you not work when you were able to work?" That is why I toil and do it to the best of my ability' [Achilles 5].

Achilles' fathoms might be traded as rope, or coiled around and sewn together with linen thread [John the Persian 2 / 6.8] using a stout needle to make baskets. Needle and thread were needed for rope-making too, it appears [Poemen 10]. The same raw materials could also be used to manufacture the rush mat, a primitive futon that served as bed and sofa in the homes of poorer folk as well as in monks' cells [Paul the Great 3 / 4.41]. A variety of baskets could also be devised by weaving palm-fronds, reeds, rushes and their like. 'They used to say of Abba Megethius that he ... never did possess any of this world's material goods other than one needle with which he would split [?] the palm-fronds. He made three baskets a day [to defray the cost] of his food' [Megethius 1]. It should be added that all the raw materials mentioned so far had to be steeped in water for some time before they could be worked. Even when steeped these were not kind to the workers' hands, hence work was not only a necessity for the monk; it was also a painful necessity.

Other Kinds of Work

Monks gained their bread in a variety of other ways:

> Some brothers once visited a great elder. He said to the first one: 'What work do you do, brother?' 'I braid rope, abba,' he replied. 'God will plait a crown for you, my son,' the elder told him. Then he said to the second one: 'And what work do you do, brother?' 'Rush mats,' he said. 'God will strengthen you, my son,' the elder said. He said to the third one: 'What do you make brother?' 'Sieves,' he replied, whereupon the elder said to him: 'God will protect you, my son.' He said to the fourth one: 'And what do you do?' 'I am a scribe,' he said. 'Then you are learned,' said the elder. Then he asked the fifth brother: 'What work do you do?' but he said: 'I weave linen.' 'That has nothing to do with me,' said the elder. 'He who braids rope, if he does it with calm persistence, plaits himself a crown in cooperation with God. He who makes rush mats needs strength, for it is hard work; the maker of sieves needs protection, for they sell them in the villages. The scribe has to

humble his heart, for his trade leads to high-mindedness. As for the linen-weaver, I have nothing to do with him because he trades. If someone sees afar off a person carrying baskets, rush mats or sieves, he says: "Now that is a monk," for straw is the raw material of the monk's handwork and it burns in the fire. But if a person sees somebody selling linen, he says: "Look, the merchants have come," for linen-working is an activity of the world, not beneficial for many folk.' [375]

The great elder was antipathetic to the linen-weaver because his product was destined for the privileged classes; it was a luxury, whereas all the other workers were producing items that were needed by all. Yet some monks undoubtedly were engaged in the linen industry. A monk who had fled into the wilderness and was living with buffalos told the elder who went looking for him: 'I was in a coenobion in the Thebaid working as a linen-weaver, but a *logismos* came upon me saying: "Go out and live alone, then you will be able to practise *hesychia* and hospitality"' [132A / 20.15]. Palladius says of the folk at Nitria: 'All these men work with their hands in the manufacture of linen so that they are all self-sufficient' [*HL* 7. 5; see also G50, S22]. He also says that the ladies Piamoun and Alexandra spent their time spinning linen [*HL* 31.1; 5.3].

The best-known case of a monk earning his keep as a scribe is Evagrius Ponticus at Kellia, but he was not alone [517; 519 / 15.129] and a reference to 'the scribes who are in this desert' [758] suggests they were not rare. One of them was very absent-minded [520]; then there is this anecdote:

Abba Abraham used to say of one of the people at Scêtê that he was a scribe and that he did not eat bread. A brother came begging him to write out a book for him. The elder's mind was wrapt in contemplation; he wrote in continuous lines without punctuation. When the brother took it and wanted to punctuate [it] he found it lacked some verses and he said to the elder: 'There are some lines missing, abba.' Said the elder to him: 'Go away, and first practise what is written; then come back and I will write the rest for you too.' [Abraham 3]

The following tale about a well-trained scribe also affords a glimpse into the working of a small religious community:

They used to say about Abba Silvanus that, at Scêtê, he had a disciple called Mark, a man of enormous obedience and a calligrapher too; the elder loved him for his obedience. He had eleven other disciples and it hurt them that he loved [Mark] more than them. The elders heard of it and were sad. The elders came to him one day and, taking them along, he went out and knocked at each cell saying: 'Brother so-and-so, come for I need you' and not one of them followed him right away. Coming to Mark's cell the elder knocked, saying: 'Mark!' and, on hearing the elder's voice, he immediately came out in haste and [Silvanus] sent him on an errand. And he said to the elders: 'Where are the other brothers, fathers?' Going into [Mark's] cell he took up his quarto and found that he had begun an *omega* but, hearing the elder's voice he did not turn the pen to finish it. So the elders said: 'We indeed love him whom you love, abba, because God loves him too.' [Mark the disciple of Silvanus 1 / 14.11]

One other story of a professional scribe is worth quoting as it also bears evidence of writing used in an unusual way:

A diligent brother came from a foreign country and lived in a small cell on Mount Sinaï. The first day when he came to stay there he found a small piece of wood that had been inscribed like this by the brother who had once lived there: 'I, Moses, son of Theodore, am here and bear witness'. The brother set the piece of wood before his eyes every day and asked the one who wrote it (as though he were present): 'Where are you now, oh man, that you can say: "I am here and bear witness"? In what kind of world and where is now the hand that wrote this?' Spending the whole day in this activity and mindful of death, he was constantly grieving. His manual activity was that of a scribe. Although he was getting paper and orders for copies from the brothers, he died without writing anything for anybody, except that he inscribed on a small tablet that he left on the paper of each one these words: 'Forgive me, my masters and brothers; I had a little business to do with somebody and, for that reason, I did not have time to write for you.' [519 / longer version 15.129]

There are some passages where it is not clear whether the monk was a writer by trade or simply one who did his own writing, e.g.: 'A monk named Philoromos who had been a monk since the time of Julian the Apostate [361–364] continued writing until he was about eighty' [*HL* 45.3; 517].

Three brothers once visited an elder at Scêtê. One of them asked him: 'Abba, I have learnt the Old and the New Testaments by heart ...' 'You have filled the air with words,' said the elder in reply to him. The second one asked: 'And I have written out the Old and the New Testaments for myself ...' 'You have filled the casements with documents,' the elder replied. Then the third one said: 'And mould has formed in my cooking-pot ...' 'And you have chased hospitality away from you,' the elder told him in reply. [385 / 10.147]

Some monks were engaged in other kinds of work. Abba Achilles was a maker of nets at Scêtê [Achilles 1 / 10.18], probably not mosquito nets, although mosquitos there certainly were at Scêtê [Macarius 21] (and no doubt elsewhere too) and one case is known of a monk making a large mosquito net [*PS* 161]. Achilles' nets would be for huntsmen [Miles 2 / 7.17], hence the 'net-making season' [59 / 10.190] would be dependent on the hunting season. A demon in disguise says: 'I am mending my nets, for I wish to catch in them the gazelles in the wilderness' [s86].

Paper-Making

> Some brothers once went off to live on the mountain of Diolcos and they learnt how to work at paper-making, working for wages. But since they were not skilled, nobody gave them work. Then one elder encountered them and he said to them: 'Why are you not working?' As they were respectful, they answered: 'Because we do bad work.' But the elder knew a godly workman and he said to them: 'Go to such-and-such an elder and he will provide you with work,' so they went and he gladly provided them with work. But the brothers said to him: 'We do bad work, father,' and the elder said: 'I trust in God that, because you are working with your hands, the rest will follow' and, overflowing with love, the elder encouraged them to work. It is true, you see, that the violent take the kingdom of heaven by force. [cf. Mt 11.12; 614]

Paper was made from the stem of the papyrus plant, the sticky fibrous inner pith being cut into thin strips that were glued together. Drying and polishing completed the process. The transportation and delivery of paper could be almost as complicated as its manufacture:

> When the blessed Seridos [directed] a coenobion at Thavatha he had a beloved Egyptian living at Ascalon who had a disciple. Once when it was winter time that person sent his disciple to Abba Seridos with a letter about bringing him a roll of paper. When the young man was coming from Ascalon there happened to be much rain, so that the river Thyathon became swollen. It was raining when he gave the letter to Abba Seridos and the young man said to him: 'Give me the paper so I can go off,' but he said to him: 'It is raining; where can you go now?' The young man said to him: 'I have a commandment and I cannot wait.' As he went on insisting, [the elder] gave him the paper and he departed with the leave and the blessing of the abba. Then the abba said to those who were present with them (among whom was Abba Theodore who is one of those with us): 'Let us go and see what he does at the river,' for the rain was beating down. When he arrived at it, he went far from them, took off his clothes, wrapped the paper in his clothes, put it on top of his head, tied [it] and said to them: 'Pray for me,' – and threw himself into the river. When Abba Seridos assured his companions [of this] they could think of nothing else but to send to the sea and find his remains but [the young man] continued struggling and resisting the rushing water and, swept downstream some distance, he arrived at the other bank of the river. Amazed at his obedience unto death,

we glorified God. This is the obedience which the fathers say is unwavering, which bestows great confidence with God upon him who was deemed worthy of it. He will deem us worthy of the same grace too so that, passing our days care-free and peacefully, we may find mercy with our fathers in the presence of God. [752]

Somebody appears to have foreseen that parchment would supersede papyrus and that some parchments would be used as palimpsests:

Here I am telling you, my son, the days will come when Christians will destroy the books of the holy gospels and of the holy apostles and of the divine prophets, smoothing away the holy Scriptures and writing *troparia* and pagan poems; and their mind will be besotted with *troparia* and pagan poetry. This is why our fathers have said that the scribes who are in this desert are not to write the lives and sayings of the holy fathers on parchment but on paper, for the forthcoming generation is going to smooth away the lives of the holy fathers and write according to their own will. [758]

The case of a curtain-maker reveals some interesting things about his living conditions:

A brother asked Abba Serapion saying: 'My father, I was so overcome by sadness that I [thought I] would go into the world and work [there].' Said Abba Serapion: 'What work are you doing that you wish to leave your dwelling place and go into the world to work?' The brother answered: 'I make these curtains.' Said the elder: 'Do you not have a mat under you when you are weaving?' I answered him: 'Yes, I have.' He said to me again: 'Do you not have another mat at your doorway?' I answered: 'I have.' He said to me: 'Do you not have a window of glass where you sleep? Do you not keep yourself warm in the winter?' I answered him: 'Yes, I do.' He said to me: 'Believe me, my son; if a man could see beyond [this world to] the inheritance, glory and rest that God has prepared for those who loved him all the days they had in this world, then, [even] if he lived in a cell full of worms up to his knees, it would not sadden him.' [E51; cf. 196 / 7.35]

Harvesting

Great though the importance might be of monks staying in their cells, there is a surprisingly large amount of evidence of them coming out to harvest, and not just to harvest monastic crops (if there were any), but of returning to the inhabited world and the cultivated lands bordering the Nile, there to hire themselves out as day labourers. 'The Scêtiotes have this custom, that they go out to the estates and reap' [*PS* 183, followed by an interesting anecdote]. Harvesting inevitably provoked an interruption in one's spiritual discipline; it has already been noted how John Colobos used to repair the damage [John Colobos 35]. 'They also used to say of him that [the wages of] all the labour he expended on the harvest he would take and bring to Scêtê saying: "My widows and orphans are at Scêtê."' [John Colobos 57]. John had the example of Abba Pior here, a disciple of Antony who lived a solitary life somewhere between the Wadi el Natrun and Nitria and was remembered for having made a new start every day [Poemen 85]:

> Having worked at the harvest for somebody, the blessed Pior reminded him that he should receive his wage; but he procrastinated and [Pior] went off to his monastery. When the season called for it, he harvested for him again and, diligently though he worked, that one gave him nothing so off he went to his dwelling. The third year came around; the elder accomplished his customary task and went away having received nothing. But the Lord prospered the house of that man; he went around the monasteries in search of the holy one, bringing his wage. As soon as he found him he fell at his feet and gave it to him saying: 'The Lord has given it to me.' But [Pior] entreated him to donate it to the priest at the church. [Pior 1]

It was said of the monks of Scêtê that 'when they went up to Egypt and wished to receive the payment for their harvests or the price of their handiwork, each one of them limited his provisions according to their needs, and they gave everything else to widows and orphans' [A25].

There were advantages other than financial accruing to the harvesters: 'Abba Benjamin used to say: "When we came down to Scêtê from the harvest they brought us a gratuity from Alexandria, for each one a *sextarius*-jar [*c.* 500cc] of oil sealed with plaster ..." (which they hardly touched)' [Benjamin 1].

The brothers at Kellia were probably less than well behaved at harvest time, for their abba, 'when he was about to go harvesting, said to them: "I am not giving you any more instructions for you do not keep them"' [Isaac of Kellia 4 / 4.22]. He must have been rather disillusioned with them:

> Abba Isaac used to say to the brothers: 'Our fathers and Abba Pambo wore old, patched up clothes made of palm-fibre; now you are wearing expensive clothing. Go away from here for you have turned this location into a desert.' [Isaac of Kellia 7 / 6.10]

But not all his charges were self-pleasing:

> Abba Isaac said: 'I know a brother who was harvesting in a field and he wanted to eat an ear of grain. He said to the owner of the field: "Will you let me eat one ear of grain?" He was astounded on hearing this and said to him: "The field is yours, father, and you ask me?" That was the extent to which the brother was scrupulous.' [Isaac of Kellia 4 / 4.22]

There are two excellent stories associated with harvest, unfortunately too long to be reproduced here. The first begins: 'Abba Sisoes used to say: "When I was at Scêtê with Abba Macarius we went harvesting with him, seven persons in all, and here there was a widow gleaning behind us who never stopped crying"' [Macarius of Egypt 7 / 19.12]. The cause of her tears is discovered and (of course) dealt with. The other story begins: 'Three brothers once went away to the harvest; they undertook to do sixty *arourai* themselves but one of them fell sick the first day and went back to his cell' [350 / 17.24]. It is a touching tale of how two men harvested about twelve hectares all alone and nevertheless insisted that their sick colleague receive a fair share of the wages.

CHAPTER 9

Eating and Drinking

By no means is the soul humbled unless you reduce its food or restrict it to feeding only when necessary. [G20]

Regular and Occasional Fasting

There was regular fasting and fasting that was exceptional. The regular fast of a monk, sometimes referred to in the apothegms as a 'dry diet', consisted of one frugal meal a day with water to drink, usually taken at the ninth hour, occasionally at sundown. The monk's meal was what today would be called strictly vegan fare and of the plainest kind. All serious monks limited themselves to this single meal, neither eating nor drinking during the heat of the day until the ninth hour, i.e. halfway between noon and sundown. Some waited longer still. Theopemptus asked a brother 'How do you fast?' 'Until the ninth [hour],' he said. The elder told him: 'Fast until evening; discipline yourself and recite by heart the Gospel and the other Scriptures' [Macarius the Egyptian 3 / 18.13]. The time between the ninth hour and sundown would of course vary in length depending on the time of year. At one season it was long enough for Antony and his companions to walk the 12 Roman miles (almost 18 kilometres) from Nitria to the site of Kellia [Antony 34]. Nevertheless, there are not a few fathers who are said to have done as this one did: 'Abba Paesios who had been living in the remotest desert for forty years ... said: "The sun never saw me eating since I started living alone"' [Cassian 4 / 4.26; Inst 5.27].

Some monks inflicted an even more severe fast upon themselves, the most common form being only to eat every second day or even every third, and in very exceptional cases, only once a week or less. John Moschos reports: 'They said that Abba Mark the anchorite who lived near the Penthoucla monastery practised the austerity of fasting all week long for sixty-nine years' [PS 13]. Less credible is the brother who said: 'I have seen elders [at Scêtê] who never ate at all, unless somebody came that way'

[*PS* 54]. Some fathers used to deny themselves anything that had been cooked (which might or might not exclude bread) or would condemn themselves only to drink brackish water.

John Moschos also makes mention of 'grazers' [*boskoi*],[1] folk who lived out in the wilderness, eating only what they could find there. He makes mention of them more times than they are spoken of in the whole of the rest of monastic literature put together, which may indicate that theirs was a particularly popular form of spiritual discipline in his time. In eleven passages, fifteen grazers are identified [*PS* 19, 21, 92, 129, 154, 159, 167, etc.]. Their way of life may have been of questionable validity; it is written of a monk who

> went into the wasteland and lived there for many years, eating wild herbs. After a while he prayed to God to let him know what kind of reward he would be giving to him. An angel spoke to him: 'Depart from this desert and go out on the road and a shepherd will meet you and, according to [what] this person [says,] you shall receive [as] a reward.' Departing straight away, he met that shepherd about whom he had been told and greeted him. When they sat down to converse with one another he saw the shepherd's bag in which were some herbs. That monk asked: 'What is this?' He said to him: 'It is my food.' He said to him: 'How long have you been eating these herbs?' The shepherd said to him: 'Thirty years more or less I have not tasted anything else except these herbs once in the evening of every day, while also drinking water in accordance with what I eat. The wage which the owner of the flock gives to me I give to the poor.' When that monk heard these things, he fell down at the feet of that shepherd and said: 'I thought I had mastered abstinence, but you through your discipline are worthy of a greater reward than me because, every herb that I encountered, I ate immediately.' Then that shepherd said to me [*sic*]: 'It is not right for rational human beings to imitate the animals, but at the correct and organised times to eat what is prepared for them and, afterwards, to observe a fast from everything until the [next] correct time.' Having profited [from this], that monk added to his labour and was perfected. He praised God, marvelling at how many holy people there were in the world, unknown to human beings. [s3]

Fasting was one more aspect of the monk's rejection of the world, possibly of his 'hating his own life' too [Lk 14.26]. He could not sever himself completely from nourishment so he did the next best thing: he reduced his intake to a minimum. And this he did with unquestioning belief in its beneficial effects, variously expressed:

[1] See John Wortley, 'Grazers [βόσκοι] in the Judaean Desert,' *The Sabaite Heritage in the Orthodox Church from the fifth century to the present*, Orientalia Lovaniensia Analecta, Leuven 2001, pp. 37–48. See *APanon* 62, 516.

> Abba John Colobos said: 'If a king wishes to capture a city of the enemy, he first takes control of the water supply and the supply of food: thus the enemy submits to him, reduced by famine. So it is with the passions of the flesh too: if a person exists with fasting and hunger, the Enemy wastes away from his soul.' [John Colobos 3 / 4.20]

Poemen said: 'Affliction, confinement and fasting: these are the working tools of the monastic life' [Poemen 60 / 1.23], and Syncletica: 'Just as the most bitter medicines put poisonous animals to flight, so prayer with fasting expels an evil *logismos*' [Syncletica 3 / 4.50]. Sisoes of Petra, the disciple of Antony, said: 'Fasting is the mother of all virtues, because it gives birth to them and leads man to all of them. But humbleness of spirit is the greatest of all virtues' [E155].

Fasting may be the mother of all virtues, but it is not the greatest, for 'Compassion is greater than prayer, and prayer is greater than fasting. Prayer emaciates the body, and fasting dries up the bile and keeping vigil reduces the bone' [A37]. Fasting is inferior to the other virtues in another way too: 'Fasting is a useful and necessary practice, but we do it by our own choice; whereas the law of God enjoins the practice of charity as obligatory' [Cassian 1 /13.2].

Every monk had to decide how much fasting he was going to do, but woe betide him who made that decision alone:

> Abba Moses said: 'A monk who is under [the supervision] of a spiritual father yet does not possess obedience and humility, who fasts or does anything else of his own accord in order to appear righteous: such a person neither acquires a single virtue nor does he even know what it is to be a monk.' [G2]

A spiritual father might explain how fasting was thought to work:

> Abba Eligius said to his disciple: 'My son, gradually accustom yourself to afflicting your stomach with fasting. For just as a [wine-] skin becomes thinner when stretched out, likewise also the stomach when receiving much food. But if it receives little, it is constrained and requests little.' [A10]

In general, the fathers seem to have been concerned to keep fasting within reasonable limits: 'A brother asked an elder: "To what extent ought one to fast?" and the elder said: "No more than is stipulated. There are many who want to go beyond that but, in the event, were not strong enough to complete even a little"' [G22]. The higoumen at Nitria said: 'To fast for two days is appropriate only for anchorites; likewise, to partake of fruit and refrain from bread is neither advantageous nor praiseworthy; it

has the appearance of vain glory' [G23]. As is so often the case, Poemen
gives sound advice:

> Abba Poemen said: 'I know a brother of Scêtê who fasted every second day
> for three years and still was not triumphant. When he stopped fasting every
> second day and deliberately fasted [every day] until evening, from that time
> on he always prevailed.' And to me Abba Poemen said: 'Eat and do not eat,
> drink and do not drink, sleep and do not sleep. Act with wisdom and you
> will find repose.' [E163]

> Abba Joseph asked Abba Poemen: 'How ought one to fast?' and Abba
> Poemen said, 'I would like the person who eats every day to stop a little
> short of eating his fill.' Abba Joseph said to him, 'Did you not fast every
> second day when you were young, abba?' 'Indeed for three and four days
> and even for a whole week,' the elder said, 'but the elders, being capable
> themselves, tested all these things and concluded that it was good to eat
> each day, but in small quantity.' [Poemen 31 / 10.61]

Bread

'They related of Abba Dioscorus of Nachiastis [Namiasis?] that his bread
was made from barley and lentils' [Dioscorus 1 / 4.13]. It is impossible to
say whether that was the normal consistency of the monks' bread ('the
only bread he ate was made from bran' [PS 17]), but it is clear that a monk
rarely ate fresh bread, except when it was provided miraculously [HL 71.3]
or by a special effort, e.g. 'A brother at Kellia brought his own fresh loaves
[psômia] and invited a table-full of elders' [155 / 4.77; cf. 348 / 17.21, 592/2].
Otherwise the word translated bread or loaf (slice in E-sayings) is paxamas,
named after a baker in ancient Athens called Paxamos. He discovered that
if bread were dried out in the oven or in the sun [see Ammoes 5], it would
last much longer than if were left the way it came out of the oven. Dried
out, it had enormous advantages for people going on long journeys (like
'hardtack' for navigators) or for those requiring provisions for a considerable length of time, such as solitary monks. Athanasius comments when
Antony laid up enough bread for six months: 'Those from the Thebaid do
this, and often the bread is stored even for an entire year without harm'
[VA 14.4]. The disadvantage is that paxamas was extremely hard; it had to
be wetted to soften it before it could be digested. Such was the staple diet
of those monks who had not renounced all cooked food, and for some of
those too, for Ammonios 'never ate anything that had been cooked except
bread' [HL 11.4], but 'There was one of the great fathers in Scêtê who did
not taste bread or drink wine' [A66].

The normal consumption was probably two loaves each day, for a brother is instructed: 'Get yourself forty pairs of loaves and enough palm-fronds for forty days, then go away into the remotest desert and stay there for forty days' [173 / 5.27]. A brother told Pambo: 'After fasting for two days I eat a pair of loaves' [Pambo 2 / 10.94]. Serinos 'only ever ate two dried loaves' [Serinos 1], while Agathon said: 'I fast every other day and then eat two dried loaves' [Agathon 20]. But some could eat more: 'If I find myself somewhere and I eat three loaves, is it a lot?' a brother asked an elder [Xoios 1], while others could eat less: 'One of the holy ones happened to visit [Megethius and asked] him: "How do you live in this desert, brother?" "I fast every second day and consume one loaf." "If you will listen to me, eat half a loaf each day." He did so and found repose' [Megethios 2 / 14.10]. Both Evagrius Ponticus [*HL* 38.10] and his mentor, Macarius of Alexandria, allowed themselves one pound of bread per day (which *might* be the equivalent of two loaves). They had a very curious way of consuming it:

> [Macarius] heard of yet another person that he ate a pound of bread. He broke his own hard loaf, put [the fragments] into vessels and resolved [only] to eat so much as the hand could lift out. He recounted with a smile: 'I laid hold of many pieces but could not lift them all out on account of the narrowness of the opening; like a tax collector it would not let me do so.' He maintained that spiritual discipline for three years, eating four or five ounces [100–125 g] of bread and drinking a comparable amount of water, [using] half a litre of olive oil a year. [*HL* 18.2]

Presumably Macarius had water in the vessel where he introduced the fragments of dry bread, for as noted already, *paxamas* had to be moistened in order to be digested, e.g. 'When it was the sixth hour he moistened some dry bread and sat down to eat' [145 / 4.71]. Thus a monk entertaining Emperor Theodosius II at Constantinople 'moistened some bread for him, adding a little oil and salt, and he ate; he gave him water and he drank' [308 / 15.85]. The wetting of *paxamas* gave rise to this curious incident:

> An event of this kind is reported of Pambo: Piôr the ascetic visited him and he brought his own bread. He was reproved by [Pambo with the words:] 'For what reason have you done this?' 'In order not to inconvenience you,' the other replied. Pambo taught him a lesson by letting the silence speak. Sometime later [Pambo] went to visit [Piôr] having wetted the [dried] bread he was bringing. Then, when he was asked, he said: 'I even wetted it so as not to inconvenience you.' [*HL* 10.8]

Salt

In another situation, an elder 'set dried loaves and salt before [his guests,] saying: "But we must make a feast in your honour" – and he poured a little vinegar on the salt' [229 / 10.150]. Of Candida, a female ascetic, it is recorded that 'she abstained completely from what had blood and life in it but she did take some fish and vegetables with oil on a feast-day. Otherwise she lived out her days satisfied with diluted vinegar and dried bread' [*HL* 57.20]. Abba Dorotheos 'used to eat six ounces [+/- 170 g] of bread [each day] and a portion of chopped vegetables, drinking a proportionate amount of water' [*HL* 2.2].

A considerable number of apothegms mention salt in connection with dry bread, e.g. 'While the fathers of Scêtê were eating only bread and salt they would say: "Pass fifty days eating bread with salt once a day …"' [291 / 14.23]. 'Go and spend this year eating bread and salt in the evening, then come back again and I will speak to you' [Ares / 14.3]. 'They used to say of the same Abba Helladius that he used [only] to eat bread and salt' [Helladius 2]. 'While the fathers of Scêtê were eating only bread and salt they would say: "Let us not oblige ourselves [to eat] bread and salt" and thus were they strong for the work of God' [John Colobos 29].

> They used to say of ... Abba Helladius that he used [only] to eat bread and salt. When Easter came around he would say: 'The brothers are eating bread and salt. I ought to make a little effort for Easter. Since I eat sitting down on the other days, now that it is Easter I will make an effort and eat standing up.' [Helladius 2]

There was scriptural justification for the use of salt:

> For if there is no connection operating between [one's] life and the truth of [one's] words it is bread without salt (as Job says) which is either not eaten at all or, if it is eaten, will bring those who eat it to a bad condition. 'Shall bread be eaten without salt?' he says, 'and is there any taste in empty words' that are not fulfilled by the witness of deeds? [Job 6.6; *HL* 47.14]

But salt was simply a physical necessity for those living in the Egyptian heat:

> Abba Achilles once came to the cell of Abba Isaiah at Scêtê and found him eating; he was putting salt and water in a dish. Seeing that he had hidden it behind the [coil of] rope, the elder said to him, 'Tell me what you were eating,' but he said, 'Forgive me, Abba; I was cutting palm fronds, and, coming back in the heat of the day, I put a morsel [of bread] in my mouth with some salt, but my throat was dry from the heat and the morsel would

not go down. For that reason, I was obliged to put a little water with the salt so that, in this way, I might be able to swallow; please forgive me.' But the elder said, 'Come and see Isaiah eating soup at Scêtê! If you want to eat soup, go to Egypt.' [Achilles 3 / 4.10]

There were probably many monks like Dioscorus: 'his practice is to eat nothing but bread, salt and water' [C14], which must mean that the following is a tale of episcopal perversity:

One of the bishops visited the fathers at Scêtê each year. A brother met him and conducted him into his [own] cell, setting before him bread and salt with the words: 'Forgive me, my lord, for I have nothing else to set before you.' The bishop said to him: 'When I come next year I don't want even to find salt.' [28 / 4.103]

We have already seen Macarius the Egyptian at supper with 'the two strangers' (see p. 24); here is a rather more lavish feast:

One of the elders was visiting another elder and he said to his disciple: 'Cook a few lentils for us' – this he did – 'and moisten some bread for us' – so he moistened [it]. They went on talking about spiritual matters until the sixth hour of the next day, then the elder said to his disciple again: 'Cook a few lentils for us my son,' and he said: 'I did it yesterday,' and then they ate. [149 / 4.69]

There was a monk at Kellia who used to cook himself a few lentils before *synaxis* so that he was not tempted to rush away after the service [L21] but usually lentils were cooked as and when they were required. 'Abba Isaiah called one of the brothers and washed his feet then he threw a handful of lentils in a pot and served them when it came to the boil' [Isaiah 6]. 'When some of the fathers visited him and he had only one small vessel of water; while he was boiling a few lentils, it was used up' [Moses 13 / 6.27]. Sisoes would not have approved: 'A brother enquired of Abba Sisoes how he ought to remain in his own cell, to whom he said: "Eat your bread and salt and let it not be necessary for you to cook anything"' [L23].

Wine

In the *Prologue* to *HL* Palladius sets out his attitude to wine at some length [*HL Prologue* 9–14]. This may be in response to a dispute in the monastic community on the subject, which would hardly be surprising. Antony only drank water himself [*VA* 7.6–7]; nevertheless, he sets out the scriptural position on drinking: 'the Apostle [Paul] said: "Do not get drunk on wine for that leads to dissipation" [Eph 5.18] and the Lord, urging the

disciples in the Gospel said: "Watch out that your hearts be not weighed
down with intoxication and drunkenness"' [Lk 21.34; Antony 22 / 5.1].
This led some monks to regard wine as a dangerous abomination: 'They
would say that where there are wine and youths, there is no need of Satan'
[545]. 'Wine and women distance one from God' [592.55]. Hence there
were monks who were determined teetotallers, e.g.: 'Once there was a fes-
tival at Scêtê and they gave a cup of wine to an elder. But he refused it,
saying: "Take that death away from me." When the rest of them who were
eating with him witnessed this, neither did they accept it' [144 / 4.63].
Another elder, offered a cup of wine at the very end of his life, 'wept when
he saw it, saying: "I never expected to drink wine until the day I died"'
[157 / 4.79].

So some monks clearly did abstain; and abstainers were to stand firm:

> If you are visiting somewhere, do not intentionally reveal your ascetic way
> of life or [say]: 'I do not eat oil or cooked food or fish,' only do not com-
> promise so far as wine is concerned if you fear the battle; and if some people
> reproach you, do not let it trouble you. [592.48]

But even serious abstainers may have made exceptions: 'They used to say
of a certain elder that he went fifty years without eating bread or *readily*
drinking wine' [Abraham 1, 10.19]. And Paphnutius is said to have had a
cup of wine *forced* on him by a kindly robber chief [Paphnutius 2 / 17.15].
Macarius the Egyptian drank occasionally, but he made himself pay for it:

> They used to say of Abba Macarius that, if he was enjoying the company of
> some brothers, he would impose a rule on himself: 'If there is wine, drink
> for the brothers' sake and in place of one cup of wine do not drink water for
> one [whole] day.' The brothers would give him wine by way of refreshment
> and the elder would take it with pleasure in order to torture himself. But his
> disciple, aware of [his] practice, said to the brothers: 'For the Lord's sake,
> do not give it to him for otherwise he is going to afflict himself in his cell.'
> When the brothers learnt [this] they did not give him [wine] any more.
> [Macarius the Egyptian 10 / 4.29]

Macarius was not the only one who punished himself for taking wine:

> Once while the brothers were eating in the church at Kellia at Eastertide,
> they gave a brother a cup of wine and obliged him to drink it. But he said
> to them: 'Excuse me fathers, for you did this to me last year too and I was
> afflicted for a long time.' [60 / 4.91]

There is one version of a saying in which total abstinence is advocated
for monks [330 / 1.34], while another version of the same saying would have
them '[refrain] from any more than a little wine' [Mathoes 11]. Elsewhere

we read of a monastery (unidentified) where 'an allowance of a single dried loaf and a cup of wine was often given to the brothers after the *synaxis*' [Isaac the Theban 2 / 11.47]. There are also various indications that wine was sometimes consumed more freely, e.g.:

> Abba Theodore was once passing some time with some brothers at Scêtê and, while they were eating, the brothers were discreetly taking cups [of wine] in silence; they were not saying: 'Forgive.' Abba Theodore commented: 'The monks have lost their manners, not saying: "Forgive."' [Theodore of Phermê 6 / 15.32]

Palladius says that at Nitria, 'They drink wine and there is wine for sale' [*HL* 7.4]. However, the custom seems to have been that monks ought not to drink any more than three cups. Thus an unnamed elder said: 'Let no monk that drinks more than three cups of wine pray for me' [465 / 4.98]. 'If I drink three cups of wine, is it a lot?' a brother asked Abba Xoios, who said to him: 'If there were no demon it would not be a lot; if there be, it is a lot, for wine is foreign to monks living a godly life' [Xoios 1]. This was obviously not what Abba Isaiah thought: 'When there was an *agapê* in the church and the brothers were eating and talking to each other, the priest of Pelusium reproved them, saying: "Be quiet, brothers; I personally saw a brother eating with you and drinking as many cups as you and his prayer is going up before God like fire"' [Isaiah 4 / 12.8].

> Once an offering [i.e. a Eucharist] took place at the mountain of Abba Antony and a *knidion* [unknown quantity] of wine was there. Taking a small bottle and a cup, one of the elders brought [some wine] to Abba Sisoes. He gave it to him and he drank it. Likewise, a second [cup] and he accepted it. He offered him a third one too but [the elder] did not take it, saying: 'Stop brother, or do you not know that it is Satan?' [Sisoes 8 / 4.44]

There is no knowing how much a cup contained. When we read, 'A *saïtês* of new wine was once brought to Kellia so a cup could be given to the brethren,' we know one *saïtês* was approximately nine litres but there is no telling how many brothers it had to serve. That particular event had unfortunate consequences:

> When one of the brothers climbed up onto the dome to escape [from …?] the dome collapsed. Running out at the crash, the others found him on the ground; they began to scold him saying: 'Show off! It served you right!' But the abba took his side, saying: 'Leave my son alone: he has done a good thing. As the Lord lives, that dome will not be rebuilt in my time, so that the world may know that the dome fell at Kellia on account of a cup of wine.' [148 / 4.64]

Really serious ascetics would nevertheless have heeded the injunction: 'If good wine comes your way, mix a little vinegar with it and say: "For the sake of Christ who drank vinegar." Do not drink your fill, but leave a little saying: "Look, Christ's share too"' [592/2]. Better, though, is never to start taking wine:

> If you are still young, flee from wine as from a serpent. If you drink a little at a love feast, desist. If your hosts bind you with an oath and even prostrate themselves before you, pay no attention to their oaths. Satan often gives monks the idea of pressing the young ones to take wine, for he knows that wine and women separate [us] from God. [592/55]

Isisdore, one of the renowned early elders at Scêtê, had a dire warning for drinkers:

> He often used to say that if a person gave himself to wine-drinking, he would not escape the onslaught of the *logismoi*; for, obliged by his daughters, Lot became drunk with wine and, on account of his drunkenness, the devil made easy work of contriving for him to commit lawless *porneia*. [cf. Gen 19.31–35; Isidore the Priest 1 / 4.23]

When some folk reported to Abba Poemen that a certain monk did not drink wine, he said to them: 'Wine has nothing whatever to do with the monks' [Poemen 19 / 4.34], but, as though this were something exceptional, 'They used to say of Abba Peter the Pionite at Kellia that he did not drink wine' [Peter the Pionite 1 / 4.43]. And, endeavouring to reconcile an alienated brother, Poemen said: 'Make a little food, get a *sextarius* of wine [*c.* 567cc] and let us go to him and eat together; perhaps we will be able to sooth him like that' [Poemen 4 / 17.11]. 'It is better to drink wine rationally than to drink water with conceit,' Palladius told Lausus. And: 'if the body is in need of it, let us prudently partake of wine like Jesus, even if they say: "Here are gluttons and tipplers"' [Mt 11.18–19; *HL Prologue* 10, 12]. Many monks appear to have adopted the same attitude; they too did not escape criticism:

> Abba Xanthias once went up from Scêtê to Terenouthis and there he broke [his journey]. They brought him a little wine as he was exhausted from his ascetic life-style. When some people heard of him they brought one possessed of a demon to him. The demon began abusing the elder and saying: 'You have brought me to this wine-bibber?' The elder did not want to expel [the demon], but because of his insult he said: 'I trust in Christ that I will not finish this cup before you come out.' As the elder began drinking the demon cried out saying: 'You are burning me, you are burning me'

and, before he had finished, the demon came out by the grace of Christ. [Xanthias 2 / 19.20]

There is a rare flash of humour in the following context:

> One of the elders said: 'We went to the mountain of the blessed Antony to [visit] Abba Sisoes, and when we were sitting down to eat, a young man came in who was asking for alms. When we were beginning to eat, an elder said, "Ask that young man if he wishes to come in and eat with us." When he spoke to him, [the young man] did not wish [to do so]. The elder said, "Let us give to him whatever is left over from us to eat outside." The elder produced a pitcher of wine which was being kept for the Eucharist, and the elder mixed for each one a cup, giving that young man two cups. I was joking and said to him, "I will also go outside: give me two [cups]!" Abba Sisoes said, "If he had eaten with us he would have drunk equally, and he would have been convinced that we do not drink more. For now he will think to himself, 'These monks enjoy themselves more than me.' It is good, therefore, that our conscience should not condemn us."' [s13]

The conscience of another elder told him: 'Since it is necessary to extinguish carefully the fire of the lusts being stirred up in us, we have need of water, and not of wine' [s71]. The good Amma's advice was: 'Do not stuff yourself with bread and you will not long for wine' [Syncletica 4 / 4.5].

CHAPTER 10

Hospitality and Neighbourliness

Love your neighbour as yourself and all your enemies will fall beneath your feet. [E85]

The Monk's Dilemma

The monk was on the horns of a dilemma for he was subject to two conflicting imperatives. On the one hand, he was constantly being encouraged to flee from folk: to live silently in isolation. Yet he could no more deny his humanity than he could avoid his erotic proclivities or the necessity of food and drink. And, being human, he was bound by the Second Commandment that stands next to the First and Great Commandment: 'and you shall love your neighbour as yourself', for 'there is no other commandment greater than these; on these two commandments hang all the law and the Prophets' [Mt 22.40]; compare Paul: 'The whole Law is fulfilled in one word, even this: you shall love your neighbour as yourself' [Gal 5.14].

This Second Commandment laid a double obligation on the monk: in addition to labouring to support his neighbour as well as himself as and when need arose, he must also be prepared to adjust his way of living accordingly if and when a guest (monk, worldling or even a woman) should come to his door. For it is the bounden duty of monks, whether living alone or in community, to practice altruistic hospitality, *philoxenia*, lit. 'love of the stranger/guest' (the word *xenos* means both). The responsibility is grave, for Jesus says: 'I was a stranger and you took me in' and 'Inasmuch as you did unto one of these my brethren, even the least, you did it unto me' [Mt 25.35, 40], and Paul writes: 'As we have opportunity, let us do good unto all men, especially to them who are of the household of faith' [Gal 6.10; see also Rom 12.13, 1; Tim 3.2; Tit 1.8]. (Presumably Paul meant one's fellow Christians, but the monks may have taken it to mean others of their kind.) 'Be hospitable to one another without complaining,' says Peter [1 Pet 4.9] and the writer of the Epistle to the Hebrews, citing Abraham's hospitality [Gen 18.1–5], says, 'Be not forgetful to entertain strangers: for thereby some have entertained angels unawares' [Heb 13.1]. These injunctions apply to Christians at large: the monks embraced them wholeheartedly, e.g.:

> Concerning receiving the brothers as guests, [Apollos] said: 'We must venerate the brothers who come by. It is not them we venerate but God; for when you saw your brother, you saw the Lord your God. We received this from Abraham,' he said; 'and when you receive [brothers] constrain them to take some refreshment. We have learnt this from Lot who constrained the angels [to enter and eat].' [Gen 19.3; Apollos 3]

This thought would eventually be expressed yet more strongly: 'Let every guest who comes be received as though he were Christ himself, for he is going to say: "I was a stranger and you took me in" [Mt 25.35]. And to all let due honour be shown, especially to those who are of the household of faith' [Gal 6.10; *Rule of St Benedict*, c.52].

Yet in his instructions to the visitors from Jerusalem in 394–395 John Lycopolis seems to suggest that really serious monks could leave the task of being hospitable to other (presumably less proficient) monks:

> So then do you too my sons pursue *hesychia*, always exercising yourselves in contemplation so you can acquire a pure mind in prayer to God. For that is a good monk who is always exercising himself in [this] world by devoting himself to good works, displaying brotherly affection, hospitality, concern for the stranger, giving alms and charitable donations, benefitting visitors, helping those who toil and remaining free of scandal. That monk is good, very good indeed, for he is practising the commandments and working at them even when he is occupied in worldly matters. *But better than him and greater* is that contemplative who withdraws from practical matters in favour of the mental. He leaves it to others to concern themselves with those matters. As for him, once he has denied himself and consigned himself to oblivion, he concerns himself with heavenly matters. He presents himself before God unimpeded by any concern and is held back by no other worries. Such a monk as that lives and has his being with God, singing unending hymns to God. [*HME* 1.62–63]

It appears that some did indeed 'shut up the bowels of compassion' [1 Jn 3.17] when visitors came by. Their niggardliness gained the monks a bad reputation, for a brother asked an elder: 'Abba, what reply should I give to those who revile us that we do not return [to the world] on account of laziness, and through our manual work [and] labour of our souls we do not give comfort to strangers?' [s43]. Fully to appreciate the following example one has to be aware that Arsenius had once been the friend of kings and the tutor of princes, Moses a highwayman:

> They used to say of one brother who came to see Abba Arsenius at Scêtê that he came into church and besought the clergy [that he might] meet with Abba Arsenius. They said to him: 'Take a little refreshment, brother and you shall see him,' but he said: 'I am not tasting anything until I meet with him.' So they sent a brother to go with him because his cell was far away. They knocked at the door and went in; when they had greeted the elder, they sat in silence. So the brother, the one from the church, said: 'I am going [back;] pray for me.' Since the brother from elsewhere was not having any communication with the elder, he said to the brother: 'I am coming with you too,' and out they went together. Then he begged him: 'Take me to Abba Moses too, the one who was a brigand.' They came to him and he received them joyfully. He treated them with honour and sent them on their way. Then the brother who was guiding him said to him: 'Here I have taken you to the outsider and to the Egyptian; which of the two pleased you?' In reply he said: 'The Egyptian pleased me so far.' On hearing this, one of the fathers prayed to God: 'Lord, show me this matter: one person avoids people in your name while another welcomes them with open arms in your name,' and here there was shown to him two great boats on the river. In one of them he saw Abba Arsenius with the Holy Spirit sailing in *hesychia* while in the other there sailed Abba Moses and the angels of God and they were feeding him honeycombs. [Arsenius 38]

One can sympathise with Arsenius. The true solitary was faced with a very difficult decision when a visitor came knocking: should he preserve his solitude, or obey the Second Commandment and risk becoming the leader of a following? Antony too could hesitate to accept visitors. This story is probably a fiction, but the dilemma is real:

> Abba Macarius the Egyptian visited Abba Antony at the mountain. When he knocked at the door [Antony] came out to him and said to him: 'Who are you?' 'I am Macarius,' he said, whereupon [Antony] closed the door, went in and left him. But when he saw his patience he opened up to him and, taking delight in him, said: 'I have been wanting to see you for a long time for I have heard tell of you.' He received him as his guest and gave him refreshment, for he was extremely exhausted. [Macarius 4 / 7.14]

The story goes on to tell how they worked and talked together, leaving one in no doubt that Macarius' visit severely disrupted Antony's normal routine: precisely what Arsenius feared and Moses welcomed. It appears from the apothegms that much discussion centred around this very point: what was the monk to do when visitors arrived?

A brother asked Abba Matoes: 'What shall I do if a brother visits me and it is a fast day or at an early hour, for I am perplexed?' The elder said to him: 'If you are perplexed but eat with the brother, you do well. But if you eat when you are not expecting anybody, you are following your own will.' [Matoes 6]

Most of the nineteen entries in section thirteen of the *APsys*, 'One should joyfully dispense hospitality and charity', are concerned with that same question, rather than with how guests should be treated:

Two brothers once came visiting an elder; it was the custom of the elder not to eat every day. When he saw the brothers he joyfully welcomed them in, saying to them: 'Fasting has its reward, but he who, out of love, eats again, fulfils two commandments: for he abandoned his own will and he fulfilled the [Second] Commandment, having refreshed the brothers.' [288 / 13.11]

A brother was visiting an elder. As he was leaving, he said to him: 'Forgive me, abba, for I have diverted you from observing your rule,' but in response he said to him: 'My rule is to refresh you and to send you on your way in peace.' [283 / 13.8]

And here once again is Moses, the ex-highwayman:

An order was once issued at Scêtê: 'Fast this week then celebrate Easter.' It happened that some brothers from Egypt visited Abba Moses and he cooked them a little food. Seeing the smoke, his neighbours reported it to the clergy: 'Look, Moses has broken the order of the fathers and cooked himself some food.' 'It is we who will speak to him when he comes,' they said. When Saturday came around, the clergy, well aware of the great discipline of Abba Moses, said to him in public: 'Oh Abba Moses, you have broken the order of men but fulfilled [the law of] God.' [Moses 5 /13.4]

The fathers are unanimous in teaching that, when a guest arrives, he must be received 'as Christ himself'. The importance of hospitality was made clear to this brother dying of thirst:

As I lay there I fell into an ecstasy and I saw a pool of water full to overflowing. Two people were standing at the edge of the pool, drawing water with a wooden vessel. I began to make a request of one of them in these words: 'Of your charity sir, give me a little water, for I am faint,' but he was unwilling to grant my request. The other one said to him: 'Give him a little,' but he replied: 'No, let us not give him any, for he is too easy-going and does not take care [of his soul].' The other said: 'Yes, yes; it is true that he is easy-going but he is hospitable to strangers,' – and so he gave some to me and also to my companions. We drank and went on our way, travelling three more days without drinking until we came back to the inhabited world. [*PS* 16]

So great was the importance of hospitality that some amazing liberties could be taken in in order to entertain guests:

> There was one of the great fathers in Scêtê who did not taste bread or drink wine. Gathering the elders, he came to the church of Isidore. When he did not find the priest there, trusting in the openness that he had with him and knowing that the fathers lived in such piety and labour, he entered inside and took what he needed and a little wine. And he himself was the first to begin to eat and drink. And they were astonished how, for the sake of God, he denied his own wishes in order that he might provide refreshment for the elders. [A66]

Fasting, work and even prayer are to be suspended (or at least modified) for the duration of a guest's stay. It did not, however, always work out quite like that though:

> Coming out of a coenobion, some brothers went visiting in the desert and there they encountered an anchorite. He gladly received them and, as is the custom among hermits, set a table before them there and then, perceiving that they were very weary. He put before them whatever there was in this cell and refreshed them. When evening fell they recited the twelve psalms and likewise during the night. While the elder alone was keeping the vigil, he heard the visitors saying to each other: 'The anchorites in the desert get more repose than we do in coenobia.' In the morning, as they were about to go visit his neighbouring elder, he said to them: 'Greet him on my behalf and tell him: "Do not water the vegetables."' When the neighbour heard this, he understood the phrase: he kept them at work, fasting, until evening. When evening fell he offered a long *synaxis* then he said to them: 'Let us break our fast for your sakes, for you are worn out,' adding: 'it is not our custom to eat every day, but let us take a little food for your sakes.' He set dried loaves and salt before them, saying: 'But we must make a feast in your honour' – and he poured a little vinegar on the salt. Then they got up and offered a *synaxis* until dawn, when he said to them: 'I could not complete the canonical service for you must take a little repose, being from elsewhere.' They wanted to leave when dawn broke but he besought them, saying: 'Stay with us for some time, at least for the three days customary in the desert.' Realising that he would not willingly let them go, they got up and slipped away secretly. [229 / 10.150]

Joseph of Panepho used to say: 'When there are brothers present, let us receive them with joy. But when we are alone, we need sorrow to abide with us' [Joseph of Panepho 1]. But what about when the visitor tried to impose his standards on the host?

A person named Eulogius was a disciple of the holy John [Chrysostom] the archbishop. He was a priest and a great ascetic who used to fast two days at a time and often went a whole week eating nothing but bread and salt; he was held in high esteem by the people. He visited Abba Joseph of Panepho expecting to see some yet more severe austerity [while staying] with him. The elder received him with joy and caused some refreshment to be served of whatever he had to hand, but Eulogius' disciples said: 'The priest does not eat anything but bread and salt.' For his part, Abba Joseph just kept quiet and went on eating. [The guests] stayed three days but did not hear [the hosts] singing psalms or praying, for their activity was in secret. So they went their way without reaping any benefit. But, by divine providence, there came up a mist; they wandered off track and came back to the elder's monastery. Before they knocked at the gate, however, they heard [those inside] singing psalms. They waited a long time, then knocked, [whereupon they within] silenced their psalm-singing and joyfully welcomed them in. On account of the great heat Eulogius' disciples put some water in the bottle and gave it to him. It was a mixture of sea- and river-water: he could not drink it. Coming to his senses, he fell down before the elder. Wishing to learn his way of life, he said: 'How is this, Abba?[1] At first you were not singing psalms; but now, after we went out, you are? And the bottle I just received, I found the water salty?' The elder answered him: 'The brother is a fool, and in his wandering [mind] he mixed it with sea-water,' but Eulogius begged the elder, wishing to learn the truth and the elder said to him: 'That little cup of wine was for the *agapê*; but this water is what the brothers drink all the time.' Then he taught him discretion regarding *logismoi*, and he detached all human concerns from him. [Eulogius] became accommodating and from then on would eat whatever was put before him. He too learned to perform his activity in secret; he said to the elder: 'Your [pl.] activity is genuine indeed.' [Eulogius 1 / 8.4]

John Cassian is formal: 'All fasting is to be set aside when guests arrive' [Cassian 1 / 13.2 citing Mk 2.19–20]. He tells of a visit to an elder who said: 'This is now the *sixth* time that I have set the table for brothers who have come by. I invited them to eat and myself ate with each one of them' [Cassian 3, *Inst* 5.25]. When guests perceive that Abba Sisoes has eaten with them in the morning (and that on a fast day too), they are reproved when they realise that he will subsequently mortify himself many days for this breach of his rule [Sisoes 15 / 8.20].

---

[1] The text may be defective here. *Synag* 3.26.8.6 continues: 'While we were with you, you did not sing psalms, but after we went out from you, then there was a great deal of psalm-singing. Likewise then, you were drinking wine in our presence, but now I tasted your water I found it saline and scarcely drinkable.'

Visiting

As we said, the monk who boasted: 'Mould has formed in my cooking-pot' was reproved by an elder: 'And you have chased hospitality away from you' [385 / 10.147]. He may have chased away visitors too for one might well conclude from reading the apothegms that monks were constantly visiting each other. The word *visit* and its cognates do occur frequently, but this is deceiving. Like those recording devices that only spring into action when something moves or a sound is made, the apothegms tend only to report unusual occurrences: they have little or nothing to say of the long, silent hours of loneliness the monks chose to endure.

A certain amount of visiting was obligatory, although this was not universally agreed: 'One elder said: "Such a habit is unnecessary"' [A34]. Yet a brother must consult with his elder from time to time. As one elder put it: 'The monk's toil is in vain if he does not visit the servants of God to learn what is profitable to his soul' [E167]. Macarius the Egyptian gives a good reason why: 'Do not neglect visiting the elders, because the days will come [when], if you wish to serve [God], you will prevail due to the words of the elders' [E72]. Conversely, an elder might not hesitate to go looking for a lost sheep, as Macarius went to investigate the two strangers when he had not heard from them for so long [Macarius the Egyptian 33 / 20.3]. Not to be able to visit their elders was a serious matter for monks:

> Abba Isaac and Abba Abraham were living together. Abba Abraham went in and found Abba Isaac weeping. 'Why are you weeping?' he said to him and the elder said to him: 'Why should we not weep? For where can we go? Our fathers have died and our handiwork is insufficient for us [to pay] the price of the boats we take to go visiting the elders. So now we are orphaned – and that is why I too am weeping.' [Isaac of Kellia 3]

The arrival of a visitor was an occasion of great importance for the monks and could be a time of celebration. This is attributed to Palladius but it is not found in *HL*:

> Once we came from Jerusalem to Egypt and went to see Apollo the Great. The brothers who were with him ran eagerly to meet us with singing, for that is the custom of all the monks. They prostrated themselves and embraced us. Then some of them preceded us, others followed singing until we came near to the father. When the father heard the singing he too came to meet us as he used to do for all brothers who arrived [there]. First he prostrated himself on the ground then got up and embraced us. Then, leading us in [to his cell] he offered a prayer and washed our feet with his own hands, inviting us to repose ourselves. It was his custom to do likewise, not for us

alone, but for all [visitors]. He said to his entourage: 'One is obliged to reverence brothers who arrive, for it is not them, but God whom you revere. When you see your brother,' he said, 'you see the Lord your God.' [*Synagogê* 3.41.1; cf. *HME* 8]

Apollo of Hermopolis[2] in the Thebaid gave his visitors from the Mount of Olives a similar message:

He said a great deal to us in private about spiritual discipline and the [monastic] way of life and would often talk about entertaining brothers as guests: 'You have to prostrate yourself before visiting brothers, for it is not them you are revering, but God. When you see your brother (he said) you are seeing the Lord your God. And this (he said) has come down to us from Abraham whilst from Lot we have learnt that sometimes we have to oblige brothers to receive refreshment – for he obliged angels in that way.' [Gen 19.3; *HME* 8.55–56; Apollo 3]

Community

The arrival of guests was so important to the monk because, by virtue of his withdrawal from the world, he had severely restricted his opportunities for practising the Second Commandment: to love his neighbour as himself. When a person came to his door, that was when he could demonstrate his love for the other. Theodoret of Cyrrus says: '[The monks of Egypt work] not only to supply their own needs but also to care for guests who arrive and for those in need' [*Philotheos Historia* 30.6]. For Poemen, the three cardinal monastic virtues are fear of God, ceaseless prayer and hospitality [Poemen 160], while another father rates hospitality second [296 / Rufus 2 / 14.29]. An unnamed elder, sending a disciple to live in seclusion far away, says to him: 'Off you go to live alone; you will be able to live in *hêsychia* and to practise hospitality' [20.15].

A monk living alone might receive a rather unusual guest:

One of the holy men of Egypt was living in a desert place. There was another [anchorite] some distance from him, a Manichee – and he a priest [or] one of those whom they call priests. As he came from visiting one of his co-religionists evening overtook him there where the orthodox holy man was. He was on the horns of a dilemma, afraid to come into his [cell] and sleep there, for he knew the elder was aware that he was a Manichee and might not receive him. However, obliged by necessity, he knocked. The elder

---

[2] Apollo is the only father who advocates daily communion. The sentence in both extracts: 'When you see your brother, etc.' was often cited as scriptural (which is not) by anthropomorphists in support of their position.

opened the door, recognised him and joyfully received him. He obliged
him to pray, refreshed him and gave him a bed. Awaking in the night, the
Manichee said: 'How come he has not shown me any disrespect? This is
[a man] of God.' He came and fell at his feet saying: 'I am an orthodox from
this day forward,' and thus he remained with him. [289 / 13.12]

Not all monks lived alone. A steadily increasing number of them were
in some measure members of a community, subsequently known as a lavra
and eventually a coenobion. The same difficulty arises here as with the
collections of apothegms: the monastic community was in a state of evolution, each community at a different stage of development [cf. Anoub
1 / 15.12]. There was little or no cooperation between the various communities. Certainly, there was nothing resembling the 'orders' into which
western monasteries would eventually be organised. Each community was
a law unto itself. At the heart of a community was the founder's cell where
the founder or his chosen successor presided as abba. As time went on the
abba was more likely to be a priest, but he could be one who had effectively imprisoned himself, with only a hole in the wall through which he
received provisions and conversed with his lieutenants. Those who had
come and remained to be his disciples lived at some distance from him
and from each other, even at some considerable distance, thus Arsenius
at Scêtê: 'They used to say of him that his cell was thirty-two miles away'
[Arsenius 21 / 2.9].

At first the cells were single dwellings, but as time went by an increasing
proportion of them housed two, three or more brothers. As enrolments
increased (which they did rapidly, e.g. at Nitria), cells were erected over an
ever-widening area. As the amount of suitable terrain was finite, in some
cases satellite communities were established, e.g. Nitria > Kellia > Phermê
and the 'four churches' at Scêtê.

The extent of suitable terrain was finite because, vast though the desert
might be, there was a limit to the number of places where humankind could
survive. Also, monks were not the only people living in the wilderness.
Tales indicating the presence of thieves and predators (men and beasts)
are plentiful. But far more dangerous were the tribal barbarians who occasionally swept in from the Libyan desert, e.g. the Mazices who devastated
Scêtê three times, killing and destroying. Their attacks led directly to some
monks emigrating, thus diffusing the ideal of Egyptian monachism far and
wide. Others stayed and rebuilt, but each time they rebuilt, the community was drawn ever closer together (for outlying cells were too easy prey)
until, in due course, a defensive wall was erected around it and the monastery became a fortress, Saint Catherine's Sinai being an excellent example.

Needless to say, this increasing concentration of the physical plant brought important changes into the life of its inhabitants. The earliest aspirants who came asking how they could be saved were expecting to be taught how to live and pray in the desert, then to be sent out to do it. The cells set up adjacent to but at some distance from the elder's were already a compromise for those living in them. Further compromise gradually became the norm, which meant that monks were brought increasingly into contact with one another. Thus it became the practice (we know not how or when) for each monk to pack up the articles he had completed on the last day of the week and make his way to a central location, a journey of several kilometres in some cases. Once the brothers had all arrived and congregated they would intone the evening psalms and then (sometimes) observe an over-night vigil (consisting of more psalms and Scripture readings) until dawn broke. That was the signal for the morning psalms, to be followed by a celebration of the Holy Eucharist and general communion if a priest were present. A communal meal [*agapê*] would follow the liturgy, accompanied by a small degree of social intercourse. Subsequently, in return for the finished items he had brought in, each monk would be given some raw materials and enough provisions for the coming week. Then, with enough time to arrive before dark, each monk would set off back to his own cell for another week of solitude.

It goes without saying that this weekly gathering implies a certain amount of infrastructure and organisation. There had to be a place where the monks could congregate to worship and to eat, even if it were no more than a roof to protect them from the sun. Somebody had to trade the monks' handiwork for the necessities of life, both for the *agape* and for the monks to take back with them. In a sense these were small seeds, but they developed rapidly: the primitive shelter into both a church and a refectory; the one trader into a whole organisation necessary for a larger community. Liturgically, the one weekly communal *synaxis* gradually became a daily occurrence,[3] the monks eventually assembling for prayer, not only once, but several times each day. There is surprisingly early attestation to this practice, significantly in Palestine where things probably evolved more quickly than in Egypt:

> It was reported to the blessed Epiphanius, Bishop of Cyprus [367–403], by the abba of the monastery he had in Palestine, 'Thanks to your prayers, we

---

[3] This, however, is *not* true of the Holy Eucharist which, probably on account of its later institution (i.e. when a priest became available), remained (and still remains) a weekly event (plus when a major feast falls on a weekday) in Orthodox monasteries.

did not neglect the rule but are diligent in celebrating both the first hour, the third, the sixth, the ninth, and at lamp lighting,' but he reprimanded them and declared, 'You are clearly deficient in prayer, desisting from prayer at the other hours of the day, for the true monk must unceasingly have prayer and psalmody in his heart.' [Epiphanius 3 / 12.6]

The method used to this day to summon monks was the *semantron*, a long wooden plank held in the player's left hand and struck with a wooden mallet in his right. The tone can be varied somewhat by striking at different distances down the plank and usually a distinctive rhythm is maintained. The sound carries very well, ideal for desert conditions. Even in the early days there would be occasions other than Saturdays when monks were required to congregate, for instance when an important visitor arrived [Theophilus 2 / 15.59] or a death occurred:

> The brother went and told the abba and [he] ordered his body to be brought into the church to be buried there. When they had placed him before the altar, [the abba] ordered the *semantron* to be struck so that the entire lavra could be assembled and his body be honourably interred. [642–643]

Other meetings appear to have taken place: a council at Scêtê is mentioned twice [Moses 2 / 9.7, 3 / 16.9] and 'Once there was a meeting at Kellia about some matter and Abba Evagrius spoke' [Evagrius 7/ 16.3]. These were not always very pleasant meetings: 'At first we used to assemble together and speak of [spiritual] benefit; we became as choirs, choirs [of angels] and were being lifted up to heaven. Now we assemble together and come to back-biting, dragging each other down into the abyss' [Megethios 4 / 238 / 10.165].

Monks might congregate for a specific purpose, e.g. 'Those of Scêtê were once assembled to enquire into the question of Melchizedech' [Coprès 3 / 15.38] and 'Some monks left their cells and gathered together in one place … Next day they all assembled in the same place and began discussing a brother who had defaulted; they began to speak ill of him' [18.43]. There is, however, no evidence of regular meetings other than for worship; nothing akin to the Benedictine chapter.

Neighbours

As monks began coming into contact with one another more often in various ways, it became increasingly important that a monk know how he ought to comport himself towards his neighbour. Of the many apothegms dealing with this subject, few cite any of the scriptural texts we might consider appropriate. It may, however, be that such texts were so well known that they were literally taken for granted – or simply referred to obliquely, e.g. the reference to Mt 25.32–33 in 307 / 15.84 is meaningless unless the reader know the significance of 'the goats'. Moreover, Antony the Great almost certainly had the 'love your neighbour' commandment in mind when he said: 'Life and death depend on our neighbour: for if we win over our brother, we win over God, but if we offend our brother, we sin against Christ' [Antony 9 / 17.2]; compare 'Owe nobody anything but to love one another; for he that loves his neighbour has fulfilled the Law' [Rom 13.8]. The same commandment is definitely being referred to in this saying:

> Abba John the Dwarf said: 'It is impossible to build the house from top to bottom, but from the foundation up.' When they said to him: 'What is this saying?' the elder replied: 'The foundation is one's neighbour to be won over and he ought to come first; for on him hang all the commandments of Christ.' [John Colobos 39; cf. Mt 22:40]

There is a certain paradox here,[4] for, even in the early stages of his career as a member of a group around an elder, a monk would not be in frequent contact with his neighbour – that is, if he obeyed the oft-repeated injunction to stay quietly alone in his cell most of the time. Hence one distinguished father says: 'The person who learns the sweetness of the cell does not dishonour his neighbour in avoiding him' [Theodore of Phermê 14]. For the monk who advanced to a more remote and solitary state, a neighbour would be even less frequently encountered. As we saw, some solitaries might even have been tempted to be averse to their neighbours: 'A brother asked an elder: "Is it good to have an aversion towards one's neighbour?" The elder said to him: "Such aversions do not have the power to break a muzzle [meaning unclear]. You have an aversion towards your brother? If you want to have an aversion, have it rather towards the passions"' [129].

But no matter how rarely a neighbour might be encountered, certain general principles are laid down concerning how a monk ought to behave on such occasions. In those principles the word *conscience* frequently recurs, [*syneidêsis*] – not a word that appears very often in the apothegms.

---

[4] There is a massive paradox in that, while Jesus preached a supremely social gospel, the monastic movement was precisely a rejection of society and a turning away from it. This was probably due to the unfortunate use of the verb μισεῖν / *odisse* / hate in Lk 14.26 to translate whatever the Lord actually said. Now the commentators assure us: '*Hair* est un hébraisme: il faut préférer le Christ à tout autre' [*Bible de Jérusalem*] and '*odiare* nei senso biblico di amar meno: qui non mi preferisce a suo padre &c.' [*Versione ufficiale*]. But Gregory, Ambrose, Cyril *et al.* did not understand this and struggled with the expression to no avail: see *Catena Aurea*, ad loc.

Yet when it does appear, it nearly always has to do with how one ought to interact with his neighbour. Above all he should 'keep his conscience clear' with respect to his neighbour, e.g. 'Deeds are good, but if you keep your conscience [clear] with respect to your neighbour, in that way you are being saved' [Pambo 2 / 10.94 end; cf. *HL* 14]. When a group of elders was asked how the brothers ought to be living, they replied: 'In great spiritual discipline and guarding their conscience with respect to their neighbour' [Pambo 11 /4.86]. This is also prescribed as one way of acquiring the longed-for repose: 'Keep a watch on your conscience with respect to your neighbour and you shall have repose' [21.60].

Judge Not

High on the list of things that might give one a bad conscience with respect to his neighbour are passing judgement on him and/or belittling him. Isaiah of Scêtê advises how these are to be avoided: 'If a *logismos* comes to you to pass judgement on your neighbour for some sin, first bear in mind that you are more of a sinner than he is. Do not believe the good you think you are doing pleased God and you will not dare to pass judgement on your neighbour.' Also: 'In not passing judgement on one's neighbour and in belittling oneself; that is where repose of the conscience is located' [9.3, 4; cf. 11.27].

Belittle oneself, yes, but he who belittles another (especially one's inferior) is in grave danger. One father warns: 'Be on your guard against the brothers who praise you, against *logismoi* and against those who belittle their neighbours for nobody knows anything' [Xanthias 1 / 11.113; cf. Poemen 100 / 10.70]. For he who belittles his neighbour is in contempt of the Lord's injunction: 'Judge not that you be not judged' [Mt 7.1]. John Colobos said: 'There is no other virtue like not belittling' [G35]. 'Abba Poemen said to Abba Joseph: "Tell me how I might become a monk." Said the elder to him: "If you want to find repose both here and there, say in every situation: 'I, who am I?' and do not pass judgement on anybody"' [Joseph of Panepho 2 / 9.8]. 'Abba Theodotus said: "Do not judge the one who indulges in *porneia* if you are chaste, for in that way you transgress the law; because he who says: Do not indulge in *porneia* [Mt 5.27] also says: Do not judge"' [Mt 7.1; Theodotus s1 / 11 / 9.15]. 'A brother asked an elder: "How does the fear of God come to the soul?" "If a man have humility, be indifferent to material goods and refrain from judging, the fear of God shall come to him," the elder said' [Euprepios 5, 137, 1/29;see also Mark the Egyptian 1 / 9.6].

Slandering

The word usually translated *slander-ing* [*katalalia*, lit. 'talking back'] is by far the most frequently mentioned offence against one's neighbour. '[Slandering] is to be ignorant of God and of his glory; it is to be envious of one's neighbour' [Isaiah 10 / 21.2]. 'To slander is death to the soul' [592/19] and Abba Poemen says: 'A person must not mention these two *logismoi* or think of them in his heart: *porneia* and slandering his neighbour. If he wish to give them any consideration whatsoever in his heart, he will reap no benefit; but if he be made angry by them he will experience repose' [Poemen 154 / 5.8]. Another elder asserted that slandering is a two-edged sword: 'By whispering, the serpent expelled Eve from Paradise and he who slanders his neighbour is like it, for he ruins the soul of him who hears and does not keep his own safe' [Hyperechios 5 / 4. 60]. When a brother asked Abba John Colobos: 'How is it that my soul, wounded though it be, is not ashamed to slander my neighbour?', he was told the infamous Parable of the Man with Two Wives [John Colobos 15 / 9.12].[5] Abba Ammon of Kellia makes a surprisingly frank confession when he says: 'I underwent all the mortifications my ear heard of, but I did not find among them a hardship [more difficult than] these two: rising from the table while you are still hungry, and forcing yourself not to say a bad word to your brother' [E117].

A good defence against speaking ill of (or to) one's neighbour is to abase oneself. 'To abase oneself is a rampart,' said one elder [21.58]. 'If you slander your brother and your conscience troubles you, go, prostrate yourself before him and say to him: "I slandered you" and make sure you be not led astray again' [592/19]. Poemen is wise as ever:

> There is no greater love to be found than for somebody to lay down his life for his neighbour [cf. Jn 15.13]. For if somebody hears a bad word, one that wounds him that is, and is capable of uttering something like it himself but struggles not to say it, or if someone is being browbeaten and bears it

[5] 'There was a man who was poor and he had a wife. Seeing another [woman] who could be persuaded, he took her too; both were naked. Now there was a fair somewhere and they begged him, saying: "Take us with you." He took them both, put them into a barrel, got into a boat and came to the fairground. When it became hot and people were resting, one of the women peeped out and, seeing nobody, ran to the rubbish dump, gathered together some old rags and made herself a skirt; then she boldly paraded around. But the other woman, staying naked inside [the barrel] said: "Just look at that whore! She has no shame to walk around naked!" Her husband was annoyed; he said: "Heavens above! At least she covers her unseemliness; are you, totally naked, not ashamed, speaking like that?" It is like that with slandering.'

without paying [his adversary] back, such a person is laying down his life for his neighbour. [Poemen 116 / 17.13]

Poemen also said: 'If you make accusations against your brother and extol yourself, that is a heavy burden. And a light burden is when you make accusations against yourself and extol your brothers' [E158] and: 'A person living with his neighbour ought to be like a pillar of stone: insulted but not getting angry, revered without becoming haughty' [Poemen S 11; cf. Anoub 1 / 15.12]. And here is a passage (already cited in part for its apparent preference of the Sayings of the Elders over Holy Scripture) recalling how the elders used to interact with one another:

> They used to say of Abba Amoun (he who lived two months on a measure of barley) that he visited Abba Poemen and said to him: 'If I go to my neighbour's cell or he visits me for some need, we are afraid to speak with each other in case some alien discourse raises its head.' 'Well done,' the elder said to him. 'Youth needs vigilance.' Abba Amoun said to him: 'So what did the elders used to do?' and he said to him: 'The elders who were advanced had nothing else in mind or any alien matter in their mouth that they might speak it.' Abba Amoun said to him: 'So if a necessity arises to speak with my neighbour, do you want me to speak of the Scriptures or of the sayings of the elders?' Said the elder: 'If you cannot keep silent, it is better to speak of the sayings of the elders and not of the Scriptures, for *there* is no small danger.' [Amoun 2 / 11.56]

The great danger in later times was that a visiting brother might speak inappropriately: here are two elders' solutions:

> A brother asked an elder: 'If a brother brings me reports from outside, do you want me to tell him not to bring me them, abba?' 'No,' said the elder to him and the brother said: 'Why?' and the elder said: 'Because we could not keep that [rule] ourselves and lest while telling our neighbour not to do it, afterwards we be discovered doing it ourselves.' The brother said: 'What then must I do?' and the elder said: 'If we are willing to keep silent, that will suffice for the neighbour.' [303 /15.77]

> If one brother speaks ill of another in your presence, see that you do not turn yourself away from him saying: 'Yes, it is so.' But either keep silent or say to him: 'Brother, I myself am a condemned man and cannot judge another.' Thus you are saving both yourself and the other person. [592/40]

Poemen says: 'A brother asked Abba Pambo if it is a good thing to praise one's neighbour, and he said to him, "It is better to keep silent"' [Poemen 47 / 4.37]. As for the neighbour's shortcomings, Syncletica says these should be passed over in silence, but it is good to lament them: 'Useful sorrow is to groan both for one's own sins and also for the weakness of [one's] neighbours; [it is] not to fall short of the intended goal in order to attain the ultimate goodness' [Syncletica s10 / 10.102]. But one should be very careful indeed about trying to rectify a neighbour's weakness, as Poemen warns: 'To teach one's neighbour is [the work] of a healthy person, free of passions; for what is the point of building a house for somebody else and destroying one's own?' [Poemen 127 /10.55]. When he was asked, 'What is a hypocrite?', the same elder said: 'A hypocrite is one who teaches his neighbour something to which he has not attained himself, for it is written: "Why do you notice the speck in your brother's eye when here there is a joist in yours?" etc.' [Poemen 117; cf. Mt 7.3–4, 4.28]. On the other hand:

> One of the saints said that there is [nothing] better than this commandment not to belittle any of the brothers, for it is written: 'With rebuke you shall rebuke your neighbour without incurring sin on his account' [Lev 19.17]. So if you see your brother committing sin and you do not speak up to make him aware of his own fault, his blood will be on your hands. But if he be rebuked and persist, he will die in his sin. So it is good for you to rebuke with love: not to deride or belittle him as an enemy would. [478]

'To the best of your ability deliver your neighbour from sins without disgrace,' advises Abba Hyperechios, 'for God does not reject those who turn to him. Let no expression of evil or of craftiness dwell in your heart against your brother, so you can say: "Forgive us our trespasses as we forgive those who trespass against us"' [Hyperechios 17.16; cf. Mt 6.12]. Elsewhere there is an excellent example of an elder 'delivering his brother from sin without disgrace':

> A brother went to draw water from the river; there he found a woman who was washing clothes and it transpired that he fell with her ... Then] he went into his cell and dwelt in *hesychia* as yesterday and before. But the Lord revealed to an elder who was his neighbour that brother so-and-so, though falling, had triumphed. So the elder came to him and said to him: ... 'God revealed to me that, though you had fallen, you triumphed,' whereupon the brother narrated all that had happened to him. The elder said: 'Indeed, your *discretion* shattered the power of the enemy, brother.' [50 / 5.47]

It was said of Abba Isidore that, when he spoke to the brothers in church, this was the only thing he said: 'Brothers, it is written: "Forgive your neighbour that you might receive forgiveness"' [Isidore s1; cf. Mt 6.14]. An unnamed father said: 'He who is gratuitously done an injustice and forgives his neighbour is of the nature of Jesus' [760]; *per contra*:

> Somebody else who loves money and pleasure but who 'shuts up his bowels of compassion' against his brother [cf. 1 Jo 3.17] and is not merciful to his

neighbour, he has denied Jesus too and serves idols, for he has the effigy of Hermes within himself, worshipping the creature, rather than the Creator; 'For the love of money is the root of all evil.' [600; cf. 1 Tim 6.10]

Some of the fathers said of one great elder that if anybody came to ask him for a saying, he would solemnly say to him: 'Look, I am taking upon me the person of God and am seated on the throne of judgement; what do you want me to do for you? If you say: "Have mercy on me," God says to you: "If you want me to have mercy on you, do you then have mercy on your brother. If you want me to forgive you, do you too forgive your neighbour." Is there injustice with God? Certainly not! But it is up to us if we want to be saved.' [226 / 10.148]

Question: How can a person know whether his prayer is accepted?

Answer: When someone is on his guard not to wrong his neighbour, he can be confident in his mind that his prayer was acceptable to God. But if he wrong his neighbour, then his prayer is an abomination and unacceptable, for the groaning of the one who is wronged will not allow the prayer of him who wronged him to come before God. [508]

Not to wrong his neighbour; but what if one did? One elder said:

Whoever does not attack or afflict or revile people, he pursues the work of angels.[6] And whoever attacks people and is angry [with them], but immediately returns to become reconciled with his brother and repents for having left him; that is truly the act of a champion. But whoever makes his neighbour sad and holds a grudge in his heart, he is a brother of Satan and cannot ask God for forgiveness. If he asks for [it], he will not receive it as long as he does not forgive and pardon his brother. [E170]

In a word, 'getting it right with one's neighbour' was the key to it all, for he who could or did not love his neighbour 'as himself' certainly did not love God with his whole being.

Abba Menas told us: 'Once when I was staying in my cell a brother came to me from afar, begging me and saying: "Take me to Abba Macarius." I got up and went to the elder with him. When he had offered a prayer for us we sat down and the brother said to the elder: "Father, I have spent thirty years not eating meat and still have a fight not to do so." The elder said to him: "Do not tell me that you have spent thirty years not eating meat but inform me about this, my son, and tell me the truth: how many days have you lived when you did not speak against your brother, did not condemn

---

[6] 'Do not be amazed that, though you are a man, you can become an angel; for a glory like that of the angels lies before you, and he who presides over the games promises [that glory] to those who run the race' [PS 152, Marcellus the Scetiote].

your neighbour and when no vain word came out of your mouth?" The brother prostrated himself, saying: "Pray for me, father, that I might make a start." ' [746]

Finally, a word of Evagrius Ponticus: 'It is impossible to love all the brothers equally; but it is possible to encounter them dispassionately, unfettered by recrimination and hatred' [*Praktikos* 100].

CHAPTER II

Women in the Desert

Women Visiting

> Abba Abraham, the disciple of Abba Sisoes, said to him: 'You have aged, father; so let us go a little nearer to where there is habitation.' Said Abba Sisoes to him: 'Let us go where there is no woman.' His disciple said to him: 'And where is there a place where there is no woman, other than the desert?' so the elder said: 'To the desert then take me.' [Sisoes 3 / 2.26]

The desert, however, was certainly not 'a place where there is no woman'. It was not unknown for women to walk about in the desert: 'A monk who encountered some nuns on the road withdrew from the road. The superior said to him: "If you were a proper monk you would not have noticed that we be women"' [154 / 4.75]. Abba Paphnutius reported the sad case of a woman he found wandering by, who said to him:

> Ask me nothing, my lord, and do not question this wretch; just take me where you will to be your slave. For two years my husband has been frequently beaten for three hundred pieces of gold owing to the public purse. He is shut up in prison and my three children have been sold into slavery; I took to my heels and am travelling from place to place. As I wander in the desert I am frequently captured and often beaten and now I have been in the desert for three days without food. [*HME* 14.6]

He dealt kindly with that unfortunate creature, but the presence of women was by no means always accepted with equinanimity:

> A ship once sailed to Diolcos and moored at the settlement of the monks. A woman got out of the ship and sat down on the hill. A brother coming for a fill of water saw her; he returned to the priest and said: 'Behold, there is a woman sitting by the river, something that never happened here!' On hearing this, the elder seized his staff and, going out at a run, cried out, saying: 'Help me, brothers, there are robbers!' On seeing him, they all came running towards the ship, staff in hand. When the sailors saw the advancing

mass of them, they grasped the situation. Dragging the woman on board they cut the mooring rope and let the ship go off with the current. [459]

This, however, may not be evidence of paranoia on the part of monks towards women, but rather a simple case of misunderstanding. The water-bearer called out 'woman', but the priest mistakenly thought he said 'robbers', quite likely in Coptic I am told [*she-meh, gee-wey*] – and called out the troops, so to speak.

Be that as it may, there were probably fewer women than men in the desert, but some women there certainly were. Even in the remote settlement of Scêtê, monks had to be warned to 'Let no woman enter your cell' [Sopatros / 14.16]. To this end, 'The custom at Scêtê when a woman came to speak to her brother or somebody else not related to her, was for them to speak with each other while remaining at a distance' [Carion 2].

Most of the women we know about were in the desert for religious reasons, but there were other women who did not hesitate to head out into the wilderness when it suited their purpose, e.g. the mother of Mark, the disciple of Silvanus, who 'came down to see him and came in great style' [Mark 3 / 14.12]. And one of the fathers told this about Abba Poemen and his brothers:

> While they were living in Egypt, their mother wanted to see them and was not able to do so. She kept careful watch when they were coming to church and confronted them; but they saw her, turned back and shut the gate in her face. She cried out at the gate, weeping with much wailing and saying: 'Let me see you, my beloved children.' When he heard her, Abba Anoub went in to Abba Poemen and said, 'What are we to do about that old woman weeping at the gate?' Standing inside, [Abba Poemen] heard her weeping with much wailing, and he said to her, 'Why are you shouting like that, old woman?' She shouted much more when she heard his voice, weeping and saying, 'I want to see you, my children; what does it matter if I see you? Am I not your mother? Did I not nurse you? Now I am all white haired, and when I heard your voice I was troubled.' The elder said to her, 'Do you want to see us in this world or in the next?' She said to him, 'If I do not see you here, will I see you there?' He said to her, 'If you steel yourself not to see us here, you shall see us there,' so she went her way. [Poemen 76 / 4.40]

That is a cruel tale, but Poemen and his brothers were probably aware that visits by relatives could have dangerous consequences, as in this case:

> An elder lived in a remote part of the desert; he had a female relative who, for many years, had desired to see him. She inquired where he was living then got up and came to the road into the desert. Finding a company of camel-drivers, she went into the desert with them. [176 / 5.28]

Alas with disastrous results, for she caused the elder to fall into sin (but
he repented and was restored). The great Arsenius, he who had once been
the tutor of princes, knew how to deal with visitors in a similar situation:

> Once when Arsenius was living at Canopus, an exceedingly rich God-
> fearing virgin of senatorial rank came from Rome to see him. Archbishop
> Theophilus received her [as his guest] and she entreated him to persuade
> the elder to give her an audience. He went to him and entreated him,
> saying: 'So-and-so of senatorial rank came from Rome and she wants to see
> you,' but the elder would not agree to meet her. She, however, when this was
> reported to her, ordered beasts to be saddled, saying: 'I am trusting in God
> that I shall see him for I did not come to see a man. There are many folk in
> our city, but I came to see a prophet.' By divine providence, he happened to
> be outside when she approached the elder's cell. She fell at his feet when she
> saw him but he angrily raised her up and, looking her up and down, said to
> her: 'If you want to see my face, take a look,' but she was ashamed to look
> him in the face. The elder said to her: 'Have you not heard of my deeds?
> You should look to those. How dare you undertake such a voyage? Do you
> not realise you are a woman and ought never to go out anywhere? Or was it
> so that you can say to the other women when you return to Rome: "I saw
> Arsenius," and turn the sea into a highway for women coming to me?' She
> said: 'If it be the Lord's will, I will not allow anybody to come here; but do
> you pray for me and ever be mindful of me.' In answer, he said to her: 'I am
> praying to God that he might expunge the memory of you from my heart,'
> on hearing which she went out deeply troubled. When she came to the city,
> she fell into a fever from her grief. It was reported to the archbishop that
> she was ill and he came to her, begging of her that he might learn what the
> matter was. Said she to him: 'Would that I had not come here, for I said
> to the elder: "Be mindful of me," and he said to me: "I am praying to God
> that the memory of you be expunged from my heart," and here I am dying
> of grief!' 'Are you not aware that you are a woman,' the archbishop said to
> her, 'and that it is through women that the enemy does battle with the holy
> ones? This is why the elder said [that,] for he is praying for your soul all the
> time.' In this way, her *logismos* was healed; she went back to her homeland
> with joy. [Arsenius 28 / 2.10]

Less-Respectable Visitors

Not all the women going into the desert were equally respectable. There are
two cases of courtesans penetrating elders' cells, in both cases apparently at
the instigation of malicious people interested in corrupting the holy ones.
The first story affords a glimpse into the living conditions of an ascetic:

> There was an anchorite in the lower parts of Egypt who was famous because
> he lived all alone in a cell in the desert. Then here, by the machination of

Satan, there was a disreputable woman who, when she heard about him, said to the young men: 'What will you give me if I bring your anchorite down?' They agreed to give her something valuable. She went out in the evening and came to his cell as though she had lost her way. He came out when she knocked. He was deeply troubled when he saw her, saying: 'How did you come here?' 'I came here having lost my way,' she cried, with tears. Moved with compassion, he brought her into his little courtyard, went into his cell and shut the door. But the wretched woman called out saying: 'Abba, the wild beasts will devour me.' Again he was deeply troubled but, fearing the judgement of God, he said: 'From where did this wrath come upon me?' – but he opened the door and brought her in.

The elder countered any possibility of rising passion by feeding his fingers into the flame of a lamp one by one.

At dawn the young men came to the anchorite saying: 'Did a woman come here last night?' 'Yes,' he said, 'she is sleeping inside.' Finding her dead when they went in, they said to him: 'Abba, she has died.' He then uncovered his hands and showed them to them, saying: 'Look what the daughter of the devil did to me; she has made me lose my fingers.' [189 / 5.42; *BHG* 1318fb, *de manu ambusta*]

The other tale of an attempted seduction has quite a different ending:

Once again when Abba Ephraim was passing by, there was a whore who approached him at somebody's instigation and she fawned on him to move him to shameful intercourse; or at least to anger, for nobody had ever seen him being angry or contentious. But he said to her, 'Follow me.' Approaching a place that was much frequented, he said to her, 'Here, in this place, come and do what you wanted to,' but she, seeing the crowd, said to him, 'How can we do it in the presence of such a crowd and not be ashamed?' He said to her, 'If you are ashamed before folk, how much more ought we to be ashamed before God who reproves "the hidden things of darkness"?' [cf. 1 Cor 4.5]. She went away ashamed, nothing accomplished. [Ephraim 3 / 10.26]

Not much is known about Serapion, to whom John Cassian attributes a fine passage on the nature of humility [*Conf* 18.11]. Humility is also the subject of the last of the four apothegms attributed to Serapion in *APalph*, while the first recounts a very curious way of capturing the soul of a courtesan:

One day, Abba Serapion was passing through a village of Egypt when he saw a whore standing at her dwelling. The elder said to her: 'Expect me this evening; I want to come to you and spend this night at your side.' 'Very well, abba,' she said in reply. She got herself ready and prepared the bed. When it was evening the elder came to her and as he entered the dwelling he said to her: 'Did you get the bed ready?' 'Yes, abba,' she said. Closing the door, he said to her: 'Wait a little; we have a rule; [wait] until I first fulfil it,' and the elder started his *synaxis*. Beginning with the Psalter, he offered a prayer at each psalm, beseeching God on her behalf, that she might repent and be saved. And God heard him: the woman stood by the elder, trembling and praying. The woman fell to the ground as the elder finished the entire Psalter. Starting with the Apostle, the elder recited a large part of it and so fulfilled his *synaxis*. The woman was pricked in her conscience; she realised that it was not to sin that he came to her, but to save her. She fell down before him saying: 'Of your charity abba, take me to wherever I can be well-pleasing to God.' Then the elder took her to a monastery for virgins and handed her over to the amma. [Serapion 1 / 17.34]

In the interests of justice, it should be pointed out that there are instances of women actually preventing monks from falling with them. In one case a young widow, having successfully diverted the unwelcome attentions of a young monk, says to him:

Look, if I had been persuaded by you, we would already have committed the sin. Then, what kind of face would you have put on to confront my father, or to return to your monastery and hear the choir of those holy ones singing psalms? So, I beg you to be virtuous in future and seek not to lose all that hard labour you have accomplished by indulging in a little shameful pleasure, only to be deprived of the benefits of eternity. [52]

John Moschos reports two instances:

Somebody said that a [brother] was bitten by a snake and went into the city to receive treatment. He was taken in by a devout woman who feared the Lord and she healed him. When he found some relief from his discomfort, the devil began sowing some libidinous thoughts about the woman in his heart. He began wanting to touch her hand, but she said to him: 'Not so, father; you have Christ to fear. Think of the sorrow and the remorse in which you shall repent, sitting in your cell. Imagine the sighs you shall utter and the tears you shall shed.' [*PS* 204]

And in this way she brought him to his senses. In the other story [*PS* 205] a godly young widow dissuades a libidinous brother with various arguments, but the heroine of yet another story is a courtesan who has been bribed by an elder *not* to corrupt the brother who is coming to her:

As soon as he came in, the prostitute said to him: 'Wait brother; for even though I am a sinner, we have a rule and we are obliged to fulfil it first.' So she told him to stand to one side and perform fifty prostrations while she at her side did likewise. After the brother had performed twenty or thirty prostrations, his conscience pricked him. 'How am I praying to God while expecting to do that abominable deed?' he said to himself. He went out straightaway, undefiled. [44]

One more example:

> A brother was sent on an errand by his abba and, coming to a place where there was water, he found a woman there washing clothes. Severely tempted, he asked her if he could lie with her. She said to him: 'It is easy to go along with your request, but then I become the cause of much affliction for you.' 'How so?' he said to her. 'After you have done the deed, your conscience will smite you,' she answered. 'You will either despair of yourself, or you will have to undergo great drudgery to regain your present status. So, go your way in peace before you receive the wound.' He was conscience-stricken on hearing this and gave thanks to God and to her shrewdness. [49]

Monks Visiting Women

Not every woman was bold enough to venture out into the desert; at least one case is known where a monk was summoned in from the desert to meet a woman, with somewhat curious results:

> Piôr, an Egyptian, renounced the world as a young man and left his father's house, giving his word to God (through an excess of zeal) never again to set eyes on one of his own people. Fifty years later, his sister (who had grown old) heard that he was alive; she was approaching a state of distraction unless she could see him. As she could not go into the great desert, she besought the bishop of the region to write to the fathers in the desert [asking them to] send him so she might see him. After much coercion had been applied to [Piôr] he decided to take another [with him]. In the house of the sister they were reporting: 'Your brother Piôr is here.' Standing outside, he perceived from the noise of the door (for he had closed his eyes) that the old lady had come out to meet him. He called out: 'Oh N—, oh N—! I am your brother Piôr, it is indeed I. Look at me as much as you like.' She was convinced and glorified God but, unable to persuade him to enter her house, she returned into her own house. But [Piôr] offered a prayer at the doorposts then removed himself into the desert again. [*HL* 39.1–2; *L*3]

Piôr died about 360.

Women who ventured into the desert in search of some physical or spiritual healing were not always peremptorily dismissed. Some were (reluctantly) granted an audience and sometimes received what they sought. Antony the Great is reported to have healed somebody's daughter on at least five occasions [*VA* 48.1–3; 58, 71, 72]. Longinus is said to have cured a woman of breast cancer [Longinus 3 /19.6] and on another occasion a woman who had an incurable wound in her right hand [*A*79]. Then there is the celebrated case (twice reported) of the restoration by Macarius the Great of a young women who had turned into a mare [*HME* 21.17; *HL* 17.6–9]. But, 'You are horses yourselves and people with horses' eyes; that is a woman, not transformed at all – except in the eyes of those who have been deceived,' says Macarius in Palladius' version [*HL* 17.8–9].

Some monks inevitably encountered secular women, but usually when they went to inhabited areas or perhaps 'by the river' where women knelt to wash clothes (49, 50), sometimes with disastrous results, e.g.: 'He encountered a woman and, tripped up by his lack of caution, he came to a remote place with the enemy in tow and fell [into sin] beside the river' [175 / 5.46]. Visits to town were particularly dangerous [179, 346].

It was not unknown for a monk to have a woman living with him, as the following rather amusing anecdote reveals:

> Abba Ammonas once came somewhere to eat and there was one there who had a bad reputation. The woman happened to come and go into the cell of the brother who had the bad reputation. They who were living in that place were troubled when they learned of it and they got together to drive him out of his cell. Knowing that Bishop Ammonas was at that place, they went and besought him to go along with them. When the brother became aware of this, he took the woman and concealed her in a large barrel. When the crowd arrived, Abba Ammonas saw what had happened and covered the matter up in the name of God. He came in, sat down on the barrel and ordered the cell to be searched. When they had searched diligently and not found the woman, Abba Ammonas said to them: 'What is this? God will forgive you' and, offering a prayer, he obliged them all to withdraw. Then, taking the brother's hand, he said to him: 'Pay attention to yourself, brother' and, so saying, he went away. [Ammonas 10]

Here is a yet more explicit case, the object of the exercise being to hold up for admiration and emulation the extraordinary persistence of the young man in diligently serving the elder, with wholly satisfactory consequences:

> A young man who wished to renounce the world went off into the desert. Seeing a tower, or rather a cell built in the form of a tower, he said to himself: 'Whoever I find in the tower, I will serve him until death.' He arrived and knocked. Out there came an elder, a monk who said to him: 'What do you want?' He replied: 'I came for the purpose of prayer.' Taking him and entertaining him, the elder said to him: 'Have you nothing to do anywhere else?' He said: 'No; this is where I want to stay,' and when the elder heard this, he left him: for the elder was living in *porneia*; he had the woman there with him. So he said to the brother: 'If you want to reap any benefit, get yourself into a monastery, for I have a wife.' The brother said: 'It is immaterial to me whether she be wife or sister; I will still serve you until death.'

Some time went by and the brother performed all the duties of a servant without the least question or complaint. Then [the monk and the woman] said to each other: 'Are we not carrying a sufficient weight of sin as it is, without taking on the responsibility for this man's soul? Let us get away from this place and leave him the cell.' They took as much as they could of their belongings and said to the brother: 'We are going away to pray: you look after the cell for us.' When they had gone a little way off, the brother realised what was their intent. He went running after them. When they saw him, they were troubled and they said: 'How much longer are you going to condemn us? You have the cell; stay there and look to your own condition.' But he said: 'I did not come for the cell, but to serve you.' Their consciences began to trouble them when they heard this; they came to the conclusion that they should repent before God. For her part, the woman went to a monastery [for women] whilst the elder returned to his own cell: thus were they both saved by the patience of the brother. [G14; *BHG* 1317s, *iunior salvat seniorem*]

Demons as Women

A demon pretending to be a women was an even greater danger than *femina ipsa* and certainly gets more frequent mention in the earlier texts, e.g. *VA* 5.5; 23,3, and 'The Tempter took the form of so beautiful a woman that John of Lycopolis was almost led into sin by her' [*HME* 1.32–35]. Also: 'A brother was enflamed by the demon of *porneia*. Four demons transformed into the appearance of beautiful women were around for twenty days, struggling with him to draw him into shameful intercourse' [188 / 5.41].

Palladius, speaking of a time when he was staying in the wilderness, says: 'I was being troubled by the desire for a woman and I was distressed in the matter both by my thoughts and by nocturnal visions.' He opened his heart to the seventy-year-old Pachôn who confessed to having been plagued by *porneia* himself almost all his life long. Having described one onslaught, he continued:

> After delaying a few days, the demon attacked me again, more forcefully than at first, until I was at the point of blaspheming. He transformed himself into an Ethiopian maiden whom I had once seen in my youth, gathering reeds in summer. 'She' sat on my knees and so excited me that I was thinking of making love with 'her'. In my fury I struck 'her' a blow, at which 'she' became invisible: for two years I could not stand the stench of my hand. Discouraged and despairing, I went wandering in the great desert. Finding a small asp, I took it up and put to my genitals so in that way I would be bitten and would die. I pressed the animal's head against my genitals (the cause of my temptation) but I was not bitten. [*HL* 23.1–5]

We should not, however, omit mention of the story of a monk in need of consolation: 'and here, during that night, the grace of God appeared to him in the form of a maiden' [215 / 7.57].

Women Disguised as Monks

Among the monks living in the desert, it appears that a few of them (probably a *very* few) were women disguised (and practising) as monks. There exists a fairly detailed account of the life of the eighth- or ninth-century Anna of Constantinople. Having suffered much personal tragedy (including the loss of her children), Anna disguised herself as a man and lived as a monk under the name of Euphemianus. She was assumed to be a eunuch but eventually her subterfuge was discovered. She was nevertheless allowed to continue her life of distinguished asceticism. In due course, she returned to Constantinople where she became a famous wonder-worker [*SynaxCP* 174^16–178; *BHG* 2027].

Anna was not by any means the first woman said to have assumed the male monastic role, but her tale is somewhat unusual: in most cases the woman's imposture is only discovered at the time of her death. One of the best-known examples is the case of Anastasia the Patrician in the sixth century. Caution is required here because (as with all the tales associated with Daniel of Scêtê) a larger than usual degree of fiction has to be suspected. The story goes that, at the end of a long solitary life in a cave, when she was dying, 'brother Anastasius' (as she was known) asked for help. Those who came to bury her discovered that 'he' was female [*BHG* (79, 80) 80e; Daniel of Scêtê 02; *Synax. CP* 523^55–528^33].

A similar story recurs from time to time. The reason why the woman in question took refuge in the desert as a monk may vary, but the last part remains constant. Bessarion, the hero of the following example, was a fourth-century monk at Scêtê. Twelve apothegms are attributed to him in *APalph*, albeit some of them rather dubiously. The following is the fourth one. One day while Abba Bessarion and his disciple Doulas were travelling in the desert,

> we walked around and came to a cave. In we went and found a brother sitting there, making rope but he paid no attention to us; did not greet us nor did he in the least want to talk with us. 'Let us leave this place,' the elder said to me; 'perchance the elder is not inspired to speak with us' … On the way back we came again to the cave where we had seen the brother. The elder said to me: 'Let us go in to him; perhaps God will inspire him to speak' but when we went in we found him dead. The elder said to

me: 'Come now, brother, let us wrap up his body; this is what God sent us here for' but as we were wrapping him up for burial we discovered that he was a woman. The elder was astounded; he said: 'See how women too over-throw Satan while we in communities act shamefully.' We glorified God, the sure protection of those who love him; then we went away from there. [Bessarion 4 / 12.3]

John Moschos tells of some monks who discovered the still-warm corpse of a brother in a cave; a brother who turned out to have been a sister [*PS* 170; *BHG* 1442t, *de muliere in deserto defuncta*]. But the best and certainly the most detailed narrative is set in the reign of Justinian. This has the unusual feature of an elder (Daniel of Scêtê) suppplying provisions to an anchorite whom he knew full well not to be a man, but he maintained the pretence. His disciple only detected that the anchorite was a female when they went to bury her, prompting Daniel to tell him her story: 'She was the first lady of patrician rank in the palatine order. The Emperor Justinian wanted to have her in the palace on account of her fine intelligence but, when Theodora learnt of this, she was angry and wished to send her into exile. When [the lady] got wind of this, she hired a vessel, put some of her things aboard by night and fled.' After several adventures, she found refuge under Daniel's protection [596.2; *BHG* 79, 80: *Anastasia patricia sub Iustiniano*]. There are other examples and much has been made of the theme of a woman passing herself off as a male recluse.[1] But the various tales resemble each other so closely that there is a good reason to suspect that this is yet another case of a single occurrence being variously reported.

Women Ascetics

There are also stories of women leading a monastic life *without* any attempt to disguise the fact that they are women – probably rather more in number than the tales of deception, e.g. John of Calamon 'had a sister who had been living in the holy estate of monks since infancy' [L4]. Unfortunately, it is impossible to say what proportion of the monks living in the desert were women. The only statistic available (and it is as unre-liable as any other ancient statistic) is that, of roughly 120 elders cited or mentioned in the alphabetic sayings, only three are women: Theodora, Sarah and Syncletica (who may never have left Alexandria). Eugenia and Sibylla of Saqqara are mentioned elsewhere [447; *Virtues of St Macarius*

[1] Evelyne Patlagean, 'L'histoire de la femme déguisée en moine et l'évolution de la sainteté féminine à Byzance', *Studi medievali*, 3rd ser., 17.2, 1976, 597–623.

377–393], while John Moschos speaks of Damiana, Joanna and 'a *monastria*' [*PS* 127, 128, 179]. To these may be added the case of the virgin of the Holy City who fled to the desert rather than allow a youth who had become enamoured of her to fall into sin with her. She fled, taking with her only a few beans in a basket. Eighteen years later, she met an abba and told him the beans had sufficed and the goodness of God had sheltered her; nor had she seen any man until him, that very day [*PS* 179; *BHG* 1440kj, *de iuniore monacho in caupona*].

There is also the tale of the eighteen-year-old daughter of a distinguished Constantinopolitan who is reported to have avoided marriage with the son of another leading citizen by asking permission to fulfil her vow to visit the Holy Places whilst still a virgin. Evading her retinue at Jerusalem, she was able to persuade an elder (with 300 pieces of gold!) to give her the monastic habit and two books. She then, for the next twenty-eight years, lived in the cave where the narrator claims to have found her. But he was never able to find her again [*BHG* 1318w, *de syncletica in deserto Jordanis*; *AB* 100 (1982), 305–317].

Elsewhere it is reported that some secular brothers once met an anchorite who was female and a virgin: a true solitary. 'The Lord sent you to bury me,' she said. 'I am a virgin in body, but I wage perpetual and inhuman warfare against *porneia*. I see angels coming for my soul, and I see Satan thrusting lascivious thoughts upon me.' Then she died; and they found that she was indeed a virgin [*BHG* 1322fa, *de moniali tentata*, unpublished].

To these may be added the following, though with the customary caution about tales dealing with Daniel of Scêtê:

> Two great elders were travelling in the desert of Scêtê. On hearing someone muttering out of the ground, they looked for the entrance of a cave. When they entered they found an aged holy virgin lying down. 'When did you come here, old lady,' they said to her, 'and who is looking after you?' – for they found nothing other than her alone, lying there, sick. She said: 'I have been in this cave for thirty-eight years, satisfying myself with weeds and serving Christ. And I never saw a man until today, for God has sent you to bury my remains.' When she had said this, she fell asleep. The elders glorified God then departed when they had buried the body. [132c / 20.12; *BHG* 1322eb, [2] de vetula in spelunca]

In another instance, an unnamed anchorite discovered what he thought to be a lion, but was in fact a naked woman, living in a hole in the desert. He had to give her his pallium before she would come out. She told how

---

[2] *BHG* 1322ed is almost identical, Cod. Lond. Harl. 5639, ff. 134v–135.

she had been a *canonica* at the Holy Sepulchre, but fell into sin with a monk. That monk bitterly wept for his sins, so she fled to do the same. One basket of provisions and one bottle of water had lasted her thirty years. Her clothes wore out, but her hair grew long enough to cover her decently. In thirty years she saw no man until the arrival of the monk. At her request, he went in search of clothing for her, but he could not find her when he returned. Sometime later, other anchorites saw and heard her. They fed from her supplies, but next morning, they found her dead [*BHG* 1449x, *de canonica nuda*[3]].

Children and Youths in the Desert

There is at least one case of a woman coming into the desert on a very special mission, in this case all the way to Scêtê, more than thirty kilometres beyond Nitria:

> There was a monk at Scêtê called Abba Carion. He had [fathered] two children and left them with his own wife when he retired [from the world]. Subsequently there was a famine in Egypt and the wife, being in tight straits, came to Scêtê bringing the children with her; one was a boy named Zachary, the other a girl. She remained at a distance from the elder, in the marsh. (There is a marsh around Scêtê, there where the churches were built and where the wells of water are located.) ... On that occasion the wife said to Abba Carion: 'Here you have become a monk and there is a famine; who is going to feed your children?' Abba Carion said to her: 'Send them here to me.' The wife said to the children: 'Go to your father.' As they were coming to their father, the girl turned back to her mother but the boy came to his own father. Then he said to her: 'See, it is well; do you take the girl and go back and I [will keep] the boy.' [Carion 2]

There are other indications of children in monasteries, e.g. 'A certain child had been given to a monastery by his parents' (the higoumen treated him badly) [A59]. 'They used to say of one elder that he brought his son, a child not yet weaned, when he came down to Scêtê; a child that did not know what a woman was' [171 / 5.25]. An unnamed elder managed to engender a child, but he did not disown it:

> After it was weaned, one day when there was a feast at Scêtê, the elder went down carrying the child on his shoulder. He entered the church in the

---

[3] Ed. J. Wortley, *Les récits de Paul, évêque de Monembasie et d'autres auteurs*, Paris, 1987, pp. 119–123. N.b. *BHG* 1449, *de tribus mulieribus* (ibid., 28–34), seems to be an expanded version of +/- the same theme.

presence of the community and they wept on seeing him. He said to the
brothers: 'Look at this child: it is the son of disobedience. Keep a careful
watch on yourselves, brothers, for it was in my old age that I did this; and
do you pray for me.' [187 / 5.40; *BHG* 1322hc, *de monacho fornicato*]

Yet the apothegms manifest a marked antipathy to children no less than
that to women. 'When you see a cell built near to the marsh, learn that
its desolation is near. When you see trees, it is at the door. When you see
children, take your sheepskins and get away,' the great founder of Scêtê
told the brothers there [Macarius the Egyptian 5 / 18.16]. At Kellia another
elder said: 'Do not bring children here; four churches at Scêtê have become
deserted because of children' [Isaac of Kellia 5 / 10.44]. 'Have no friendship
with a child, no relationship with a woman, no heretic as your friend'
[Matoes 11 / 330 / 1.34]. 'He who stuffs himself and speaks with a child
has already indulged in *porneia* with him in the *logismos*' [John Colobos
4 / 5.3]. 'Desire is kindled more fervently in him as he continually sees
women and children and hears worldly discourse. Thus he commits adul-
tery every day' [G5].

Some, however, were more tolerant. We already noted Poemen reproving
those who complained of children's voices: 'You want to get away from
here because of the angels' voices?' [Poemen 155]; and another elder who
said: 'If I do not stand this little [disturbance], how am I to withstand
severe temptation if it comes upon me?' [338 / 16.23].

No such tolerance is ever expressed for the presence of women: rather,
there is a marked antipathy towards their sex in general:

> A brother was travelling with his own mother who was elderly. When they
> came to a river the old woman was unable to get across. Taking her shawl,
> the son wound it around his own hands so he would not have contact
> with his mother's body. Carrying her in that way, he carried her over to the
> other side. 'Why did you wrap your hands, my son?' his mother asked him.
> 'A woman's body is fire,' he said, 'and from this would come the recollection
> of other women. That is why I acted as I did.' [159 / 4.83]

An elder said: 'Children, salt comes from water. But if it comes back to
water, it is dissolved and disappears. So the monk comes from woman;
and if he comes back to a woman, he is undone and, insofar as his being
a monk is concerned, he dies' [*PS* 217]. Archbishop Theophilus [*ob* 412]
said: 'It is through women that the enemy does battle with the holy ones'
[Arsenius 28 / 2.10]. 'Never put your hand in a dish with a woman to eat
with her,' another elder warned [Daniel 2 / Evagrius, *Prakt* 96]. 'Wine and
women separate [us] from God,' said a third [592/55].

But there was an even worse danger: 'Abba Eudaemôn said of Abba Paphnutius, the father of Scêtê: "I went down there as a young man and he would not let me stay there, saying regarding me: 'I will not let a woman's face stay at Scêtê because of the battle with the enemy'"' [Eudaemôn]. 'Again, they would say that youths are a worse snare of the devil for monks than women are' [544], and 'where there are wine and youths, there is no need of Satan' [545]. 'The fathers used to say that God does not tolerate youths in the desert but that Satan does, in order to subvert those who wish to live a godly life' [458, e.g. 341 / 16.24], hence the following injunction:

> Never in your life sleep at all close to anyone; do not give a kiss to a beardless youth, neither in the church itself nor to one coming from abroad. Laugh not with a youth lest your soul be lost; do not sit beside him or go for walks with him or get close to each other. [592]

'An elder said: "A man living with a youth falls if he is unable [to resist]. If he is able, he does not fall, but neither does he progress"' [123 *bis*]; cf. 'An elder said: "Do not be friendly with a higoumen, have no commerce with a woman neither exchange any favours with a young man"' [125 / cf. 10.124].

> They said of a great elder that, visiting a convent, he saw a youth there and would not sleep at that place. The brothers accompanying him said to him: 'Are you afraid, abba?' 'Of course I am not afraid, children,' he said, 'but what need is there of an unnecessary struggle?' [456]

This antipathy to youths is something of a paradox: for angels are sometimes portrayed as handsome youths. Here are two good examples:

> An elder named Hellê, embarrassed by lack of the wherewithal to entertain some guests, said: 'God is able to set a table in the desert' [cf. Ps 77.19] and right away, while they were praying, there was a youth, a fine looking young man, knocking at the door with a large basket full of loaves and olives. These they accepted and, after offering thanks to the Lord, shared them around – while the youth instantly became invisible. [*HME* 12.15]

> They used to say of Abba Zeno that when he was staying at Scêtê he came out of his cell by night meaning to go to the marsh but he lost his way; he spent three days and three nights walking around. Exhausted, he became faint and fell down to die. Then here there stood before him a youth with bread and a bottle of water. 'Get up and eat,' he said to him. Up he got and prayed, under the impression that it was a vision but, in response, the other said to him: 'Well done,' so he prayed again a second time and likewise a third and he said to him: 'Well done,' so the elder got up, took and ate. After that [the youth] said to him: 'The more you walked around, the further you were from your cell, but get up and follow me.' Immediately he found himself at his cell, so the elder said to him: 'Come in and

offer a prayer for us.' When the elder went in the [youth] disappeared. [Zeno 5 /18.8]

Compare: 'a young man whose appearance was brighter than the sun' [*PS* 66], 'two men, wearing mantles and clothed in white' [*PS* 105a] and 'an extremely handsome young man' [*PS* 108]. In later tales the angelic youths are portrayed as handsome eunuchs.

Women's Monasteries

Palladius states his explicit intention to write 'of both male *and female* ascetics' [*HL* 41.1] and he advises Lausus (for whom he was writing) to 'seek the acquaintance of holy men *and women*' [*HL* Prologue §15]. Palladius obviously knew that there were at least some women living in the desert on the same footing as the men, for he says: 'This Ammonios ([Pambo's] disciple) together with three other brothers and his two sisters, excelling in love for God, went to live in the desert, the women making themselves a dwelling and he one for himself, a sufficient distance apart from each other' [*HL* 11.1]. Yet most of the women of whom Palladius writes were not ascetics, but rather persons living godly lives 'in the world', two outstanding examples being Melania the elder and her eponymous grand-daughter.

Palladius also includes a surprisingly large number of references to monasteries for women [e.g. 1.4, 29–30, 33–34, 45.5, 49.2, 70.3], not to mention amazing statements such as: 'There are twelve monasteries for women in the city of Antinoe' [59.1] and 'In that city of Ancyra there are many other spinsters,[4] about two thousand[5] or more, also women distinguished in their continence and decency' [*HL* 67.1]. He also provides some indication of what at least one monstery for women was like:

> Elijah, whose spiritual discipline was severe, was quite devoted to spinsters [*philoparthenos*] for there are such souls to whom the virtuous goal they pursue bears witness. Feeling compassion for the order of females who were practising spiritual discipline, he built a large monastery [*monasterion*] in the city of Athrib[6] where he owned some property. He gathered all the wandering women into the monastery then went on caring for them. He secured their complete comfort, providing gardens, household utensils and furniture and whatever life requires.

---

[4] 'Spinster' here translates *parthenos* which can mean *virgo intacta*, a female monk, a holy woman, etc.
[5] Palladius' statistics must be treated very cautiously.
[6] Athribis or Tell Athrib was the capital of the 10th Nome of Lower Egypt located on a branch of the Nile Delta.

But, drawn as those women were from various ways of life, they were continually at odds with each other. Since he had to hear them out and pacify them (for he had gathered up about three hundred of them) he had to intervene for two years. Being a young man (he was thirty or forty years old) he was tempted to take pleasure in them. He withdrew from the monastery and went wandering in the desert for two days, fasting, making this supplication: 'Lord, either kill me so I do not see those afflicted women, or take the passion away from me so I can look after them rationally.' He fell asleep in the desert towards evening and three angels came to him (as he himself told it). Laying hold on him they said: 'Why did you come out of the women's monastery?' He related the matter to them: 'I was afraid of harming both them and myself.' They said to him: 'If we relieve you of the passion, will you go back and look after them?' He agreed to those terms and they made him swear an oath. The oath (he used to say) was like this: 'Swear to us that by him who looks after me I will look after them,' and he swore to them. Then they took hold of him, one his hands and one his feet; the third [angel] took a razor and cut off his testicles, not in reality, but in appearance. He seemed to be in an ecstasy as you might say and to have been cured. 'Did you feel any benefit?' they asked him and he told them: 'I was greatly relieved and I do believe I am delivered from the passion.' They said to him: 'Off you go.' Returning after five days, he found the monastery in mourning. In he went and there he stayed from then on in a cell to one side from which (being close by) he was continually rectifying the ladies' behaviour, insofar as he was able. He lived another forty years and he firmly asserted to the fathers: 'No passion arose in my mind.' Such was the spiritual gift of that holy one who took such care of the [women's] monastery. [*HL* 29.1–5; cf. *PS* 3]

But there is a sequel to the above:

[Elijah's] successor was Dorotheos, a man of great experience who grew old living a life of goodness and activity. Unable to live in the monastery itself as [Elijah] had done, he shut himself up in an upper-storey and made a window (which he used to open and close) looking onto the women's monastery. He would sit at that window all the time, guaranteeing [the women] freedom from quarrelling. He grew old doing this, up there on the upper storey, with neither the women going up to him nor he being able to go down, for there was no ladder. [*HL* 30]

There is some indication that women's monasteries may have been more plentiful in Upper Egypt:

There [at Tabennesi] are other monasteries of two or three hundred [men], of which I entered the one in the city of Panos[7] and found three hundred men.

---

[7] Akhmin today, on the right bank of the Nile in Upper Egypt.

In that monastery I saw fifteen tailors, seven metal-workers, four carpenters, twelve camel-drivers and fifteen fullers. They practise every trade, *supplying women's monasteries* and prisons from their surplus products. [*HL* 32.9]

Speaking of the Tabennesi, Palladius goes on to speak of one women's monastery there:

They also have a monastery for about four hundred women; these have the same rule and the same way of life except for the cloak. The women are across the river, the men at this side. When a sister dies, the sisters who have prepared her for burial bring her and lay her on the river bank. The brothers cross over with a boat and take her to the other shore with palm- and olive-branches and psalm-singing then they bury her in their own tombs. With the exception of the priest and the deacon (and they only on Sundays) nobody crosses to the women's monastery. [*HL* 33.1–2]

But if the monastery at Athrib was afflicted with quarrelling, something quite dreadful happened at this one:

A worldling who was a tailor in search of work crossed over in ignorance. A younger sister came out (for the place is desert) and unintentionally ran into him. 'We have our own tailors,' she told him. Another sister witnessed this encounter. Time went by, then an altercation arose and, by devilish supposition, from much perversity and seething rage, she made a false accusation against the sister before the community and a few other sisters gave their support to the accusation out of spite. Overcome with grief at being falsely accused of something that had never even entered her mind, that sister, unable to bear it, threw herself into the river when nobody was looking and perished. She who had made the false accusation was aware that it was out of perversity that she had made the accusation and brought about this blood-letting. She went and hanged herself, unable to bear the matter. The remaining sisters declared the matter to the priest when he came and he ordered that no offering of the Eucharist be made even for one of those [two sisters]. And as for those who had failed to reconcile them, since they were aware of the false accusation and had still given credence to what was said, he excommunicated them, imposing a period of seven years. [*HL* 33.3–4]

Palladius follows this with a story about the same monastery concerning a sister who pretended to be insane.[8] Of the four hundred women living there, none would have anything to do with one women who appeared to be deranged. In reality the woman was feigning insanity; she was 'fulfilling by her behaviour that which is written, "If anyone among you seems to be wise in this world, let him become a fool in order to be wise"' [1 Cor 3.18; cf. 120 / 21.39]. 'She never

---

[8] A similar story occurs at least twice elsewhere: 596.7 / 18.24 = Daniel of Scêtê 07; *BHG* 2101, *de virgine quae ebrietatem simulabat*, where the monastery is identified as Jeremiah's, located at Hermopolis.

insulted anybody, did not complain, did not speak a little or at length although she was punched and insulted, cursed and loathed.' Her status was eventually discerned and revealed by the intervention of a holy man.

> On hearing this, [the sisters] fell at his feet, all confessing different things: one that she had poured the washbowl on her, another that she had punched her, another that she had rubbed her nose in mustard. In a word, they all confessed various offences ... After a few days, unable to tolerate the esteem and respect of the sisters and weighed down by their excuses, [that woman] went out of the monastery. Where she went, where she hid away, or how she died, nobody knew. [*HL* 34 1–7]

In the light of the above, there can be no doubt that women's monasteries existed, or that they were establishments of some importance. There is a tale that speaks of a monastery on the outskirts of Antioch whose inmates number 60 in one version, 260 in another,[9] that was walled about and protected, truly a fortress. Like that one, most women's monasteries appear to have been located at or near some urban centre, hence they cannot really be said to have been in the desert. They also seem to have been places where bad things could happen. This is not unknown in male establishments, but with them it is a rare occurrence (to judge from the extant reports) [e.g. Daniel 6 /10.23; 339 /16.28; 642–643], whereas an unfortunate occurrence appears to have been a marked feature of the women's houses. This rather leaves one wondering whether 'women's monastery' really means what we think it means today. It is not impossible that some of those monasteries were more of the nature of refuges for unattached women, rather than seminaries of piety. The polyvalence of the word 'monastery' is notorious, covering as it does everything from the hermit's shack to a vast congregation of ascetics. The one distinguishing feature of 'monastery' is that its inhabitants spend their lives in separation from the world at large. That would be equally true of single women in need of protection.

While there undoubtedly were some institutions where women made a serious attempt to pursue the Royal Road, even so the nomenclature can be confusing:

> In Thessaloniki there used to be a monastery [*askêtêrion*] of virgins, one of whom was forced by the working of the enemy to come out of the monastery [*monastêrion*]. When she came out she fell into *porneia* under the influence of the demon who had deceived her into coming out. Once she had

---

⁹ 'De latrone converso: the Tale of the Converted Robber (BHG 1450kb)', *Byzantion* 66, 1996, 219–243.

fallen, she spent a considerable amount of time in *porneia*. After coming to regret this through the good God assisting her towards repentance, she came to her convent [*coenobion*] where she repented and, falling down before the gate, she died. [751; *BHG* 1450xa *de silentio*]

Palladius has only praise for Sisinnius the Cappadocian, but he introduces yet another term:

> [Sisinnius] has gathered together a brotherhood of men and women; by his devout way of life he has both driven out his own masculine desire and silenced the femininity of the women by continence, with the result that the scripture was fulfilled: 'In Christ Jesus there is neither male nor female' [Gal 3.28]. [*HL* 48.2]

If by *brotherhood* Palladius meant a cohabitation, then this is the only mention of a 'double monastery' so early. It is more likely that he meant some sort of association such as the term 'order of virgins'. There was, however, one women's monastery he knew and praised highly:

> There are twelve monasteries for women in that city of Antinoe. [At one of these] I made the acquaintance of Amma Talis, an old woman who has spent eighty years under spiritual discipline, according to herself and her neighbours. There are sixty young women living with her who loved her so much that no key exists to the courtyard of the monastery (as at other monasteries): they are held there by their love of her. [*HL* 59.1]

Such hints hardly make it possible to say how many women were living in institutions called monasteries, or what proportion of those who were in them were truly ascetics. Against this the brother who wrote up the visit of the monks from the Mount of Olives who visited Egypt in the winter of 394–395 provides an interesting piece of information. Speaking of Oxyrhynchus, a city of the Thebaid, he asks:

> And how might one state the number of monks and spinsters since they cannot be counted? We reported here what we were apprised of by the holy bishop who is there: that he has ten thousand monks and two thousand spinsters under his supervision. [*HME* 5.5–6]

We may not be able to say how many of the inmates of women's monasteries were holy women, but we can say that not all holy women were living in monasteries, as the following tale of how Macarius was brought into line makes clear:

> Once when Abba Macarius was praying in his cell, a voice came to him, saying: 'Macarius, you have not yet attained the stature [*metron*] of those two women of this city.' The elder got up early, took his palm-wood staff

and began to make the journey to the city. When he got there and identified the place, he knocked at the door. One of the women came out and invited him into the house. He sat there for a little then the other woman came. When he invited them to approach, they did so, seating themselves bedside him. The elder said to them: 'It is on your account that I have put myself to the trouble of undertaking the journey, coming in from the desert; tell me now, what kind of a rule of life do you follow?' 'Believe us, Father,' they told him, 'we were never absent from our husbands' beds to this very day; what sort of a rule of life do you expect of us?' The elder apologised to them and asked them, saying: 'Show me the way you live,' at which they told him: 'We are unrelated to each other in the worldly sense, but it happened that we were married to two sons of the same mother and, behold! Now we have been living in this house for fifteen years. It crossed our mind to leave our husbands and to join the order of the virgins but, even though we persisted in our request, our husbands would not agree to release us. Frustrated in that project, we took an oath to each other and before God that we would indulge in no secular conversation until we died.' When Abba Macarius heard this, he said: 'Indeed, there is no distinction between dedicated virgin and married woman, monk and layman; God is looking for good conduct and he gives the Holy Spirit to everybody.' [489 / 20.21;[10] *BHG* 999yb, *de praestantia mulierum duarum*]

In this tale, although the two ladies here are well and truly married, they contemplate joining 'the order of virgins'. The term is almost identical with the one used of Elijah the *philoparthenos* when he built his large monastery for 'the order of females who were practising spiritual discipline'. Does this mean (1) women like the two whom Macarius visited, living a godly life quietly at home; (2) women living in a specific location under spiritual discipline; or (3) single women in need of protection? What Elijah did for the women of Athrib resembles what Pachomius is said to have done for the pious men of the Thebaid after he had a vision of an angel telling him: 'The will of God is to minister to the race of men, to reconcile them to him' (see Chapter 14). But there the resemblance ends. Pachomius clearly gathered up men seriously engaged in the ascetic life: Elijah 'gathered all the wandering women into the monastery' and, 'drawn as those women were from various ways of life, they were continually at each others' throats', so much so that their benefactor had to spend a great deal of time and effort pacifying them. His successor was similarly engaged it seems, since he was at pains to keep the women at arm's length. None of this sounds like a family of God-loving sisters dwelling together in unity,

---

[10] 20.21 simply says 'a certain elder'. Which Macarius is intended we do not know; neither version names the women or the city.

such as Amma Talis is said to have presided over at Antinoe. And perhaps it was not; perhaps it (along with many another women's monastery) was an *asile* where unmarried and orphaned women, widows and wives separated from their husbands could find the safety they were denied in society. Orphanages, hospitals, poor-houses and homes for the aged were certainly provided by Christian charity; it would hardly be surprising if that charity were also extended to the relief of women in need of care and protection.

CHAPTER 12

Literacy

Reading the divine Scriptures terrifies the demons. [21.44]

Reading and Meditating

Reading and meditating are not always clearly distinguished in the texts; witness the priest far advanced in spiritual discipline who 'did his meditation with extensive reading of the sacred Scriptures' [18.49]. This is because both meditating and reading were normally *audible* activities, so much so that it was noted as exceptional when either activity was done in silence [127 / 5.29]. John Cassian speaks of an elder at Scêtê who, going to a brother's cell, 'heard him inside muttering something. Wanting to know what he was reading from Scripture or what, as the custom is, he was repeating by heart while he worked' [*Inst* 11.16]. Antony appears to attest to reading being done aloud when he warns his disciples: 'There are times when, whilst we are reading, [the demons] often immediately utter what has been read like an echo' [*VA* 25.2].

Those who could not read for themselves would hear the Scriptures being read out in church and would learn the psalms from the chanting of their fellow monks. Antony urged his followers: 'Recite/sing psalms before and after sleeping; learn the precepts in the Scriptures by heart and be mindful of the acts of the holy ones' [*VA* 55.3].

There is also one (but only one) somewhat enigmatic indication that there was reading at meal-times, possibly at Panepho. Here is a portion of a rather long piece:

> We are in such an uproar sitting at the table that nothing being read to us is heard due to the noise of unprofitable conversation which we are conducting with one another ... For many of us desire to hear the stories and commandments of the fathers which are read at table or between one sitting and the next, but we are not able to hear the sound of their speaking. [s53]

There may have been other opportunities to hear works read aloud. When Antony was preparing for his life in the desert, he paid careful attention to certain elders skilled in various ways, including 'one given to vigils and ... one who was a scholar' [*philologos*] [*VA* 4.1]. Presumably he received oral instruction from this *philologos* and listened to him reading books other than the Scriptures. Athanasius' closing injunction, 'So read these [chapters] to the other brothers that they might learn what the life of monks ought to be' [*VA* 94.1], suggests that public reading was not an unusual activity. Antony could easily master what he heard read, says Athanasius: 'He was very intelligent and the amazing thing was that, although he had not learnt letters, he was a shrewd and sagacious man' [*VA* 72.1]. In his opinion: 'There is no need of letters for him whose mind is whole' [*VA* 73.3].

Literate and Illiterate Fathers

While the validity of Athanasius' allegation of Antony's illiteracy has been challenged, that is how he depicts the man to whom many monks looked up: an illiterate yet learned man whom they considered to be their father [*VA* 88]. What can be said of his many disciples and followers? The story 'Of the Roman' [Roman 1 / 10.110] is informative. A monk who was formerly a high imperial official encounters one who had been a common herdsman. The story contrasts the meagre comforts of the Roman (austerities for him) with the improved physical condition of the Egyptian. It also contrasts the sophisticated, Hellenised, bourgeois culture of the one with the rural simplicity of the other. Clearly education and literacy were equally important characteristics of the former as the absence of them was of the latter. This must have caused some to question the value of education for those who aspired to 'leave all and follow' their Lord. This is told of Arsenius who abandoned a brilliant career at the imperial court in 394 to live in austerity at Scêtê until it was devastated yet again in 434:

> An elder said to the blessed Arsenius: 'How is it that we have nothing from so much education and wisdom, while these Egyptian peasants have acquired such virtues?' Abba Arsenius said to him: 'We have nothing from the world's education; but these Egyptian peasants have acquired the virtues from their own labours.' [Arsenius 5 / 10.7]

The brother in the following tale may well have been an educated person consulting one who was not:

> A brother visited some elder and said to him: 'Abba, tell me a saying [indicating] how I might be saved,' but he said to him: 'If you wish to be saved,

when you visit somebody, do not begin speaking until he questions you.'
Pricked in his conscience by the saying, he prostrated himself before him
saying: 'I have indeed read many books, but never knew such teaching.' He
went his way improved. [Euprepius 7 / 10.24]

It should be noted, however, that there was no such ambivalence towards
books and learning in the Pachomian tradition (see Chapter 14). In con-
trast, some (and maybe many) of the desert-dwellers had no books to hand:

> Abba Bessarion's disciples recounted his life to have been like this: he lived
> out the time of his life untroubled and carefree like a bird of the air, a fish or
> a land-animal. In his case he was not concerned with care about a house and
> it did not seem that his soul was in prey to longing for lands, a sufficiency of
> luxury, building dwellings or the provision of books. [Bessarion 12]

Things may have been rather different in Palestine though, for Epiphanius
(bishop of Salamina) said: 'The possession of the Christian books is a
necessity for those who have [the means] for the sight of the books itself
renders us more averse to sin and rather impels us to aspire to righteous-
ness' [Epiphanius 8]. Julian 'possessed nothing of this world's goods other
than a hair shirt, a cloak, a book of the gospels and a wooden bowl' [*PS* 51].
Those were the basic necessities.

Theft and Possession of Books

Gelasius made quite sure that the monks of his monastery at Nicopolis in
Palestine had access to Holy Writ:

> They used to say of Abba Gelasius that he had a book on parchment worth
> eighteen pieces of gold; it had the whole of the Old and the New Testaments
> written in it. It lay in the church so that any of the brothers who wished to
> do so might read it. A brother coming from abroad visited the elder, saw
> the book and coveted it; he stole it and went away. But, although the elder
> noticed, he did not pursue him. [The thief] went into the city and tried
> to sell it. When he found somebody willing to buy it, he asked a price of
> sixteen pieces of gold for it, but the would-be purchaser said to him: 'First
> let me validate it then I will supply the price,' so he gave him the book. He
> took it and brought it to Abba Gelasius to validate it, telling him the price
> the seller was asking. The elder said to him: 'Buy it; for it is good and worth
> the price you stated.' The fellow came and spoke differently to the one who
> was selling it and not as the elder had spoken, saying: 'Look, I showed it to
> Abba Gelasius and he told me that it was dear and not worth what you are
> asking for it.' When he heard that he said: 'Did the elder say anything else
> to you?' 'No,' he said. 'I do not want to sell it,' the brother said and, pricked
> in his conscience, he went to the elder, apologising and begging him to

accept [the book] – but [the elder] did not want to take it. Then the brother said to him: 'If you do not take it, I shall have no repose.' He said to him: 'If you have no repose, see then, I will take it.' The brother stayed there until his death, edified by the action of the elder. [Gelasius 1 / 16.2]

Theft by monks is by no means unknown and more often than not it is a book that is taken, presumably because a book was likely to be the only object of any market value in a cell. Monks were warned: 'If you possess a book, do not decorate its binding; do not possess an expensive vestment [to wear] in your worshipping' [592/11]. This is a sure indication that some monks *did* decorate the binding of books, thus rendering them even more attractive and valuable. A book-theft might also be faked:

Abba [John] Cassian said that in the time of Isidore the Great, the priest of Scêtê, there was a deacon called Paphnutius whom, on account of his virtue, they made a priest to succeed [Isidore] after his death. He, however, through piety, did not exercise his ordained status but remained a deacon. One of the elders (through the machination of the enemy) was jealous of him and, when everybody was in church for the *synaxis*, he went and placed his own book in the cell of Abba Paphnutius then came and reported to Abba Isidore: 'Some one of the brothers stole my book.' Abba Isidore was amazed; he said that nothing like that had ever happened at Scêtê. The elder who had placed the book said to him: 'Send two of the fathers with me to search the cells.' Off they went; the elder took them to the cells of the others then finally to the cell of Abba Paphnutius; they found the book and brought it to the priest at the church. In the presence of the entire congregation Abba Paphnutius prostrated himself before Abba Isidore the priest, saying: 'I have sinned; give me a penance.' He gave him the penance of not receiving communion for three weeks. Coming at the time of each *synaxis* in front of the church, he would fall down before the entire congregation saying: 'Forgive me, for I have sinned.' After the three weeks he was received [back] into communion and right away the elder who had falsely accused him was possessed of a devil. Then he began to confess: 'I falsely accused the servant of God.' There was prayer on the part of the entire church on his behalf but he was not cured. Then Isidore the Great said to Abba Paphnutius for all to hear: 'Pray for him. It was you who was falsely accused and he will not be cured other than through you.' He prayed – and the elder became whole forthwith. [16. 29; alternative version G33]

The reference to 'his own book' is interesting for there is some suggestion in the following saying attributed to Abba Poemen that at least some monks had their own personal *synaxis*-books: 'At the weekend, after prayers, Isaiah would first go to his own cell to deposit his *leviton* and his book' (this is mentioned three times), then he would go to Paesios' cell for the weekend. [E79; cf. 53 on p. 30 above]. There is mention elsewhere of a brother breaking into an elder's cell and appropriating his books (plural), his vessels and his *leviton* [*PS* 211]. Theodore, a distinguished monk who lived at Scêtê until it was devastated in 407 then at Phermê, also possessed books worth stealing. While visiting Abba Macarius he said to him: 'I have three fine books and I benefit from them; the brothers borrow them and benefit [from them]. Tell me what I ought to have done.' In answer, the elder said: 'The deeds are good, but poverty is greater than all.' 'On hearing this he went and sold them, giving the proceeds from them to the needy', the text continues [Theodore of Phermê 1 / 6.7]. He must have subsequently replenished his stock:

> Three brigands once came upon him. With two of them holding him the one began making off with his goods. When he had taken the books he wanted to get the *leviton* too, then [the elder] said to them: 'Leave that,' but they would not. He put out his hand and tore it in two. They were afraid when they saw that [so] the elder said to them: 'Have no fear; divide it into four pieces: take three and leave me one' – and so they did. Because he got his piece, [this was all] the *leviton* he wore for *synaxis*. [Theodore of Phermê 29]

Nothing is said of the brothers who would now be deprived of Theodore's library, but then it may have been that books were routinely circulated within a monastery:

> The elders used to say that the *logismos* of *porneia* is a book: if, when it is disseminated among us we are not persuaded by it and cast it away from us, it is excised with ease. But if we are delighted by it as though won over by it when it has been disseminated; transformed, it becomes iron and is excised with difficulty. Discretion is necessary in the case of this *logismos*, for there is no hope of salvation for those who are won over by it, whilst a crown awaits those who are not won over by it. [185 / 5.38]

Disposing of Books

Theodore of Phermê is not by any means the only one who is said to have divested himself of his books because they might not be the best way to salvation, e.g.:

> Abba Eulogius of Enaton used to say that there was a brother living at Kellia who, having spent twenty years applying himself day and night to reading, one day got up and sold all the books he possessed and, taking his sheepskin, went off to the inner desert. Abba Isaac met him and said to him: 'Where are you going, my son?' 'I have spent twenty years only hearing the words of the [sacred] books, father,' the brother answered him, 'and now

I finally want to make a start on putting into action what I have heard from the books.' The elder offered a prayer for him and dismissed him. [541]

An interesting anecdote concerning the disposal of a book makes its first known appearance in the writings of Evagrius Ponticus (*ob* 399): 'One of the brothers possessed a single Gospel; he sold it and gave the proceeds to feed the poor with these memorable words: "I have fulfilled the saying that tells me: *Sell your possessions and give to the poor*"' [Mt 19.21; *Praktikos* 97; 392 / 6.6]. The same anecdote reappears fully fledged in connection with Serapion Sindonios (mentioned above), so called, says Palladius,

> because he never wore anything other than a sheet [*sindonê*]. He was largely indifferent to possessions but well educated; he had memorised the entire Scriptures. With his utter indifference to possessions and his recitation of the Scriptures, he would not accept to stay in a cell, thus not being troubled by material [objects] but, going around this habited world he practised virtue. [*HL* 37.1]

There is considerably more of him elsewhere:

> They used to say of Abba Serapion that, such was his life that it was like that of one of the birds. Not a thing of this world did he possess, nor did he remain in a cell. He used to go around like an incorporeal being, wearing a sheet and carrying a little gospel [book]. They would often find him sitting by the roadside outside a village, weeping bitterly. They would ask him: 'Why are you weeping like this, elder?' and he would answer them: 'My Lord-and-master entrusted me with his wealth; but I have lost and squandered it and he wants to take vengeance on me.' As they listened to this they used to think that he was talking about money and often, throwing him a little bread, they would say: 'Take this and eat it brother; and, regarding the wealth you lost, God is powerful enough to send it [back] to you,' to which the elder answered: 'Amen.' Then another time [Serapion] met a pauper in Alexandria shivering with cold. Coming to a standstill, he thought to himself: 'How can I who am supposed to be a monk be wearing a smock while this pauper (or rather, Christ) [Mt 25.35–45] is dying of cold? If I leave him to die, naturally I shall be judged to be a murderer at the Day of Judgement.' Like a good athlete, he took off the tunic he was wearing and gave it to the pauper. Then he sat down with the little gospel [book] he always carried tucked under his arm. When the so-called 'guardian of the peace' came by and saw him naked, he said to him: 'Abba Serapion, who stripped you?' – producing the little gospel [book], he said to him: 'This one stripped me.' Getting up from there, he met a person who was being seized for debt by somebody else, because he had nothing to give him. This immortal Serapion sold his little gospel [book] and, giving [the proceeds] for the debt of the man who was being violated, went naked into his cell. When his disciple saw him naked, he said to him: 'Abba, where is your little

smock?' The elder told him: 'I sent it on to where we shall need it, my son.' 'And where is the little gospel [book]?' he said. The elder replied: 'Well, naturally, he being the one who says to me every day: "Sell all that you have and give to the poor" [Mt 19.21], I sold him and gave the proceeds to him, so that we shall enjoy greater freedom of speech with him at the Day of Judgement.' [565, 566 / 15.116, 15.117]

It could be argued that, once a person had memorised the contents of a book, it might as well be sold off for charitable purposes, but such was not always the case. Palladius encountered a monk at Ancyra so given to charitable works that

> the type of clothing he wears is not worth a penny and his food is of like value. He is not persistently bending over a writing-tablet since his philanthropic activities take him away from readings. If any one of the brothers made him the gift of a book, he sold it, saying to those who expressed amazement at it: 'How could I convince my Teacher that I have learnt his trade if I do not sell that thing in order to put his trade into action?' [*HL* 68.4]

This, however, is an *urban* monk attached to the local bishop, not to any monastic organism.

Other Literature

There is little doubt that the majority of monks did read (or learn by heart) and that their main reading material came from the Bible for, at least in the earliest days, nothing else was available in Coptic. A Coptic translation of the Scriptures is well attested by manuscript fragments from the end of the third century, but in addition to the written text of the Scriptures, the oral tradition of the tales and sayings of the elders was emerging in the fourth century. An unnamed elder said: 'Talking about the faith and reading doctrines dry up a man's sorrow for sin and obliterate it, whereas the lives and sayings of the elders enlighten the soul' [553]. Another unnamed elder said: 'Let us take our delight in the word of God and rejoice in stories of the holy fathers, not taking delight in the belly but spiritually making merry' [4.93]. 'The blessed John Chrysostom said: "When you are sitting to read the sayings of God, first call upon him to open the eyes of your heart, so as not only to read what is written, but to do it too, lest it be to our own condemnation. Let us go through the lives and sayings of the saints in detail"' [702]. John Moschos heard the following said: 'An elder of great virtue visited us and we were reading the sayings of the holy fathers in [the book called] *Paradise*, for that elder was always very fond of going through [its contents]. He inhaled them as it were, and from that [seed] he produced the fruit of every virtue' [*PS* 212]. Unfortunately it did not always work out that way. Another elder said:

> There are some who, while wasting the days of their life in negligence, seek to be saved in word and mind, but make no effort in deed. They read the *Lives of the Fathers* but do not imitate [the fathers'] humility, their indifference to possessions, their self-control, watchfulness, prayer, kneeling, sleeping on the ground, their *hesychia* and the rest of their spiritual discipline. But in their own opinion and negligence [such people] make the *Lives of the Fathers* a fiction, it being impossible (they say) for a man to endure such things – they failing to consider that where God dwells through the grace of baptism and the keeping of the commandments, supernatural gifts exist and actions take place. [G67]

Other literature must have made its appearance in due course for it is noted that there was danger of monks reading less improving books too: Sopatros warned a brother not to read apocryphal writings [Sopatros 1 / 14.16]. Cyriacus of Calamôn had experience of such literature:

> I rose up and laid hold of a book, intending to read it, thinking that perhaps reading would alleviate my distress. It was a book I had borrowed from Hesychios, priest of Jerusalem. I unwound it and found two writings of the irreligious Nestorius written at the end of it and immediately I knew that he was the enemy of our Lady, the holy Mother of God. So I rose up and went off and gave the book back to him who had given it to me. I said to him: 'Take your book back, brother, for I have not derived as much benefit from it as it has brought adversity upon me.' When he asked me how it had caused me adversity, I told him what had happened. When he had heard about it all, he immediately cut the writings of Nestorius off from the scroll and threw the piece into the fire, saying: 'The enemy of our Lady, the holy Mother of God, shall not remain in my cell either.' [*PS* 46]

Reading Time

How much reading a monk did each day is difficult to estimate, for no doubt it varied considerably from one monk to another; indeed, directors were enjoined to exercise discretion in adjusting the monk's burden to the man's ability. But while it is sometimes difficult to distinguish between reading and meditation, there is this distinction: time had to be set apart for reading while meditation was possible no matter what else one might be doing. A monk afflicted with *accidie* says: 'I am going to read a little and then eat' [195 / 7.34; cf. Arsenius 11], as though this was normal for him. On the other hand, there were those who wanted to read all the time rather

than work. Such folk had to be corrected; the person in the following anecdote was probably one of the Messalians, also known as Euchaites:

> A brother visited Abba Silvanus at Mount Sinai; he saw the brothers working
> and said to the elder: ' "Labour not for the meat which perishes" [Jh 6.27];
> "Mary has chosen the good part" ' [Lk 10.42]. The elder said to Zachariah,
> his disciple: 'Give him a book and put this brother in a cell with nothing in
> it.' When the ninth hour came around, [the brother] was watching by the
> door to see whether they would send and call him to eat. But as nobody
> said anything to him, he got up, came to the elder and said to him: 'Did
> the brothers not eat today, abba?' 'Yes,' said the elder, and the brother
> said: 'Then why did you not call me?' 'You are a spiritual person,' the elder
> said, 'and you do not need this food. But we, being physical [creatures],
> we want to eat; it is for that reason we also work. But you "have chosen
> the better part," reading all day long, and you do not want to eat physical
> food.' When he heard this, he prostrated himself saying: 'Forgive me, abba,'
> and the elder said to him: 'Mary certainly needs Martha and it is thanks to
> Martha that Mary gets the praise.' [Silvanus 5 / 10. 99]

Even moderate reading, however, was not without its dangers and
temptations, for Abba Amoun of Raïthou asked Abba Sisoes: 'When I am
reading Scripture my *logismos* wants to compose a fine speech so I have an
answer to questioning.' The elder said to him: 'There is no need for that;
do you rather acquire the ability to think and speak out of the purity of the
mind' [Sisoes 17 / 8.21]. Abba Mark said:

> The law of freedom teaches all truth. Most people read it in the light of
> what they know but a few think of it as an analogy for the fulfilling of
> the commandments. Do not look for its perfection in human virtues, for
> nobody is found to be perfect in them; its perfection is encrypted in the
> cross of Christ. [1.17]

Whether a monk sat or stood or walked around as he read we do not
know. We know of one who actually lay down: 'Another of the elders held
a book above him when he lay down so that when he fell asleep the book
would fall [upon him] and wake him up' [s81].

Location of Books

Presumably books eventually became more plentiful for we can learn a
little about how they were stored:

> They used to say of Abba Ammoes that he baked fifty measures of grain
> for future need and set them out in the sun and before they were well
> dried he saw something in [that] place that was not beneficial for him.

He said to his young helpers: 'Let us go from here' and they were severely grieved. When he saw them grieving he said to them: 'Are you grieving for the loaves? In truth, I saw some people fleeing leaving the casements with parchment books [in them] open. They did not close the casements but went off leaving them open.' [Ammoes 5]

The word twice translated 'casement' can also mean window or door, also a shelf or plank. The most likely meaning is that there were recesses in the walls, closed on the outside, serving as cupboards inside. A nineteenth-century visitor to El-Sourian monastery on the Nitrian lakes says he went 'into an upper room in a great square tower where we found several Coptic manuscripts. Most of these were lying on the floor but some were placed in niches in the stone walls.'[1] The 'upper room' appears to be the library but, as no such facility as a library is ever mentioned in the apothegms, one assumes that the casements were located in individuals' cells. In the saying of Ammoes cited above, the casements could be closed with doors on the inside; but other references to such storage places make no mention of doors:

A brother asked Abba Serapion [Sindonios]: 'Tell me a saying.' The elder said: 'What am I going to tell you? That you took the goods of widows and orphans and set them in this casement?' – for he saw that it was full of books. [Serapion 2 / 6.16]

An Elder said: 'The prophets made the books; our fathers came and practised them. Those who [came] after those memorised them. Then there came this generation; they wrote them out then set them in the casements, unused.' [228 / 10.191]

---

[1] Robert Curzon, *Visits to Monasteries in the Levant*, London 1849, 1865, repr. London 1955, p. 108. At an Abyssinian monastery books in leather cases were hung from pegs in the wall (115).

CHAPTER 13

Heresy

Form no friendship with a woman, with a child or with a heretic.
[Matoes 11; 330]

The Christological Controversies

There was freedom of religion under the old Roman Empire – to a point.
One was free to practise any (or several) of the numerous religions that
were permitted under the law. But to practise any other than the permitted
religions was to risk falling foul of the law. That is why there were sporadic
persecutions of Christians in the first three centuries of their existence: they
were illegal. Hence they were restricted in a number of ways, e.g. they
could not corporately own property. Nevertheless, Christians flourished
and multiplied, to the point that emperors realised something had to be
done about them. Persecution only seemed to make them stronger, other
measures were no more successful, so Emperor Constantine took the bold
step of allying himself with the Christians: he declared Christianity a legal
religion. In doing so he may not have been aware that the *exclusive* nature
of Christianity ensured that it would eventually become the *only* legal religion of the empire.

Now if something were to be declared legal, there had to be a clear
idea of what was being legalised: a precise definition. This was something
of which the Christians themselves had not yet felt the need; they had
been content to allow various ideas to co-exist, even though these may
have been mutually exclusive. Now Constantine required precision. He
required it not least because he was about to endow 'his' church with a
considerable amount of real estate: the properties of defunct cults that
had come into his possession as *pontifex maximus* (chief high-priest). His
lawyers had to know how to describe the new proprietor on the title-deeds.

To this end, in 325, Constantine (who may or may not even have been
a Christian at this stage) summoned the Christian bishops to a council at

147

Nicaea (modern Iznik, on the east coast of the Sea of Marmara). Presiding over their sessions, he required them to provide a definition. The result was something very like what is now known as the Nicene Creed; it was meant to be a statement of the *orthodox* (i.e. 'correct') faith. Unfortunately, this, which was meant to be a panacea, drawing all Christians under one banner, had almost the opposite effect; anybody who thought there was a consensus underlying the superficial diversity of Christian belief was disappointed. Nicaea might only have touched a flame to a fire waiting to burn, but burn it did, sometimes quite furiously, over the next three centuries.

The main bone of contention was the person of Christ: how could one say Christ was God when the commandment is formal: 'Thou shalt have no other gods before me?' On the other hand, how could one say Christ is saviour if he were merely a man like all others? The confrontation raged on, with emperors taking now one side, now another, or attempting the hopeless task of striking a compromise.

Foremost in defence of the Nicene definition that Christ is 'of one [and the same] substance' [*homo-ousios*] with God the Father was Athanasius of Alexandria [296–373]. The champion of the opposite position was Arius, a priest of Alexandria [256–336], who asserted of Jesus that, in contra-distinction to God the Father, 'there was a time when he was not'. This controversy rocked both church and state with astounding violence, much of it centred on Alexandria. The resulting disturbance clearly affected the desert to a certain extent, for Antony (who taught that frequenting heretics 'led to damage and destruction of the soul' [*VA* 68.2]) took especial excep-tion to the followers of Arius, whose words were 'worse than serpents" [*VA* 68.3]. He was so incensed by them that he left his retreat and marched into Alexandria to condemn them, probably in 338 [*VA* 69]. Later on in the controversy, in 373–375, Macarius the Egyptian, Macarius of Alexandria and some other leading monks were exiled to an island in the Delta by Lucius the Arian for their support of what would eventually be proclaimed the orthodox faith.

Yet no matter how the storm raged 'in the world' or, for that matter, in the desert, there is little indication in the apothegms that monks in general were much affected by it. Here is a rare exception:

> Some Arians once came to Abba Sisoes at the mountain of Abba Antony and began speaking ill of the orthodox; the elder answered them not a word. He summoned his own disciple saying: 'Abraham, bring me the book of the holy Athanasius and read it.' While they kept silence their heresy became apparent. He sent them on their way in peace. [Sisoes 25]

It might be that 'concerning the image' in the following apothegm refers to the Christological disputes troubling Lower Egypt at the end of the fourth century, but one cannot be sure:

> Somebody asked Abba Sopatros: 'Give me a commandment, abba, and I will keep it.' 'Let no woman enter your cell,' he said; 'do not read apocryphal writings and engage in no discussions concerning the image, for this is not heresy, but hair-splitting and quibbling on both parts. No creature is capable of comprehending this matter.' [Sopatros 1 / 14.16]

For some of the Desert Fathers (not, of course, the Hellenised ones at Kellia), the distinctions were probably too subtle; hence they considered the matter to be beyond human comprehending and left it severely alone.

If, however, the rank and file of the monastic world were relatively undisturbed by Arianism, this was certainly not the case in the next stage of the Christological controversy. In order to assert the *divinity* of Christ, the title 'God-bearer' [*theotokos*] was devised for his mother, Mary. This title was assailed by Nestorius, Patriarch at Constantinople 428–431, and that provoked the ire of some monks [Gelasius 4; Phocas 1], a clear indication that the Holy Mother was already dear to monks. An even more severe reaction erupted when in 451 the Council of Chalcedon pronounced that there were two natures to Christ's person, human and divine [*dyophysite*]. This was seen as an assault on Christ's divinity and it provoked a massive schism of what used to be called *monophysites*, now known as *miaphysites*, i.e. believers in *one* nature only, a schism which persists to this day. Most monks, indeed almost the whole of Egypt and the east, took up the miaphysite stance against Constantinople and the west. But the monks were not unanimous, at least not everywhere: 'At Kellia there are two churches: one for the orthodox [i.e. the miaphysites] and one for the schismatics' [Phocas 1].

The First Origenist Controversy

However, to return to the fourth century: while the monks may have remained aloof (or detached) from the early stages of the Christological question, they were nevertheless deeply troubled by what is known as the Origenist controversy. This was occasioned by certain Hellenistic monks, mainly at Kellia, who were thought to have become too involved in the teaching of Origen.[1] Origen Adamantius [184/5–253/4] was born and

---

[1] Origen is only mentioned once in the apothegms [Lot 1], never in *HME* and only in passing in *HL* 64.1.

raised in Alexandria under the influence of Clement of Alexandria and of Ammonius Saccas. Having revived the catechetical school of his native city, he taught there for the first half of his life. But his audacious attempts to blend Greek philosophy with Christian teaching made him so unpopular that he was forced to flee. He went to Caesarea in Palestine and stayed there for the rest of his life, teaching and writing prolifically. His work was highly influential among thinking Christians, but there was always a suspicion that in his attempts to adapt Greek philosophy to Christianity he might have adjusted the latter to fit the former to a certain extent, thus exceeding the bounds of what was beginning to be considered the orthodox faith.

The first Origenist controversy probably began with the arrival of Evagrius of Pontus at Nitria in 381. He and other educated Hellenes like him were already under the influence of the Cappadocian Fathers in addition to being familiar with, if not actually addicted to, the ideas and writings of Origen. After a period of probation at Nitria, Evagrius migrated to Kellia and stayed there until he died in 399. By then there was a significant group of monks not only at Kellia but elsewhere too who shared his admiration for Origen. These included Isidore the Guest-master at Kellia and the four 'Long Brothers' (for they were all quite tall): Ammonius, 'the one-eared', Dioscorus, Euthymius and Eusebius. We may not greatly err in supposing that, under the leadership of Macarius of Alexandria, Kellia had attained a distinctly Hellenic character and a degree of intellectual sophistication totally at variance with the simplicity of the Egyptian *fellayin*, e.g. at Scêtê.

For many of those at Scêtê (probably most of the folk in the desert) were relatively simple people: Coptic speakers, many of whom were at best semi-literate, they had no tradition of learning among them. When such people thought of the Deity, they thought in human terms. They were, after all, only a generation or so removed from folk who revered Horus, Osiris, Amun and Thoth: gods whom men had created in their own image. Understandably, the heavenly Father of the native Egyptians was one who thought and felt and saw as humans do.

For the cultured Hellenes at Kellia such *anthropomorphism*[2] was anathema, totally at variance with their conception of the Deity. For them God was essentially The One, 'without body, parts or passions'. Insofar as the simpler brothers were capable of understanding what was being taught at Kellia, they were alarmed by it and suspected the Origenists of trying

---

[2] See Cassian, *Conf* 10.3.1–4.

to steal their God. Those at Kellia were probably equally appalled at the contradictions inherent in the simple faith of their neighbours, but Kellia was a good distance from Scêtê and monks were well aware of the dangers of passing judgement on one another. So, all might have been well had not Theophilus become the twenty-third Pope of Alexandria in 385, an event that was to precipitate the fathers of the desert into the maelstrom of ecclesiastical politics.

Gibbon characterised Theophilus as 'the perpetual enemy of peace and virtue, a bold, bad man, whose hands were alternately polluted with gold and with blood'.[3] An ardent supporter of the Origenists at the outset of his pontificate, he proposed Isidore the Guest-master at Kellia as a candidate for the patriarchate of Constantinople in 390, but it was John Chrysostom who acceded to that title. This was particularly offensive to Theophilus as John was translated from Antioch to Constantinople. Meanwhile Theophilus was courting the monks, eliciting their support for the destruction of the pagan temples, apparently with some success for 'Some fathers once went into Alexandria at the invitation of Theophilus the archbishop to offer prayer and tear down the [pagan] temples' [Theophilus 3 / 162 / 4.76]. The great Serapeum and other temples were duly destroyed and (as a reward?) two of the Long Brothers were incorporated into Theophilus' retinue.

However, in 399, just when the Pope of Alexandria seemed to have the monks eating out of his hand, he succeeded in alienating the greater part of them by formally condemning their anthropomorphism. His Paschal Letter which did this was welcomed by the Origenists at Kellia and some at Nitria, but it was soundly rejected as highly offensive by three of the four congregations at Scêtê. A significant number of monks took the unusual step of marching on Alexandria and harassing the Pope. Their action appears to have had the desired effect, for Theophilus now did a remarkable *volte-face*: he agreed to condemn the works of Origen. This amazing piece of chicanery was not, however, undertaken for the sole purpose of propitiating the monks; *a fortiori* it was intended as a weapon for use in Theophilus' campaign to ruin John Chrysostom, whom he both hated and envied.

The suppression of Origenism in Egypt now became his goal. Very soon a synod at Alexandria formally condemned Origen's writings, whereupon Theophilus ordered the expulsion of three of the Long Brothers

---

[3] Edward Gibbon, *The History of the Decline and Fall of the Roman Empire*, ed. John Bagnell Bury, 12 vols., New York 1909–1914, vol. III, p. 120.

(Dioscorus was now Bishop of Hermenopolis) and bitterly reviled them when they appealed his verdict. He then proceeded to poison the minds of the simple monks against the Origenists (which was no easy matter for there were some highly respected ascetics among the latter). The result (probably intended) was that he was invited to intervene, whereupon he convened a general synod at Nitria. This was no peaceful conclave: its sessions were frequently interrupted by stormy episodes and some violence. Nevertheless, Origen's works were again condemned and three of the Long Brothers were excommunicated. The Prefect of Egypt having made an ineffectual attempt to execute this sentence, Theophilus gathered up a rabble, put down Dioscorus from his episcopal throne at Hermopolis and marched by night on the Mountain of Nitria. A brutal paroxysm of destruction and burning ensued, which caused about 300 monks of Nitria and Kellia to flee in various directions together with their clergy. Three of the Long Brothers may have already escaped to Palestine for eventually they and some like-minded people, about fifty in number, arrived at Constantinople under the leadership of Isidore. They found a sympathetic ear in John Chrysostom and even gained an audience with Empress Aelia Eudoxia – who undertook to summon a council at which Theophilus would have to answer for his actions. This was the infamous Synod of the Oak, so called after the suburb of Constantinople in which it took place in 403. But far from dealing with the refugee monks and their Origenism, the synod was turned into a prosecution of John Chrysostom by Theophilus, possibly with the connivance of the empress. John was not only condemned; he was deposed and sent into exile where he subsequently died (407). Dioscorus and Ammonius had died just before the synod and Isidore expired immediately afterwards, whereupon the first Origenist controversy came to an end. This was because Theophilus had now achieved his goal: the destruction of John Chrysostom. Origen's works, however, remained suspect and so did those who admired them. A second and more serious Origenist controversy erupted in the sixth century with disastrous results for Origen's reputation.

Heresy of Individuals

Cases of individual heresy appear to have been rare among the monks, but then monks were at least twice warned that fraternising with heretics was every bit as dangerous as having anything to do with women and children [Matoes 11, 330]. Palladius counselled Lausus:

Avoid heretics especially, for their hypocrisy is damaging, even though they seem to be dragging out their old age with their white hair and wrinkles. And even though you suffer no hurt from them on account of your noble behaviour, you will become puffed up and conceited through laughing at them, which is hurtful to you. [*HL Prologue* §15]

One major elder said that to be a heretic was to cut oneself off from God [Agathon 5 / 10.12], while another advised:

If you are friends with somebody and it happens that he fall into temptation to [commit] *porneia*, give him a hand if you can and draw him up. But if he fall into heresy and be not persuaded by you to turn away [from it], quickly cut yourself off from him lest by delaying you be dragged down into the abyss with him. [Theodore of Phermê 4 / 10.32]

On the whole, the fathers show a marked reluctance to engage in discussion concerning scriptural and doctrinal matters [Antony 26; Arsenius 42 / 15.11]. Pambo was fairly typical in this respect: 'If he were asked about a phrase in Scripture or some spiritual matter, he did not answer immediately, but would say he did not know the answer. And if he were pressed further, he would not give an answer' [Pambo 9 / *HL* 10.7]. Elijah warned the brothers: 'Be on your guard against disputations, cogitations and reflections, knowing that it is [the demons] who cast up such things to befoul the soul with inappropriate thoughts so that they can distract the mind from its sins and from God' [Elijah 4].

Melchizedek

Nevertheless, two matters are mentioned in connection with which some monks appear to have strayed. One of them concerns Melchizedech, the somewhat enigmatic king of Salem and priest of the most high God who brought bread and wine and blessed Abram and his God [Gen 14; Ep Heb *passim*]. A meeting at Scêtê to deal with this matter has already been noted [Coprès 3]. Cyril, Pope of Alexandria 412–444, dealt with it in a different way:

Another great elder living in lower Egypt used to say in his simplicity that it is Melchizedek who is Son of God. This was told of him to the blessed Cyril, archbishop of Alexandria, who sent for him. [Cyril] was aware that the elder was a wonder worker, that whatever he asked of God was revealed to him, and that it was in simplicity that he made the statement [about Melchizedek]. [Cyril] shrewdly said to him, 'Abba, I have a request: my *logismos* tells me that it is Melchizedek who is Son of God, while another *logismos* says he is not [that] but a man and a high priest of God. Since

I am in two minds on this matter, I have sent for you so that you may pray to God so that he may reveal [the solution] to you and we may know the truth.' Trusting in his own way of life, the elder confidently replied, 'Allow me three days; I will personally ask God about this and report to you who he is.' Off he went and interceded with God concerning this matter. Three days later he came and told the blessed Cyril: 'Melchizedek is a man.' The archbishop said to him, 'How do you know, abba?' He said, 'God showed me all the patriarchs passing before me, one by one, from Adam to Melchizedek. An angel said to me, "This is Melchizedek; make no mistake that this is how he is."' The elder went away and, of his own free will, announced that Melchizedek was a man. The blessed Cyril was very gratified. [Daniel 8 / 18.8]

Some of the fourth-century Gnostic texts found in 1945 do propose that Jesus and Melchizedek are one and the same person. But Epiphanius, the meddling Bishop of Cyprus, dismissed this notion: 'Melchizedek, the icon of Christ, blessed Abraham, the root of the Jews [Gen 14.19]. Much more so does Christ, who is truth itself, bless and sanctify all who believe in him' [Epiphanius 5].

Eucharistic Questions

The other matter has to do with the nature of the eucharistic species:

Abba Daniel the Pharanite related that our father Abba Arsenius said of one of those at Scêtê that he was a great one in deeds but a simpleton in belief. He erred in his ignorance, saying that the bread that we receive in Communion is not really the body of Christ but a representation.

Two fathers who tried to correct him at least persuaded him that they would all spend a week in prayer then see what happened. The following Sunday as they stood together in church:

Their inner eyes were opened, and when the bread was placed on the holy table, it appeared to the three individuals alone as a child. When the priest put forth [his hand] to break the bread, here there came down from heaven an angel of the Lord; he had a sword and he sacrificed the child, emptying its blood into the chalice. When the priest broke the bread into small pieces, the angel cut some small pieces from the child too. When they went to receive the holy mysteries, bleeding flesh was given to the elder only. He was terrified when he saw it and cried out, saying, 'Lord, I believe that the bread is your body and the chalice is your blood.' Immediately the meat in his hand became bread, as in the sacrament, and he partook of it, giving thanks to God. The elders said, 'God knows that human nature is such that it cannot eat raw flesh, and for that reason he transformed his body into bread and his blood into wine for those who partake in faith.' They gave thanks to God for not allowing the elder to lose his toil; the three [elders] went to their cells with joy. [Daniel 7 / 18.4]

This is not the only time this story of the 'divided infant' turns up [cf. 761B / 18.48] for it passed into the current of the spiritually beneficial tales [*BHG* 248, 1448y] and no doubt into the *Exempla*. It may well have been in reaction against such gross literalism that Paschasius Radbertus (785–865) would devise the embryo of the doctrine of Transubstantiation.

CHAPTER 14

The Pachomian Experiment

Pachomius, a man of great experience who had the spiritual gift of prophecy. [*HL* 18.12]

Pachomius Again

Most of the characters mentioned in the foregoing chapters lived in the fourth and fifth centuries of our era, many of them in Lower (i.e. the north of) Egypt. Meanwhile developments were taking place in the Thebaid, an area of Upper Egypt centred on the city of Thebes, some 700 kilometres farther south. That Theban monastic movement appears to have been on a grander scale than the one in the north but, unfortunately, we are significantly less well informed about it. The extant sources portray Antony's younger contemporary Pachomius (292–348) as its founder. This is how it came about.

As we saw in Chapter 1, as a very young man Pachomius was pressed into military service, probably to serve in Maximin's last war against Licinius. That war only lasted a few months so he was soon released and able to return home to Chenoboskia in the Thebaid. There, motivated by the kindness he had received at the hands of Christians when he was a recruit, he requested baptism. Once he was baptised, for reasons unexplained, he promptly sought to embrace the lonely life of a monk. The Greek *Life* tells how he sought out an aged monk called Palaemon to teach him the way. Palaemon tried hard to discourage him with stories of the rigours of the monastic life, but he finally capitulated and clothed Pachomius in the monastic habit. He then proceeded to train the neophyte.

One day whilst Pachomius was performing the task of collecting thorns (no doubt for fuel) in the wilderness, he came across the deserted village of Tabennesis. He heard a voice telling him to stay there and found a monastery, 'for many will come to you to become monks'. Palaemon not only acquiesced, he came and assisted his disciple to construct a cell before returning to his own cell. The elder and his disciple continued to visit one another occasionally until Palaemon died. Meanwhile Pachomius knew a sustained period of spiritual struggle with the powers of darkness, not unlike the struggle attributed to Antony. Then, as in the case of Antony, Macarius, Amoun and others, he attracted followers. Eventually, an increasing number of brothers congregated around him. A day came when Pachomius and some of the brothers were away cutting rushes with which to make mats and so on. As they worked, Pachomius had a vision of an angel who said to him: 'The will of God is to minister to the race of men, to reconcile them to him.'

Palladius' Testimony

Palladius now takes up the story. His *Lausiac History* [*HL*], which has been a faithful companion in the foregoing chapters, is our main informant concerning Pachomian monachism. Palladius was twice a bishop: first of Hellenopolis, then of Aspuna. For seven years between his episcopates (probably *c.* 407–414) he lived in the Thebaid, probably at one of the monasteries there (for he was an experienced monk before he became a bishop) and he says he visited others. Although he speaks from personal experience, some of what he reports must be hearsay. He tells a somewhat different story of how it all began:

> There is a place called Tabennesi in the Thebaid and that is where there lived Pachomius, a man among those who lived righteously and so were deemed worthy of foreknowledge and of visions of angels. This man became immensely devoted to folk and to his brothers. While he was residing in the cave an angel appeared to him and said: 'You have set your own matters to rights; you live too much in the cave. Come on out; gather together all the young monks and live with them. Lay down laws for them according to the rule that I am giving you.'

From this it can be seen that from the outset Pachomian monachism was fundamentally different from that of the north. The first concern of a monk in, for example, the Nitrian Desert was: 'How can *I* be saved?' Pachomius was to devise a way for folk to seek their salvation *en commun*, living together, *viz.* 'How can *we* be saved?' He was 'to minister to the race of men, to reconcile them to [God]'.

In obedience to his encounter with the angel, Pachomius is said to have invented the coenobion: the social unit in which persons cohabit as an organised family. In truth he was no innovator in this respect. John Cassian says that when he was in Egypt there were coenobia existing in the Nile Delta region which claimed descent from the first Christians at Jerusalem who held everything in common [*Conf* 18.5; *Acts* 2.44; 4.32]. One may doubt their origin but still accept that Christian coenobia had already been in existence for some time. Some subsequently heretical groups, e.g. Meletians, also appear to have maintained coenobia and, as we have seen, in spite of the fact that early Christian monachism was originally focused on the solitary existence, it assumed certain characteristics of the coenobion willy-nilly.

There were a number of reasons for this transformation. First, not every person who came to an elder would be suitable material for the lonely life. A perceptive elder being aware of this would be a harsh elder indeed (and such there were) who sent a person like that packing. By allowing the less-robust brothers to remain in his vicinity, an elder might very well find himself becoming the father of a troop of would-be ascetics. As these grew accustomed to living, working and praying together under his guidance, they would gradually evolve into a sort of coenobion *malgré-soi*.

Second, the desert was not by any means a safe place in which to be. A wall would provide sufficient protection against wild animals, but not against wild men: bandits who would pillage and barbarians who destroyed. Hence monks tended to draw closer together for mutual protection. Maybe they also found the experience of the weekly assembly to their liking and sought to increase occasions of contact with one another. In such ways their lives would tend to become more integrated and communal.

There is a third consideration. Whether the angel's message was 'The will of God is to minister to the race of men, to reconcile them to him', or 'gather together all the young monks and live with them', it would have alerted Pachomius to the possibility that there were far more persons desirous of leading a somewhat ascetical life than were capable of enduring the physical and mental rigours of the solitary life (whose origins, as we saw, may well have been pre-Christian, hence perhaps somewhat *un*-Christian). He may also have been aware that congeries of monks' cells (lavras) were already developing a communal aspect in some places. Pachomius therefore set out quite deliberately to found a monastery where a well-organised cohabitation was the norm from the outset. According to Palladius, he was prompted to do this by a remarkably meticulous divine initiative:

> [An angel of the Lord] gave him a bronze tablet on which these things had been written: 'You shall allow each one to eat and to drink according to his energy. Entrust tasks to them in proportion to the energies of those who eat and do not prevent them from either fasting or eating. Thus, entrust

the more vigorous tasks to those who are eating [substantially], the less-demanding ones to the more spiritually disciplined [brothers]. Build discreet cells in the courtyard and let them live three to a cell; but let them all look for their food in the one house. They are not to sleep lying down; let them sleep sitting up, having made chairs built with sloping backs and put their covers on them. At night let them wear the linen *leviton* with a girdle. Let each [brother] have a cloak made from a goat-skin and let them not eat without it. When they go for Communion on Saturdays and Sundays let them loosen the girdles and set aside the cloak; let them go in [wearing] only a cowl.'

In this way the principle 'To each according to his need, from each according to his ability' made its appearance, to become a permanent feature of monastic economy. The accommodation of the monks three to a cell rather looks as though the rigid insistence on individual cells in Antonine teaching was abandoned, but apparently this was not so, for Palladius writes a little further on:

When Pachomius protested to the angel that the prayers were few ['they were to offer twelve prayers in the course of the whole day, twelve in the evening, twelve during the vigils and three at the ninth hour'] the angel said to him: 'I set the rule like that so that even the young ones can fulfill it and not grieve; the fully instructed ones have no need of direction. *On their own in their cells* they devoted their entire life to the contemplation of God. I laid down laws for those who do not have an understanding mind so that, fulfilling the ordering of the way of life, they might have a confident disposition.'

There is a good description of a Theban coenobion as it appeared to the eyes of the visitors from Jerusalem in 394–395:

In the Thebaid we saw a monastery of Isidore the Great; it was protected by a brick wall and it contained a thousand monks. There were wells and gardens in there and all the necessities of life. Not one of the monks ever went out; a priest was the doorkeeper and he allowed no one to go out nor anybody to come in, unless it were somebody who wished to stay there until death, never going out.

In a small guest-house at the gate he offered hospitality to those who came that way, making them gifts in the morning and sending them on their way in peace. There were two members of the community, priests who were supervisors of the brothers' tasks and they alone went out, to acquire what was needed for those tasks. The priest who remained at the gate told us that those within were so holy that they could all perform miracles and that not one of them fell ill before he died. When each one's hour of death drew near he would tell everybody then lie down and die. [*HME* 17.1–2]

From a practical point of view, the new monasteries were to be strictly organised along lines which may have owed something to Pachomius' military experience:

> [The angel] ordered there to be twenty-four orders and to each order he applied a letter of the Greek alphabet, *alpha, beta, gamma, delta*, etc. When he enquired about or did business with such a multitude the superior would ask his second-in command 'How is the *alpha*-order?' of 'How is it with the *zeta*?' or 'My compliments to the *rho*.' 'Following some particular letter-sign you shall apply the letter *iota* to the more simple and guileless ones and apply the *xi* to the more complicated and difficult.' And, in this way, he accommodated the letter to each order according to the state of their intentions, their characters and their lives, with only the spiritual [fathers] knowing the significance.

The experiment was highly successful, for Palladius continues:

> There are [now] several monasteries adhering to this rule, embracing seven thousand men. The first and great monastery, the one that brought the other monasteries into being, is where Pachomius himself lived; in it are one thousand three hundred men … There are other monasteries of two or three hundred, of which I entered the one in the city of Panos[1] and found three hundred men. In that monastery I saw fifteen tailors, seven metal-workers, four carpenters, twelve camel-drivers and fifteen fullers. They practise every trade, supplying women's monasteries and prisons from their surplus products. They raise hogs too … Those who are on duty for the day rise at dawn; some are in the kitchen, others in the refectory. They are at their posts, getting things ready until the appointed hour. They put loaves on the table, mixed charlock,[2] olives, vegetables, cheese from cows' milk, the best cuts of meat and small vegetables. There are some who come to eat at the sixth hour, others at the seventh, others at the eighth, others at the ninth, others at the eleventh; others late in the evening, others every second day. ['Let them cover their heads with their cowls when they are eating so no one brother can see another chewing. They are not to speak whilst eating nor to let their eyes wander anywhere beyond their plate or the table.'] So each letter [of the alphabet] knows its appointed time.

The mention of hogs and cows points to farming. Whereas most of the monastic communities in Lower Egypt were at least partly and often wholly in the desert, each monk supporting himself by his own handiwork, the monasteries of the Thebaid appear effectively to have been farms, established on (or adjacent to) arable land with a reliable supply of water. This was because a large monastery required several hectares of land

---

[1] Akhmîn today, on the right bank of the Nile in Upper Egypt.
[2] *Sinapis arvensis*, a wild mustard.

on which to be self-sustaining. Many of the monks (including the camel drivers?) would be engaged in farming, a largely cooperative operation before the coming of machinery. Those who did not work on the land were engaged in a variety of occupations:

> One worked the earth as a farmer; another in the garden, another in the smithy, another in the bakery, another in the carpenters' shop or the fullers' shop; another braided large baskets, another worked in the tannery or in the cobblers' shop or in the scriptorium, another at braiding small baskets. ['I was in a coenobion in the Thebaid working as a linen-weaver' a monk remarks elsewhere [132A / 20.15]] But they were learning all the Scriptures by heart.

(All the words of Palladius above are from *HL* 32.1–12.)

Pachomian Rules

No single rule for monasteries by Pachomius has survived, probably because whatever he did write had no permanent status and was frequently revised to meet changing circumstances and differing locations. There does, however, exist a series of fragments of rules, the general consensus of which is not at all at variance with Palladius' observations. The most informative fragment is a list of 141 'Precepts of our Father Pachomius' [*Pr*], but, like all precepts, these define what ought to be and do not necessarily reflect reality.

A trumpet (as in the army?) rather than a semantron summoned brothers to assemble. On hearing the trumpet, a brother was 'to leave his cell, reciting something from the Scripture until he reached the door of the synaxis' [*Pr* 3]. 'When the synaxis is dismissed, each one shall recite something from the Scripture while going either to his cell or to the refectory' [*Pr* 28]. Bell-ringers, food-dispensers and bakers are to recite while they discharge their tasks [*Pr* 36, 37, 116]. The rule Palladius mentioned about not speaking at table should not suggest that free speech was allowed at other times for, when brothers meet, 'they shall not speak to each other, but each one shall recite something from Scripture' [*Pr* 59]. The saying about Abba Marcellinus of the Thebaid noted above (Chapter 6, p. 64) may be pertinent here too [567 / 18.19].

There was a much more favourable attitude towards books and learning in the Thebaid than in the north. Pachomius is credited with directing:

> Whoever comes to the monastery must first learn what he should observe. Then, after this first instruction, when he has consented to it all, he shall be

given twenty psalms to learn, or two of the Apostle's [i.e. Paul's] epistles, or part of another book of Scripture. If he is illiterate, he shall go at the first, third and sixth hours to find someone appointed for this [task] who can teach him. He shall stand before him and learn very carefully, with great gratitude. Then the letters of the syllables shall be written for him and he shall be forced to read, even if he refuses. Everyone in the monastery shall learn letters and memorise something of the Scriptures, at least the New Testament and the Psalter. [Pr 140]

'If they seek a book to read, let them have it; and at the end of the week they shall put it back in its place' [Pr 25], viz., 'the alcove in which books are placed' [Pr 82].

There were several subdivisions or houses within a monastery; presumably these are the lettered 'orders' that Palladius mentions. Each order had its own *oikiakos*, a rare word meaning a familiar or intimate domestic, which is quite misleading here. This was a 'housemaster', a father superior who held sway over many aspects of the lives of the monks in his order, e.g. he was responsible for at least part of the education and training of his charges:

> In the morning, in the individual houses, after the prayers are finished, they shall not return right away to their cells, but they shall discuss among themselves the instruction they heard from their housemasters … An instruction shall be given three times a week by the housemasters. [Pr 19–20, repeated at 138]

In addition to farming, Pachomian monks did a number of things in common which were usually undertaken alone at, for example, Scêtê. Certainly, prayer was largely a communal activity in the Thebaid, not only at the weekend, but two or three times every day, in a prayer-hall furnished with mats, where each had his assigned 'cushion' [*embrimion*]. As we have seen, the monks took their meals in common, the main meal at noon, not at the ninth hour as in the north. Although speaking was forbidden at mealtimes, sign-language was permitted in case of need [Pr 33]. There is no mention of public readings. One of the visitors from the Mount of Olives in 394–395 affords a brief glimpse of an unidentified monastery in the Thebaid at table:

> In the Thebaid we saw another man whose name was Ammôn, the father of three thousand monks called Tabennesiotes. They had a great way of life; they wore sheepskins and ate with their faces hidden, looking down so no one could see another. They maintain a profound silence as though they were in the desert and each one leads his own way of life in secret. They only go through the motions of sitting at table so they might appear to eat,

deliberately deceiving each other. Some of them, once they have sampled bread, oil, or something of what is on the table, bring their hands up to their mouths once or twice and are satisfied with that food after having tasted each dish. Others chew [their] bread slowly regardless of the others and persevere in that way while others still only take three spoonsful of soup, abstaining from the other dishes. [*HME* 3.1–2]

No wine or broth was allowed other than in the Infirmary [*Pr* 45], but the brothers were served some food in their cells, restricted to the dried loaves and salt on which the true anchorite subsisted [*Pr* 79].

Work also appears to have been largely a communal activity in the Thebaid, mostly the traditional manufacture of mats and so forth from steeped reeds. But whether the brothers were labouring on the land or toiling in a workshop, 'At work they shall talk of no worldly matter but either recite holy things or else keep silent' [*Pr* 60]. 'Holy things' probably means both Scripture and elders' apothegms.

The most striking difference is the sheer size of the southern communities and their self-contained-ness behind forbidding walls. From what is said of the organisation, it appears to have had a military character: a well-defined chain of command, not unlike centurions, decurions, etc. Pre-modern statistics are always suspect, but even so it is clear that the buildings housed large numbers of men; each monastery was a city in miniature, a fully functioning economic unit. Nothing is known of what the coenobion looked like, except that it was surrounded by a wall in which there was a gatehouse. It too may have had much in common with the kind of military establishment Pachomius would have known as a youth, but as it was almost certainly constructed of sun-dried brick, nothing has survived. It is not even known where the monasteries were located.

The monastery at Tabennesi was so successful that eventually a second one was founded at Pabau (Faou); after 336, that was where Pachomius spent most of his time. Faou became the largest of several monasteries that were established up and down the Nile, including one for women (this is mentioned in 596.10). By the time Pachomius died (*c.* 345), there were eight monasteries and several hundred monks following his guidance. The coenobitic way of life spread remarkably quickly to Palestine and the Judean Desert, Syria, North Africa and eventually to western Europe.

Pachomius was visited by Athanasius in 333 and offered ordination, but he refused. He was also visited by Basil of Caesarea who took many of Pachomius' ideas back to Annesi with him. Some of them were widely diffused by his ascetic writings, eventually to be incorporated in *The Rule of Saint Benedict*.

Upper and Lower Egypt

In considering the differences between the two monastic traditions, it is well to note that they were located at some considerable distance from one another (fifteen days on foot, see below) and that different forms of Coptic were spoken: *Sahidic* in parts of Upper Egypt, *Bohairic* in Lower Egypt. There is frequent mention of Theban monks and persons in the apothegms. In addition to Macarius' alleged visit to Pachomius, the apothegms provide some evidence of contact between Scêtê and the Thebaid, even though there was an entire province (Arcadia) between the two. For example, 'A great elder from the Thebaid came visiting Abba Achilles' at Scêtê. [Achilles 6], John Colobos' first abba at Scêtê was an elder from the Thebaid [John Colobos 1 / 14.4] and there is note of at least one Theban coming to Scêtê to seek counsel [Joseph of Panepho 3 / 10.38]. Five of the persons to whom sayings are attributed in *APalph* are identified as Thebans: John, Isaac, Joseph, Sisoes and Xoios; it may be mere coincidence that two of the Thebans mentioned in the apothegms appear to have been pioneers: John of the Thebaid, who first [?] linked humility with the First Beatitude [Mt 5.3; John of Kellia 2 / 15.36], and Abba Marcellinus, who would *silently* meditate a passage from Scripture on his way to church [567 / 18.19].

Evidence of persons going south is less plentiful. There is mention of a 'Paul, originally from Lower Egypt but residing in the Thebaid' [Paul / 19.15] and 'An experienced brother once came into the Thebaid from Scêtê and stayed at a coenobion' [549]. Also the linen thread which was needed by monks working rushes, palm-fronds and so on had to be fetched from the Thebaid [Arsenius 26]; this must have occasioned some coming and going.

Yet in spite of such contacts, many monks may have lived in ignorance of how the others lived, while, for those who had some awareness, a certain amount of rivalry may have obtained. Competition was by no means absent from the desert: indeed, Athanasius manifestly wrote his *Life of Antony* to encourage it [*VA* Preface, 1; cf. 203 / 7.42]. It could have been in the spirit of competition that a fertile imagination produced the following curious anecdote:

> When [Macarius of Alexandria] heard that the folk at Tabennesi had a great way of life, he disguised himself, taking on the appearance of a working-class secular person. He travelled the desert for fifteen days and came to the Thebaid. When he got to the monastery [*askêtêrion*]

of the folk at Tabennesi he sought out their archimandrite whose name was Pachomius, a man of great experience who had the spiritual gift of prophecy [although] it was hidden from him who and what Macarius was. When he encountered him, Macarius said to him: 'I beg of you to take me into your monastery [*monê*] so I may become a monk.' Said Pachomius to him: 'Anyway, you are advanced in age and cannot undertake spiritual discipline. The brothers practise it; you will not endure their toil. You will be offended and go off speaking ill of them,' and he did not take him in either the first or the second day. This went on for seven days but [Macarius] persisted, fasting; and finally he said to him: 'Take me in, abba, and if I do not fast and work as they do, order me to be thrown out.' Then [Pachomius] persuaded the brothers to take him in among them. Now the population of the one monastery is fourteen hundred men to this day. So in he went. A short time went by and Lent was at hand; [Macarius] saw that each one practised spiritual discipline by different ways of life; one ate in the evening, one every second evening, one every fifth [evening]. Then again, one stood all night long then sat during the day. So [Macarius] steeped a large quantity of palm fronds and stood in a corner; he touched neither bread nor water until the days of Lent had run their course and Easter had come and gone. He neither bent his knees nor reclined. He would take nothing but a few leaves of cabbage, and that on Sunday – to give the impression that he was eating. If ever he went out for personal needs he quickly came in and took up his position, neither speaking to anybody nor opening his mouth but standing in silence. Apart from the prayer in his heart and the fronds in his hands he did nothing. When all the monks [*askêtai*] had seen, they rose up against the higoumen, saying: 'From where did you bring us this fleshless man to condemn us? Either get rid of him or be aware that we are all taking off.' So when he heard the details of [Macarius'] way of life he prayed to God for it to be revealed to him who this was. It was revealed to him and, taking [Macarius'] hand, he led him into the house of prayer where the altar was, saying to him: 'Come now, venerable one: you are Macarius and you concealed it from me; I longed to see you for many years. I am grateful to you for smiting my children so they do not have a high opinion of their spiritual discipline. Do you now go to your own place (for you have sufficiently edified us) and pray for us.' So [Macarius] went away as requested. [*HL* 18. 12–16; cf. Macarius of Alexandria 2 / 10.46]

Another possible indication of rivalry is the almost complete silence of the apothegms concerning Pachomius and the Theban monasteries. Pachomius is hardly mentioned in *APaph* and never in *APanon*. One of his successors, Orsisios (351–386), fares a little better; two very striking apothegms of his are included [Orsisios 1 / 15.60, Orsisios 2 / 11.78] and one attributed to Psenthaisios ('Let us then die and live with [Pachomius] for he is leading us straight to God'). The only other mention of Pachomius may have been included as an implied rebuke:

> When (at the instigation of God) Abba Gelasius came to set up the coenobion, much land was offered to him. He also acquired beasts of burden and oxen for the needs of the coenobion. He[3] who at first revealed to the godly Pachomius that he should set up a coenobion was working with this [father] too in all that concerned the setting up of the monastery. The above-mentioned elder, seeing him [immersed] in these things and maintaining a sincere affection for him, said to him: 'Abba Gelasius, I am afraid that your *logismos* is attached to the lands and the rest of the property of the coenobion,' to which he replied: 'Your *logismos* is more attached to the needle with which you work than is the *logismos* of Gelasius to the property.' [Gelasius 5]

These are the only Pachomian elements to be found in *APalph*. The following piece from *APanon* is more complimentary:

> An experienced brother once came into the Thebaid from Scêtê and stayed at a coenobion. Almost all the men at the coenobion were saints of those known as Tabennesiotes. When he had stayed there a few days, he said to the archimandrite: 'Offer a prayer for me, abba, and send me on my way, for I cannot stay here.' 'Why is that, my son?' the father said to him. 'Because there is no struggling here, no reward,' the brother said, 'because all the fathers are [accomplished] combatants, while I am a sinful man. I would rather go where I find myself being insulted and despised, for these are what save a sinful man.' So the higoumen, amazed, and perceiving that this was a serious worker, sent him on his way, saying: 'Go forth, my son; "Be strong and he shall comfort your heart, and wait upon the Lord."' [Ps 26/ 27.14; 549]

One has to conclude that Pachomius was a very successful leader who created a vast and closely knit organisation. Unfortunately, that organisation had its day and then rather quickly faded away, leaving very few lasting remains. And yet some of the very elements which distinguished it from Antonine monachism were incorporated into and indeed formed the backbone of the Benedictine tradition of western monachism: an integrated organisation and chain of command, a rigorous timetable of praying, communal living, regular instruction with discussion and a marked emphasis on intellectual development.

---

[3] An angel; see *HL* 32.

Notes on the Sources

Athanasius of Alexandria, *The Life of Antony, the Coptic Life and the Greek Life*, translated by Tim Vivian and A. N. Athanasakis, Kalamazoo MI 2003 [*VA*]

Certainly the earliest and probably the most important of our sources, this book was written by someone who, although he spent some of his life among monks, was not one of them: the Pope (archbishop and patriarch) of Alexandria, Athanasius the Great (*c.* 297–373). He is believed to have written *VA* shortly after Saint Antony's death in 356 and certainly no more than a decade later. Athanasius makes it clear at the outset that he is writing *VA* to encourage monks elsewhere to emulate and even to surpass the monks of Egypt in their ascetic endeavour [*VA* Preface §1; cf. 4.3]. In the course of its ninety-four sections, details of the life of Antony are interspersed with lengthy passages allegedly of the saint's teaching. There are also several anecdotes, about half of which record visions seen by Antony, e.g. the Ascent of Amoun [*VA* 60; cf. *HL* 21]. It goes without saying that only Antony himself could have revealed what he saw in visions, whereas the other tales could have originated in observations by his followers. Athanasius was in an excellent position to compose *VA*, for, unlike most hagiographers, he had direct knowledge of his subject. He was not only personally acquainted with Antony ('I saw him often'), he also had as his informant one who had been Antony's 'long-time companion', Bishop Serapion of Thmuis, *c.* 330–*c.* 360 [*VA* Preface §5], and as primate of Egypt he must have been well aware of what was being said about Antony among those many monks and visitors who looked to the saint as their father and elder before and, *a fortiori*, after his death in 356.

Superbly written, *VA* has been a profoundly influential work in the evolution of many branches of Christian literature, especially of hagiography. One has to ask, however, whether *VA* may have been more influential than it ought to have been. There is no doubt that Athanasius used the work in several ways to strengthen his own position as primate of Egypt by enhancing the reputation of monks. And no other monk had his life written up by so eminent a person, and few so soon after their deaths. Jerome certainly felt that Athanasius had overdone it: he is thought to have produced his fictitious *Life of Paul of Thebes* (see below) in order to 'tone down' the effect of *VA*.

> *The History of the Monks of Egypt* [*HME*], translated by Russell, Norman *The Lives of the Desert Fathers: the Historia Monachorum in Ægypto*, Oxford 1981.

Next come two very different works, contemporary with (but very different from) each other. *Historia monachorum in Ægypto* [*HME*], 'An Investigation of the Monks in Egypt', tells how seven brothers from the monastery associated with Rufinus of Aquileia and Melania the Elder on the Mount of Olives at Jerusalem travelled up the Nile as far as conditions would then permit (to Lycopolis, now Asyut), then made their way down to the coastal region during the winter months of 394–395, visiting ascetics and monastic communities on the way. When they returned to Jerusalem, one of their number was prevailed upon to write about 'the ways of life of the monks of Egypt that I have witnessed, their great love and intense spiritual discipline [*askêsis*]' [*Prologue* 2]. He may have been the member of the group who was a deacon [1.14] and may have been named Timothy, eventually archdeacon of Alexandria.[1] He wrote in Greek but a Latin translation, probably by Rufinus of Aquileia, quickly made its appearance. The book consists of a Prologue, twenty-six sections varying enormously in length and an Epilogue. The Epilogue is strikingly different from the rest of the text for it is where the many misfortunes the brothers encountered in the course of their travels are eloquently lamented. They undertook that perilous journey in order to verify the amazing reports of refugee monks from Egypt seeking security in Palestine: tales about the accomplishments of their predecessors and contemporaries in the practice of spiritual discipline in the land they had left behind. Given the element of competition in early monachism, monks from the west recently installed in the Holy Land needed to know how their way of life compared with that of the original settlements in the Thebaid and in the Nitrian Desert. A number of the ascetics they encountered are *said* to have offered beneficial discourse, but John of Lycopolis is the only father of whose spiritual instruction more than a little is recorded. It is said of Evagrius Ponticus: 'He gave us many other addresses concerning spiritual discipline, fortifying our souls' [20.16], but

---

[1] E. Cuthbert Butler, *The Lausiac History of Palladius*, 2 vols., Cambridge 1898, 1904, vol. 1, pp. 276–277.

none of his teaching is recorded. In the only other section of any length Apollo provides some practical instruction for monks, exhorting them to *apatheia* and *anorexia* [8.14–16]. He (alone) strongly advocates daily communion (at the ninth hour) [8.51, 56] and gives guidance on how to reconcile fasting and hospitality [8.58]. '[Apollo] often spoke with us alone for a whole week', but then, 'How can one speak of all his teachings … when one is incapable either of writing them down or of speaking of them adequately?' the writer laments [8.60, 61]. Nevertheless the text provides descriptions of several monks, some of whom were subsequently seen to be of importance in the evolution of eremitic monachism.

There is a wealth of detail concerning the places and the people visited, how the visitors were entertained and what they saw. Particular emphasis is placed on the disciplines the Egyptian monks endured and the wondrous works they were believed to perform: 'many of them have arrested flowing rivers, have walked upon the Nile, have killed wild beasts and have accomplished cures: wonders and mighty deeds such as the holy prophets and apostles performed' [*Prologue* 9]. Hence there is a considerable quantity of anecdotal matter here, some of which puts a severe strain on one's credulity. Probably aware of this, the author says: 'We did not write everything down on account of excessive wonder, not because they were untrue, but on account of some folks' disbelief' [13.12]. Nevertheless, he records the curious anecdote of the woman turned into a mare [21.17] and the fantastic tale of the Garden of Jannès and Jambrès [21.5–12], both of which recur (somewhat altered) in Palladius' *Lausiac History* [*HL* 18.5–9, 17.6–9].

Of the more than thirty characters who figure in *HME* some were directly connected with Antony, e.g. Amoun [22] and Paul the Simple [24; see *HL* 22], whom Antony tested most sorely. A few were only recently dead (e.g. Macarius the Egyptian), while Pityrion was still living [15] and so too was Cronides, allegedly aged 110 [20.13]. The greater part of the work [1–20] describes the brothers' experiences in the Thebaid where most of the people encountered were fathers of large monasteries, e.g. Ammôn [3] had 3,000 monks, Apollo [8] 500, Isidore [17] 1,000, Serapion [18] 10,000, while a bishop at Oxyrhynchus told the brothers he had 10,000 monks and 2,000 nuns under his care [5.5]. Here too they encountered solitaries, Ôr [2], Theonas [6], Elijah [7] and John [13.3]. Unfortunately, only towards the end of their journey did the brothers reach that portion of monastic Egypt most familiar to modern readers: the Nitrian Desert [20–26]. Here the information provided is rather superficial and sometimes wrong, e.g. it was Macarius the Egyptian (not the Alexandrine) who founded Scêtê, where they did not go [23.1]. From Nitria they made their way down to Diolcopolis on the coast and then presumably took shipping from Alexandria back to Palestine.

Palladius of Aspuna, *The Lausiac History* [*HL*], translated by John Wortley, Collegeville MN 2015

The other work to consider here is also a travelogue, the fruit not of one winter, but of a lifetime's experience: the so-called *Lausiac History* [*HL*] This work resembles *HME* in a number of ways, both in form (Prologue, seventy-one sections each about a person, Epilogue) and in content: again, forty-some tales, including four (two already noted) also found in *HME*. *HL* is the work of Palladius who includes a considerable amount of auto-biographical material. Born in Galatia in the 360s, he enrolled as a monk on the Mount of Olives in his early twenties and stayed there for about three years, encountering the founders, Rufinus of Aquileia and Melania the elder. It may have been on their advice that he left for Alexandria to learn the practice of Egyptian monasticism from a hermit named Dorotheos [*HL* 2]. He subsequently spent nine years living at Kellia, first with Macarius of Alexandria, then with Evagrius of Pontus, whose influence on him is palpable [*HL* 38]. Palladius fell ill about the time Evagrius died [399] and withdrew, first to Alexandria, then to Palestine, for his health [*HL* 35, 11–12]. He took up residence first with Poseidon at Bethlehem (where he encountered Jerome) [*HL* 36], and second with a hermit near Jericho [*HL* 48.2], until John Chrysostom appointed him Bishop of Hellenopolis in 400. But after John fell, Palladius was deposed and imprisoned for eleven months in a dark cell [*HL* 35.13]; he was then sent into exile. For seven years he lived with monks in the Thebaid until he was able to return to Galatia after the opposition to John Chrysostom subsided. In due course, he was appointed to the see of Aspuna, where he may have remained until his death, possibly in 425. It was in this last stage of his life that he composed *HL*.

Palladius was very well qualified to write this book, for he must have spent about twenty years as a monk before he became a bishop, then seven or eight years in the Thebaid during his interregnum. He lets it be known in various ways that he occupied no mean position in the social order. The elegance of his language alone attests to this; of the monastic writers only his mentor, Evagrius, and Athanasius wrote Greek of similar sophistication. It is clear too that he habitually moved in exalted circles 'in the world', rubbing shoulders with persons of senatorial rank. His book has come to be known as *Lausiac* because he wrote it at the request of (and dedicated it to) the eunuch Lausus, his friend since 391 [*HL* 71.6]. Lausus served

Emperor Theodosius II and his sister, 'the blessed Pulcheria', as chamberlain [*praepositus sacri cubiculi*] from 420 to 422. At that time the emperor was not yet twenty, while his sister (who was only two years older) had already more or less gathered the reins of power into her capable hands. Palladius makes no secret of his hope that, through the minister, his book might influence the sovereigns and the entire government. Thus Palladius' is the only one of the major monastic writings written not for monks to inspire them with models for their emulation, but rather for a man very much in and of the world with the explicit intention of exerting *political* (albeit religious) influence. To what extent it contributed to the exemplary piety of the Augousta Pulcheria (who effectively ruled the empire until her death in 453) we may never know.

There are other features of *HL* that distinguish it from most monastic writings. Palladius insists on speaking of both male *and female* ascetics [*HL* 41.1] and he advises Lausus: 'Seek the acquaintance of holy men *and women*' [*Prologue* §15]. Both the elder and the younger Melania receive comprehensive treatment, while several other women are accorded honourable mention, e.g. Piamoun [31], Olympia [56], an anonymous ascetic [60] and Magna [67]. For the rest, *HL* largely consists of a series of portraits of other significant people Palladius encountered or heard about. He tells us a great deal about some of them, but he rarely has anything to say about what or how they taught. He does not restrict himself to writing about shining models for emulation: 'In order to praise those who lived well, I am not going to omit from the narrative those who have lived contemptuously, [but will include them] as a warning to those who read it,' he says [*HL* 6.1]. And, after recounting the career of the indifferent Valens, he continues:

> Just as among the sacred plants of paradise there was the tree of the knowledge of good and evil, I have to include the lives of people like that in this little book for the security against stumbling of those who read it; so that, if ever some success befall them, they do not become high-minded on account of that virtue. [*HL* 25.6]

There follows a series of bad examples of various kinds. One concludes that Palladius encountered not a few unpleasant characters in the course of his travels, among whom was the great Jerome at Bethlehem: 'He was so jealous that this obscured his literary skill' [*HL* 36.6]. Elsewhere he says:

> A certain Jerome from Dalmatia became a stumbling-block for [Paula the Roman, 'a woman greatly advanced in her spiritual way of life']. She was capable of flying higher than everybody for she was very talented but in his

jealousy he stood in her way, having won her over to his own point of view.
[*HL* 41.2]

Palladius concludes his work with a few words about 'the brother who
has been my companion from my youth until today'. As he never uses the
first-person plural when describing his travels, one concludes that he did
not have a travelling companion in the way that John Cassian travelled
with Germanus or John Moschos was accompanied by the future patriarch
Sophronius two centuries later. It is now generally (but not universally)
agreed that Palladius is here speaking of himself, as is St Paul in the passage
from which the quotation a little further on is taken. 'On behalf of such a
one I will glory' [*HL* 71.4; 2 Cor 12.5]. *HL* stands out as a work of considerable literary sophistication; indeed, it may safely be said that Palladius
brought the art of portraying the Desert Fathers to heights it would never
attain again.

'Sayings' of the Desert Fathers

By far the most important literary source for any study of the Desert
Fathers is their so-called Apothegms or Sayings [*apothegmata patrum: AP*].
Sayings is an inadequate word, for the apothegms consist of tales *about*
the fathers as well as words they uttered; 'tales and sayings' would be a
more appropriate title for what was the nearest thing those early monks
had to a training manual. Tales and sayings came into existence when a
neophyte or even a more senior person seeking counsel visited an elder
with the request so often repeated, e.g. 'Abba, tell me a saying [showing]
how I am to be saved' [e.g. Euprepios 7 / 10.24]. The reply (for which one
might be kept waiting) would usually be a laconic statement such as: 'Take
away temptations and nobody is being saved' [Evagrius 5]. But it could be
a tale, e.g. 'They used to say of so-and-so that …', a tale with a moral of
course, possibly leading up to a saying. Once the elder had spoken, what
he had said would be treasured, repeated, meditated upon – and passed
on to others to be cherished in the same way by them. In due course, a
significant and increasing corpus of tales and sayings of the fathers would
be circulating among the monks, a folklore of the desert in which tales
and sayings were intermixed like sand and gravel. Not surprisingly, as with
sand and gravel, it is not always easy to say where one ends and the other
begins.

A mere glance at the surviving material reveals that the several *narratives*
or tales interspersed with the sayings generally demonstrate the sort of life

an elder led and the kind of actions he performed. Thus while, for their part, the sayings tend to define the theory, the tales describe the practice of eremitic monachism. There are exceptions, but on the whole the distinction is a valid one.

In the beginning and for a long time this 'folklore of the desert' was exactly that: a wholly *oral* tradition circulating in a Coptic dialect, for that was what the first Christian monks spoke, being native Egyptians. The earliest evidence of sayings appears already in *VA* where it is recorded (in Greek) that Antony (who knew no Greek) would utter an apothegm on rare occasions, e.g. 'The sensitivity of the soul is strengthened when the pleasures of the body are weakened' [*VA* 7.9]. Nothing of this kind is to be found in *HME*, but there are passages in *HL* that are similar [e.g. *HL* 14]. But Evagrius Ponticus, who spent the last fourteen years in association with the leading monks at Nitria and Kellia before he died in 399, produced an important guide to the ascetic life called *Praktikos*. He concluded that book with a short series of apothegms [91–100], one attributed to Antony, two to Macarius the Egyptian; these constitute the earliest evidence of apothegms being collected in writing.

It is significant that Evagrius, living among Copts, set down his apothegms in Greek. From the time when Alexander the Great founded Alexandria and advanced up the Nile *c*. 332 BC, Egypt began to acquire an increasingly bilingual and bicultural nature. And as Alexandria became the prosperous capital of the Ptolemaic kingdom and a very important centre of Hellenic culture, Greek became the common tongue in the Delta region and who knows how much further south. Towards the end of the fourth century Greek speakers, both native and from overseas, were beginning to make their presence felt in the Coptic-speaking monastic communities, Evagrius being one of the best-known examples. And since (as certainly seems to be the case) the first monks were distinctly Egyptian and not very sophisticated, once the Hellenised people of the Delta and farther afield began to join them, a subtle transformation began to occur. The most palpable symptom of this transformation was the increasing use of the Greek language, most of all for writing. Thus, Evagrius, who thought and wrote in Greek, set down some apothegms in Greek, and so it would be thereafter.

The Alphabetic-Anonymous Collection

Nothing remains of the collections of apothegms that are said to have been composed in the century following Evagrius' death, but towards the end of that century (*c.* 490–500) a very determined effort was made to codify the extant material. That the effort was successful is testified by the large number of manuscripts remaining. But they are manuscripts which vary, sometimes considerably from each other. In all probability, this means that there never was and never will be a stable text of the tales and sayings, because, whereas there lies at the origin of most works a text which some-body sat down and wrote or dictated and an editor's task is to reconstruct that *Urtext* as far as possible, no such foundation underpins the tradition of the apothegms. For not only do its roots lie buried in the shifting sands of oral transmission, there is every reason to suppose that, far from it being immediately silenced as soon as the matter was committed to writing, transmission by word of mouth continued in vigorous existence for some centuries, constantly contaminating the written tradition and *vice versa*. This double-transmission partly explains a further complication: even scribes who, under normal circumstances, would reproduce the exemplar before them with the greatest possible accuracy, appear to have accorded themselves extraordinary editorial licence when the matter was of an apo-thegmatic nature. This may well have been because, when faced with a dis-crepancy between the dead letter of the exemplar on his desk and the living voice of some charismatic elder, the scribe preferred the latter. He might also adjust or augment the text a little to make what he perceived to be its meaning more clear. And if he recalled some tale or saying that seemed appropriate, he would not hesitate to include it in his copy or, on occasion, to omit an item that he felt to be less than appropriate. That is why the apothegmatic texts survive in a bewildering array of manuscripts under a variety of names, all consisting of tales and sayings, but all differing from each other to a greater or a lesser degree: in the wording of the items, in the items they include or exclude and in the order in which the items are presented. The best one can say is that such-and-such a manuscript represents the state of the tradition at one particular time and place, rather like a snapshot of something on the move.

> *Give me a Word: the Alphabetic Sayings of the Desert Fathers*, translated by John Wortley, Yonkers NY 2014 [*APalph*], cited by name + number, e.g. [Antony 14]

> *The Anonymous Sayings of the Desert Fathers*, edited and translated by John Wortley, Cambridge 2013 [*APanon*], cited by number, e.g. [416]

We can observe four major collections of apothegms. Of these, the first two to be considered are contemporary and very closely related: the Alphabetic [*APalph*] and the Anonymous [*APanon*] collections. These are best thought of as first and second volumes of one 'Alphabetic-Anonymous Collection'.

While Egyptian monks enjoyed the reputation of being the most advanced in spiritual discipline and they of the Nitrian Desert to be the best of the Egyptians, the Nitrian Desert was by no means the safest place to be. The four churches of Scêtê in the Wadi Natrum were devastated in 408; there were further deadly attacks by the Mazics in 434 and 444. Each time many monks were killed. Some no doubt returned to rebuild, but many also withdrew to safer locations, for instance (as we saw) Abba Poemen and his entourage to Terenouthis after 408. In addition, theological controversy also caused others to migrate elsewhere. Thus, in due course, a number of refugee communities of Egyptian monks arose outside Egypt, e.g. in Palestine, some of them along what is now the Gaza Strip. That may very well be where the major codification we are about to discuss was executed, almost certainly by refugees from the Nitrian Desert. Abba Irenaeus testified:

> When barbarians came to Scêtê, I withdrew and came into the district of Gaza, where I accepted a cell for myself at the lavra. From the abba of the lavra I received a book of sayings of the elders. The same day I set myself to read it and, as soon as I unrolled the book, I found a passage in which a brother visited an elder and said to him: 'Pray for me father.' The elder said: 'When you were with us I used to pray for you. Now you have gone away to your own homeland I pray for you no longer.' When I read this, I rewound the book and said to myself: 'Oh wretched Irenaeus, to have fled to your own homeland – and the fathers no longer pray for you!' I immediately gave the book [back] to the abba, left [that place] and came to Kellia. And that, children, is why I am here.' [*PS* 55]

It is not hard to imagine why the project of codification was undertaken. The dislocation of a community would raise fears for the integrity of its oral tradition, especially if that tradition were in a language foreign to what was spoken in the new homeland. Hence Greek, the *lingua franca* of the Mediterranean basin, was the obvious choice as an alternative. It is more than likely that some (if not all) of the apothegms were already circulating in both languages, especially at Kellia where there was a distinctive element of Hellenised monks.

Those who addressed the task of codification were not dissimilar. That they had something of a classical education is revealed by the manner in which they proceeded. This seems to have been inspired to a certain extent by Plutarch's *Sayings of the Spartans* [*Apothegmata Laconica*] where persons' names are ranged in alphabetical order with the alleged sayings and anecdotes of each Spartan entered accordingly. The monks borrowed both the word (apothegms, which never occurs in the apothegms themselves, only in the editorial matter) and the method used by Plutarch. Intending to impose some sort of order on the confusing mass of oral material in circulation, they adopted Plutarch's very sensible principle of gathering all the sayings or activities attributed to a certain person under one head; then, by reference to the initial letter of that person's name, of setting the heads in the order of the letters of the Greek alphabet. Thus they started with Antony, Arsenius, Agathon and concluded with Cheremon, Psenthaisius and Ôr (X, Ψ, Ω). The monks had the advantage over Plutarch that their matter was of relatively recent origin, whereas he was reaching back several centuries. It had nevertheless been circulating orally for some time and must therefore be treated very cautiously. Numbers vary from one manuscript to another, but generally speaking there are about a thousand items in *APalph*. The various entries vary in length, sometimes consisting of only one or two items (e.g. Theodore of Scêtê, Theodotus), sometimes as many as fifty, with one outstanding example: Poemen (see below).

The Anonymous Sayings

We come now to the second part of (or an appendix to) that first collection. After explaining the alphabetical arrangement of the items, the writer of the *Prologue* to *APalph* continues:

> Since there are also other words and deeds of the holy elders that do not indicate the names of those who spoke or performed them, we have set them out under headings after the completion of the alphabetic sequence. But, after searching out and looking into many books, we set down as much as we were able to find at the end of the headings. [*Prologue* to *APalph*]

This claim by the compilers to have created a supplement or appendix to the first collection and the three things they say about that appendix are of especial interest, *viz.* that its contents are *anonymous*, that they are arranged under headings and that anything else coming to their notice was added at the end, i.e. after the section with headings. These data leave no doubt that the series of sayings formerly known as *Nau* (the name of its first editor, Frédéric Nau) is indeed the second part or supplement to which they refer, especially since, in the principal manuscripts containing *APalph*, the text of *APanon* follows directly after. Moreover, whereas the contents of the former are in nearly every case clearly linked to the name of a person, the contents of more than the first half of the latter are sharply distinguished from those of *APalph* precisely by recording the deeds and sayings of *unnamed* persons. Additionally, in the same section of *APanon* the contents are indeed set out under headings, *viz.* 'Concerning imperial officials' [37], 'Concerning the holy habit of monks' [55], 'Concerning anchorites' [132A], 'That we should pursue *hêsychia* and grief for sin' [133]. There are eleven more such headings ending with: 'On those who have the gift of second-sight' [359]. The contents of the latter part of the collection are very mixed and might well be whatever the compilers were able to scrape together from various sources, as they say in the passage cited above. There is little doubt that subsequent copyists added other material, much of which cannot be dated any earlier than the seventh century.

APanon contains only about eight hundred items, but many of them are longer than the average item in *APalph*. Sayings generally exceed tales in number, as tales exceed sayings in length, but the proportion of tales is somewhat higher in *APanon* than in *APalph*. This is noted here because tales tend to have a more general appeal than sayings, which usually address the monastic state. Many of the tales eventually made their way into the preachers' handbooks called *Exempla* in the medieval west.

The Poemen problem

An entry that far exceeds all other entries in length is the one containing sayings and deeds attributed to Poemen, credited with more than two hundred items in *APalph* alone. If similar items found elsewhere and all the items where Poemen is mentioned were added, that number would be significantly increased. But it is not only the quantity, but also the quality of these sayings that is remarkable: 'Your sayings are full of grace and glorious,' Tithoes told Poemen [391 / 10.51]; many readers would agree.

There are those who believe that Poemen was every bit as much a real person as were Macarius, Pambo and the rest of the early fathers. They also believe that he is to be identified with the monk of Scêtê of that name who migrated to Terenouthis after 408. This view is shared by the Orthodox church where Poemen is revered as a saint. The difficulty with this is that, when all the evidence is assembled, the Poemen of the apothegms appears to have been still alive well into the following century. There are others who observe that *poemen* is the Greek word for shepherd, hence *pastor*. These folk allege that, when the collectors found themselves with an item to which no name was attached, they simply classified it under 'the Pastor'. The difficulty with this is that a very large number of the sayings attributed to Poemen have a distinctive characteristic that sharply distinguishes them from the greater part of the apothegms: his tolerance of the weakness of others and his readiness to forgive. And, as we have seen, the collectors had another way of dealing with items of unknown provenance. Briefly, the 'Poemen problem' remains unsolved.

> *The Book of the Elders: Sayings of the Desert Fathers, the Systematic Collection*, translated by John Wortley, Collegeville MN 2012 [*APsys*], citation by section and item, e.g. [16.22]

It would appear from the Introduction to *APalph* that the two parts of the collection just described were made by the same person(s) at more or less the same time. Another major collection began to emerge probably a generation or so later. It is easy to see why it was made; those attempting to live the monastic life needed to be able to consult as many of the available tales and sayings as possible on any one topic without having to search through the former collection, originally contained in several scrolls. The partial attempt of the editors of *APanon* to sort by topic was apparently appreciated; now that procedure was extended to the entire corpus. Thus there was generated the *systematic* collection [*APsys*]. Twenty-one chapter-heads were identified, each of them a monastic virtue or *desideratum*; then much of the extant material was arranged under those heads. A typical chapter of *APsys* as it now stands contains, first, a selection from *APalph* (often preserving the original alphabetic order of the items), then maybe some extracts from the *Spiritual Discourses* of Isaiah of Scêtê and/or sundry other items, mainly anonymous (for instance, the curious 'medical' items, 16.17–20). Every chapter concludes with a considerable number of selections from the 'anonymous' apothegms [*APanon*], to which some additional matter is appended in a few cases. Some of the chapters are quite short; No. 19, on miracles, has only twenty-one items, while No. 10, on discretion, is the longest with almost two hundred. The entire collection now contains about twelve hundred items, thirty-six of which are sayings of Isaiah of Scêtê (mainly located in chapters 1–3), while a further ninety items (mainly in the later chapters) are from sources other than *APalph* / *APanon*.

> *More Sayings of the Desert Fathers*, edited by John Wortley, Cambridge 2019 [*MSDF*], citation by letter (for language) and number, e.g. [S20] = item 20 in Syriac sayings.

Widely though the Greek compilers cast their nets, they did not succeed in catching all the extant apothegms; nor of course could they have included sayings that were generated after their time. Dom Lucien Regnault (1924–2003) and his colleagues at Solesmes succeeded in isolating and translating a large number of items found in other collections and/or in other languages, items, that is, which do not appear (or only appear in a very different form) in the major Greek collections. Their work was published as *Les Sentences des Pères du Désert, nouveau recueil* (Solesmes 1970, 2nd edn 1977); it made an invaluable contribution to apothegmatic studies. Their work is now available to the English reader, but with certain important differences. Over the past half century there have been advances in the field from which the English translators have been able to profit, most significantly where better editions of the original texts have appeared. But of greatest importance is the fact that, whereas in several cases the monks of Solesmes were obliged to make their translations from translations of the original (usually into Latin), the English translators, using the best editions available, have worked directly from the languages in which the material has been preserved: Greek, Latin, Syriac, Coptic, Armenian and Ethiopic.

It will readily be appreciated that there is an obvious (and lamentable) omission in that list: Arabic. While it is well known that a considerable amount of apothegmatic material has been preserved in Arabic, nobody has yet had the *courage* to determine how much of that material has not been preserved in any other language and to translate it. That is a task which awaits a future generation.

More Sayings contains more than six hundred items. When these are added to the 1,800 items of *APalph/APanon*, the 126 of *APsys*, the 10 of Evagrius Ponticus and the 14 of John the Solitary, there appear to be a total of about 2,550 apothegms at our disposal.

> 'The Life of Paul of Thebes by Jerome', in *Early Christian Lives*, translated by Carolinne White, Harmondsworth 1998, pp. 71–84.

Shortly after the death of Athanasius in 373, Jerome (*c.* 347–420) wrote his *Life of Saint Paul the First Hermit*, in Latin, possibly his first composition subsequent to his decision to dedicate himself to theological studies. Clearly aware of Athanasius' *Life of Antony* and probably resenting its influence, he devised what is now universally regarded as a fictitious *Life* in order to counter Antony's growing (and false) reputation as 'the first monk'. Born *c.* 227, Paul is said to have taken refuge in the desert near Thebes during the persecution of Decius and Valerian, thus around 250. He lived in that desert until he was forty-three, then in a cave until his death *c.* 342, at the age of about 115. Warned by a dream, Antony is alleged to have visited Paul and to have conversed with him for a day and a night. There is no mention of any such meeting in *VA*: Jerome's intention appears to have been to allege that a monk yet greater than Antony once walked the earth. However, fiction though this *Life* may be, its *couleur locale* is not to be discounted, for Jerome had probably learned many things about the monastic life through his association with Rufinus at Aquileia and with the companions who travelled with him through Thrace, Asia Minor and Syria in 373 and 374.

> John Cassian, *Conferences*, translated by Boniface Ramsey, New York 1997; John Cassian, *Institutes*, 2000. Also John Cassian, *Institutes* and *Conferences*, translated by C. S. Gibson, *Nicene and Post-Nicene Fathers, Second Series*, vol. II, www.newadvent.org/fathers/3508.htm

John Cassian (*c.* 360–435) was born on the lower Danube. He embraced the monastic life in his youth, first at Bethlehem, then (together with his life-long friend Germanus) for about fifteen years at Kellia and Scêtê. In 399 he went to Constantinople where he was made a deacon by John Chrysostom. In 405 he migrated to Rome, then in 410 to Provence where he founded and spent the last twenty years of his life as superior of the Abbey of Saint Victor near Marseilles. This was an unusual establishment for, although it was planned on Egyptian models, it included quarters for both men and women.

Sometime after 425 John produced the two works for which he is famous: the *Institutes of the Coenobia* (twelve books) and the *Conferences* [*collationes*] (twenty-four books). In these works, he sought to set out and adapt the theory and practice of Egyptian monachism for monks in Provence. The works (*Conferences* especially) may have originated as addresses to the men and women in his monastery. The first part of *Institutes* is largely a description of monastic life in Palestine and in Egypt. The second part warns the monk of the eight vices he must avoid, not unlike the eight sins of Evagrius Ponticus. *Conferences* is in the form of a series of conversations with noted Egyptian monks concerning the question of how one is to be saved, almost certainly fictional, and very much under the influence of the apothegms of the fathers. But, unlike the apothegms, John's books are sustained discourses, written in Latin, which may have been his mother tongue, for he was probably born and raised in the west, possibly in Provence.[2] Much of what he writes is put into the mouth of one or other of the Desert Fathers he had known in Egypt, or even one of their predecessors, e.g. Antony (whom one of them claimed to have heard speaking.) But, bearing in mind that it must have been at least a quarter of a century since John had been in Egypt when he set himself to writing

---

[2] Owen Chadwick, *John Cassian, a Study in Primitive Monasticism*, 2nd edn 1968, 9.

about the way they lived and taught there, and also that he was adapting his material to the needs of the west, the question arises of how accurately his work portrays Egyptian ideals. After considering all the available evidence, Owen Chadwick concludes: 'Cassian's testimony therefore is not far from the original Egyptian tradition.'[3]

> Dorotheos *of Gaza, Discourses and Sayings*, translated by Eric P. Wheeler, Kalamazoo MI 1977

Dorotheos of Gaza was a monk and an abbot who lived in Palestine in the early sixth century. In spite of the great popularity of his writings, no account of his life is known nor does his name occur on any list of saints. Much can nevertheless be learned of his life from three sources: the *Letters* of Barsanuphius and (especially) of John; the *vita* of Dositheus (who lived for three years under Dorotheos' direction); and Dorotheos' own writings. It is now generally agreed that Dorotheos was born in Antioch in the first decade of the sixth century, that he founded his own monastery shortly after 540 and that he died there between 560 and 580. He must have hailed from the leisured classes for he tells us that, as a young man, he was an avid reader and there is clear evidence that he received a decent education in secular letters. This may well have been completed in Gaza, where he may have been the student of Procopius of Gaza. He may even have taught there himself for a while. He probably made contact with Seridos and his coenobitic monastery at Thabatha (only 3 kilometres away) while so employed. Certainly, he had property to dispose of when he entered that monastery and he brought his own library with him. The monastery of Abba Seridos (of whom little is known) was distinguished by the presence of two illustrious monks from Egypt, former colleagues who lived in solitary confinement apart from one another at Thabatha for eighteen years: Barsanuphius and his sometime disciple, John 'the Prophet'. Neither of them was ever seen other than by the monk who served as his personal disciple, attendant and amanuensis: Abba Seridos in the case of 'the great elder', while Dorotheos worked with the lesser (the Prophet) for the nine years preceding his death, *c.* 540. Famous for their written responses to innumerable questions asked of them concerning many aspects of the monastic life, the solitaries' counsel (contained in more than eight hundred letters) had a profound influence on Dorotheos (to whom some of them were addressed), and also on the entire world of eremitic monachism. In spite of his indifferent health Dorotheos was charged with a number

---

[3] Ibid., p. 13.

of responsibilities by Abba Seridos. He served as the monastery's guest-master for some years. Meanwhile Barsanuphius and John were getting older and, together with other members of that community, had good reason to regret that their monastery had no infirmary. Probably aware that Dorotheos could command the necessary resources (he had an affluent brother living in the world), they prevailed upon him not only to build an infirmary but also to take personal responsibility for it. An infirmary was built and Dorotheos (who apparently had some knowledge of medicine) duly took charge of it, personally caring for the patients there for some years. He may well have begun to perform some of Abba Seridos' functions too, but he was not destined to succeed him as superior. After John died and Barsanuphius withdrew completely from the world, *c.* 540, Dorotheos left Seridos' monastery to found his own close by ('Near to Gaza and to Maiouma', *PS* 166) and it was to the community he assembled there that he delivered the celebrated *Instructions Beneficial to the Soul* on which his reputation rests. Of these, seventeen remain in addition to sixteen letters to various monks and a collection of eighteen sayings. The entire *oeuvre* is characterised by Dorotheos' secular learning before he became a monk, the teaching of Barsanuphius and (especially) of John, his own experiences as a monk at Seridos' monastery, and a profound acquaintance with the apothegms, in addition to not a few other patristic texts. The *Instructions* are the very epitome of what an address to a captive audience ought to be. Written in a simple, direct (but not inelegant) style, a typical *Instruction* probably took less than an hour to deliver. One aspect of monastic life and discipline is addressed in each *Instruction*, e.g. humility [2], lying [9] and fasts [15]. The point is made with frequent illustrations, e.g. 'When I was in [Seridos'] monastery ...' and 'One of the fathers said ...' Dorotheos never 'talks down' to his monks; he addresses them as his colleagues and friends and as one facing the same trials they are experiencing. The *Instructions* have sometimes rightly been compared with the *Institutes* and *Conferences* John Cassian wrote (in Latin) a century earlier but there are two important differences. Dorotheos had no personal experience of Egyptian monachism and, although he frequently cites the sayings of the Desert Fathers, he does not deliver his teaching in the form of a dialogue with them.

> *The Spiritual Meadow of John Moschos; [Pratum Spirituale] with the additional tales edited by Nissen and Mioni,* translated by John Wortley, Kalamazoo MI 1992, 1996 and 2001 [*PS*]

This is a collection of well over two hundred tales (the number is unsure as there is no critical edition of the text) composed by John Moschos

(Eviratus), born in Damascus in the earlier part of the sixth century. As a young man John became a monk at the monastery of Saint Theodosius, five miles west of Bethlehem, where he was eventually joined by Sophronius (the future Patriarch of Jerusalem), his friend and disciple for the rest of his life. In due course, the two of them withdrew to a more remote location in the Judaean desert where they stayed for ten years. Then *c.* 575 they undertook a journey to Egypt to collect the lore of the great elders whom they believed to be guardians of a monastic tradition which was fast being eroded by the slackness of the new generation of monks. They travelled extensively then came to stay at the monastery of the Æliotes on Mount Sinai where they remained for ten more years before undertaking further travels, this time in Palestine, then north to Antioch and Cilicia, before sailing to Alexandria where they appear to have been taken into the service of the Pope, Eulogius. With the fall of Jerusalem in 614 and the subsequent Persian advance on Egypt, the pair migrated to Rome where John was able to complete his book before he died, probably in 619.

The Spiritual Meadow only resembles any of the former works in that it purports to be a travelogue, yet it does include some apothegms (about thirty-two). There is a great deal of hearsay, but this is not to be quickly discounted, for monks had long memories and there may be genuine reminiscences here of times already long past. For the most part, *PS* is a collection of tales, some of them highly entertaining and in some cases with no evident connection to the monastic endeavour. These are a natural development of the kind of tale found among the sayings in *APalph* and (even more so) in *APanon*, usually characterised as 'tales beneficial to the soul' (even though it is not always clear wherein the benefit lies). Not by any means all the tales relate to the personal experiences of the travellers; they have been culled from a variety of sources, but the story of Gerasimos' Lion (at least) seems to be original here [*PS* 107].

Bibliography

Primary

Apothegms

The Anonymous Sayings of the Desert Fathers (*APanon*), ed. and tr. John Wortley, Cambridge 2013.

The Book of the Elders; Sayings of the Desert Fathers, the Systematic Collection (*Apsys*), tr. John Wortley, Collegeville MN 2012.

Give me a Word: the Alphabetical Sayings of the Desert Fathers (*APalph*), tr. John Wortley, Yonkers NY 2014.

More Sayings of the Desert Fathers; an English translation with notes (*MSDF*), ed. John Wortley, Cambridge 2019.

Other Works

Anon., *An Investigation of the Monks in Egypt* (*HME*), tr. Norman Russell, in *The Lives of the Desert Fathers*, Oxford and Kalamazoo MI 1981.

Athanasius of Alexandria, *The Life of Antony, the Greek Life and the Coptic Life* (*VA*), tr. Tim Vivian and A. P. Athanassakis, Kalamazoo MI 2003.

The Life and Regimen of the Blessed and Holy Teacher Syncletica, tr. Elizabeth Bryson Bongie, Toronto 1995.

Cassian, John, *Conferences and Institutes*, tr. Boniface Ramsey, New York 1997.

Dorotheos of Gaza, *Discourses and Sayings*, tr. Eric P. Wheeler, Kalamazoo MI 1977.

Evagrius Ponticus, *Praktikos and Chapters on Prayer*, tr. J. E. Bamberger, Kalamazoo MI 1981.

Isaiah of Scêtê, *Ascetic Discourses*, tr. John Chryssavgis and Robert Penkett, Kalamazoo MI 2002.

Jerome, 'The Life of Paul of Thebes by Jerome', in *Early Christian Lives*, tr. Carolinne White, Harmondsworth 1998, 71–84.

John Moschus, *The Spiritual Meadow*, tr. John Wortley, Kalamazoo MI 1992, repr. 1996, 2001.

Pachomius, *The Life of Saint Pachomius and His disciples*, tr. Armand Veilleux, Kalamazoo MI 1980.

Pachomian Koinonia: the Lives, Rules and Other Writings of St Pachomius and his Disciples, vol. II: *Pachomian Chronicles and Rules (Pr)*, tr. Armand Veilleux, Kalamazoo MI 1981.

Palladius of Aspuna, *The Lausiac History (HL)*, tr. John Wortley, Collegeville MN 2015.

Paul Evergetinos, *Synagogê [Synag]*, Venice 1783; 6th edn, 4 vols., Athens 1980.

Regnault, Lucien, ed., *Les Sentences des Pères du Désert, nouveau recueil*, Solesmes 1970, 2nd edn 1977.

Saint Macarius the Spirit Bearer: Coptic Texts Relating to Saint Macarius the Great, tr. Tim Vivian, Crestwood NY 2004.

Theodoret, *Religious History*, tr. R. M. Price, in *A History of the Monks of Syria*, Kalamazoo MI 1985: *Precepts*, pp. 145–67.

Wortley, J., ed., *Les récits de Paul, évêque de Monembasie et d'autres auteurs*, Paris 1987.

Secondary

Butler, E. Cuthbert, *The Lausiac History of Palladius*, 2 vols., Cambridge 1898, 1904.

Capozzo, Mario, *I monasteri del deserto di Scêtê*, Todi 2009.

Chadwick, Owen, *John Cassian, a Study in Primitive Monasticism*, 2nd edn, Cambridge 1968.

Chitty, Derwas J., *The Desert a City*, Oxford 1966, repr. Crestwood NY n.d.

Chryssavgis, John, *In the Heart of the Desert: the Spirituality of the Desert Fathers and Mothers*, Bloomington IN 2003.

Colegate, Isabel, *A Pelican in the Wilderness: Hermits, Solitaries and Recluses*, Berkeley CA 2002.

Curzon, Robert, *Visits to Monasteries in the Levant*, London 1849, 1865, repr. 1955.

'*De latrone converso*: the Tale of the Converted Robber (*BHG* 1450kb)', *Byzantion* 66, 1996, 219–243.

Evelyn White, H. G., *Monasteries of the Wadi'n Natrûn*, Part II: *The History of the Monasteries of Nitria and Scetis*, New York 1932–1933.

Frankfurter, David, *Christianizing Egypt: Syncretism and Local Worlds in Late Antiquity*, Princeton NJ and Oxford 2015.

Gibbon, Edward, *The History of the Decline and Fall of the Roman Empire*, ed. John Bagnell Bury, 12 vols., New York 1909–1914, vol. III.

Gould, Graham, *The Desert Fathers on Monastic Community*, Oxford 1993.

Goutagny, Étienne, *Saint Macaire et le moines du désert de Scété*, Paris 2017.

Harmless, William, *Desert Christians: an Introduction to the Literature of Early Monasticism*, New York 2004.

Kingsley, Charles, *The Hermits*, London 1869.

Michel, Julian, *Voyage aux déserts de Scété et de Nitrie à la recherche de l'Arbre sorti du Bois Sec*, Lyons 1882, repr. 2013.

Patlagean, Evelyne, 'L'histoire de la femme déguisée en moine et l'évolution de la sainteté féminine à Byzance', *Studi medievali*, 3rd ser., 17.2, 1976, 597–623.

Ramfos, Stelios and Norman Russell, *Like a Pelican in the Wilderness: Reflections on the Sayings of the Desert Fathers*, Brookline MA 2000.

Regnault, Lucien, *La Vie quotidienne des Pères du Désert en Égypte au IVe siècle*, Paris 1990; tr. as *The Day-to-Day Life of the Desert Fathers in Fourth-Century Egypt*, Petersham MA 1999.

Swan, Laura, *The Forgotten Desert Mothers: Sayings, Lives and Stories of Early Christian Women*, New York 2001.

Williams, Rowan, *Silence and Honey Cakes: The Wisdom of the Desert*, Oxford 2003.

Wortley, John, 'Grazers [βόσκοι] in the Judaean Desert', in *The Sabaite Heritage in the Orthodox Church from the Fifth Century to the Present*, Orientalia Lovaniensia Analecta, Leuven 2001, pp. 37–48.

The following work came into the author's hands after he had completed the present volume:

Wipszycka, Ewa, *The Second Gift of the Nile: Monks and Monasteries in Late Antique Egypt*, tr. Damian Jasinski, Warsaw 2018.

Index